QUEER ART

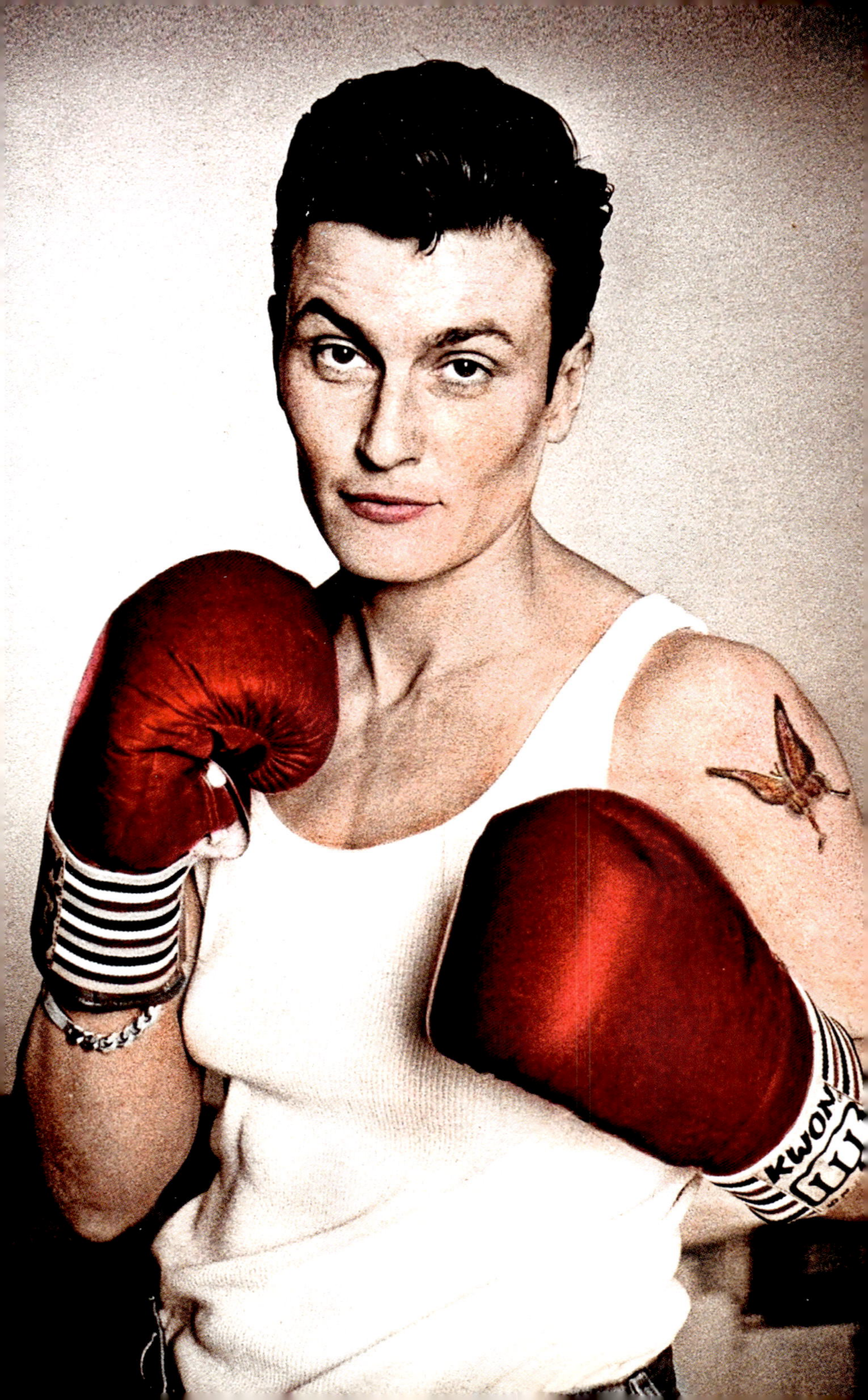

QUEER ART

—

MOLLIE E. BARNES

GEMMA ROLLS-BENTLEY

—

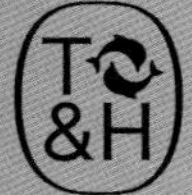

CONTENTS

INTRODUCTION

Art is almost always entwined with identity, whether due to the person creating the work, its subject, the context in which it is exhibited or the audience engaging with it. Some (mostly historical) conversations about queer art have tended towards direct representation, with an expectation to see bodies, specifically sexually explicit bodies. That approach feels outdated and reductive.

Queerness can exist in art explicitly or implicitly. Explicitly, queerness appears in depictions or references to queer life, relationships and identities. However, it can also be coded, abstracted or expressed in a way that subverts heteronormative expectations. Queerness can be expressed through unconventional aesthetics, subject matter or artistic strategies that challenge dominant social and artistic norms. The scope of queer art is expansive.

This book seeks to illuminate some of the key concerns of queer art, beginning with the recognition that queer art is not a genre, but a gesture; a refusal to be pinned down by fixed identity categories. It is shaped by fluidity, contradiction, resilience and desire. The themes explored – queer selves, resilient histories, love, liberation and queer futures – do not intend to define queer art, but to trace some key motifs that move through it. Our groupings are non-linear and overlapping, reflecting the experiences they draw from. This is by no means a definitive canon. It is offered as a starting point for thinking about a kind of art that defies categorization – an invitation to consider queer art as an open, inclusive force.

The language we use to talk about LGBTQIA+ (lesbian, gay, bisexual, transgender, queer, intersex or asexual) identity and queer expression has evolved significantly over time. Many artists lived and worked before terms like 'queer', 'gay', 'lesbian', 'trans' or 'non-binary' were used, let alone embraced. Where possible, we've used the terminology that artists used to describe themselves. At the same time, we recognize that we are interpreting historical work through a contemporary lens, one that is shaped by today's understandings of gender and sexuality. This approach is not about imposing labels on artists or artworks but about creating space to acknowledge queerness in all its complexity, even when it went unnamed.

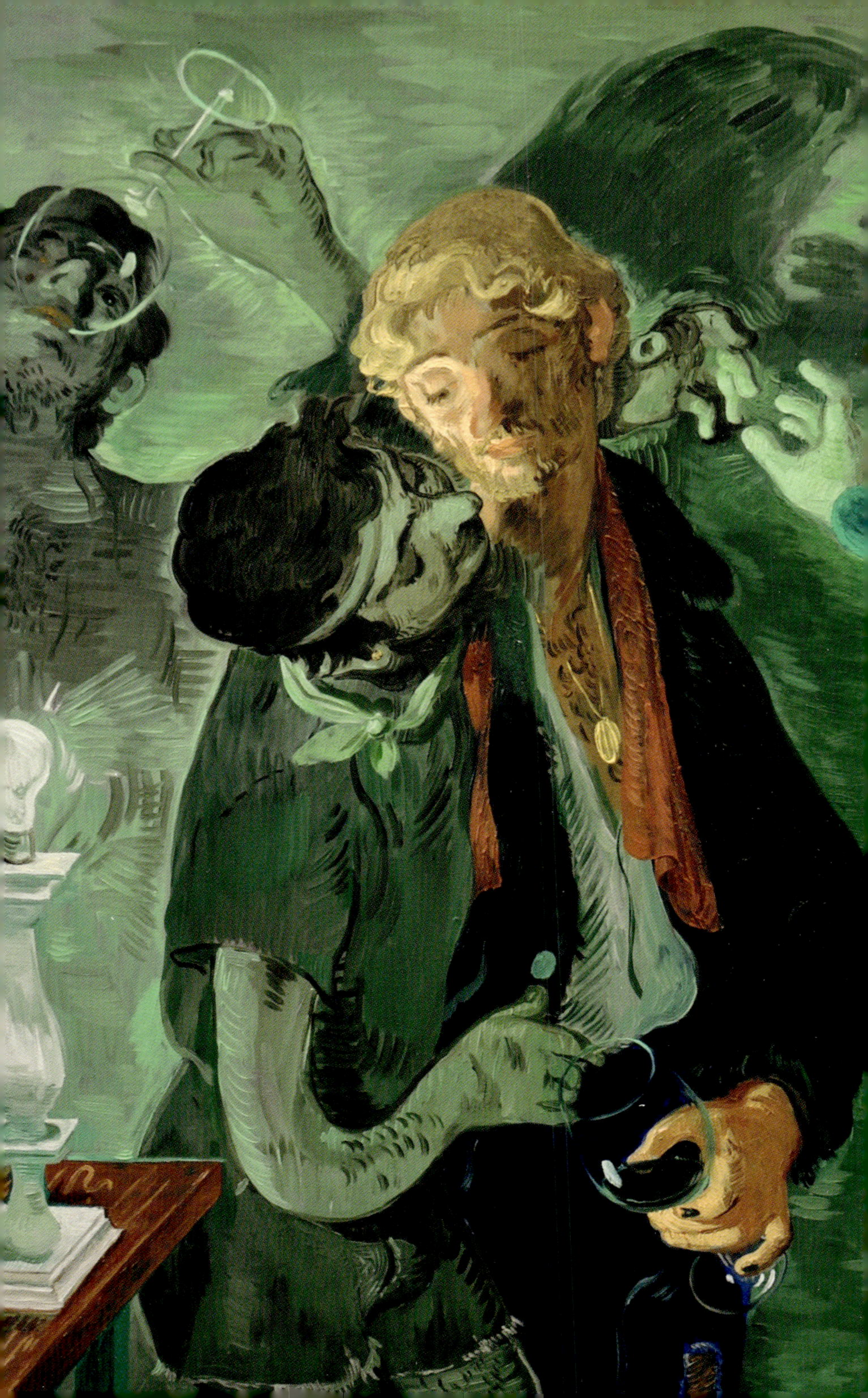

WHY TALK ABOUT
QUEER ART?

-

Traces of queer life appear throughout art
history, and we'll find them if we look for them,
but the study of art history has not always
acknowledged their existence

-

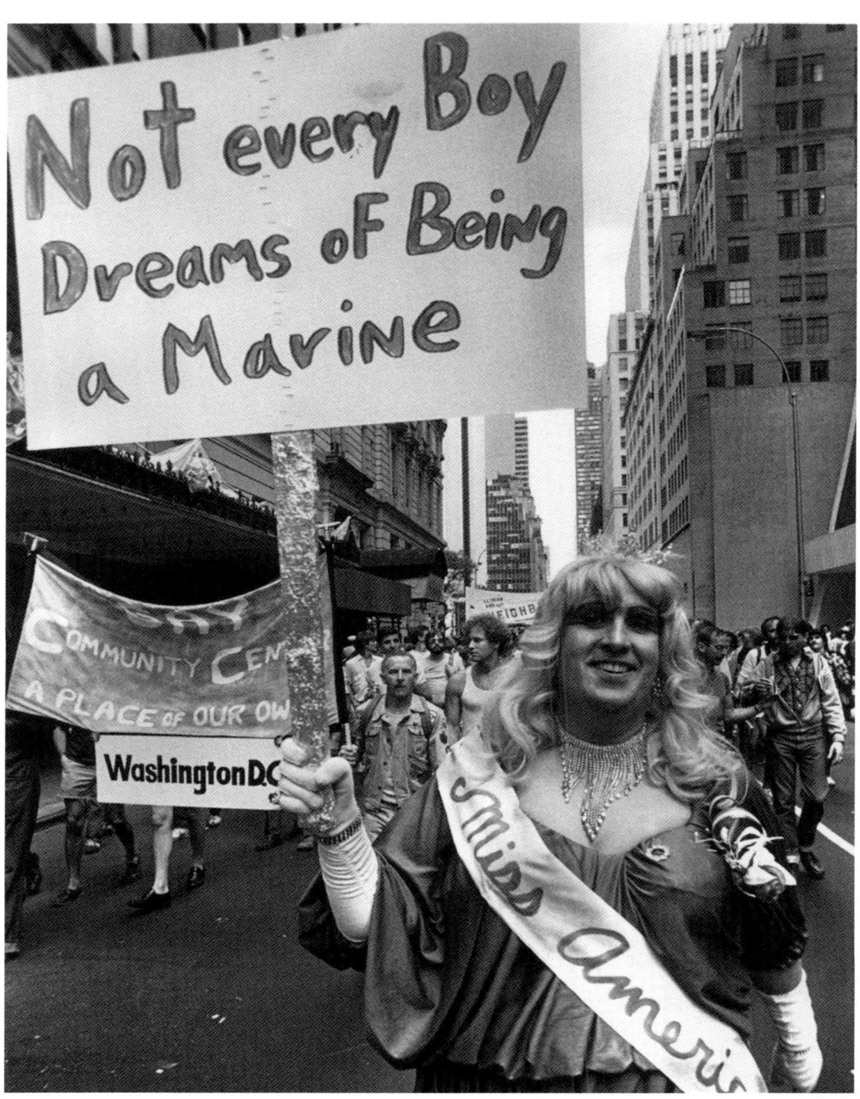

**7 July 1979,
New York City**

A protestor in drag carries
a banner during a gay rights
march from Fifth Avenue
to Central Park

WHAT DO WE MEAN BY 'QUEER'?

'Queer' has been in the English language for more than five centuries. Originally meaning strange, unusual or eccentric, people began using 'queer' to describe men who experienced same-sex desire in the late nineteenth century. By the middle of the twentieth century, the word had become established both as a derogatory term and as a label sometimes used, predominantly by gay men, to self-identify. This continued for several decades, reaching a boiling point during the early 1980s, at the beginning of the HIV/AIDS crisis, when 'queer' became common parlance within mainstream media. Its frequent use as a slur, particularly during this period, alongside other forms of violence against the LGBTQIA+ community, has made the contemporary use of the word difficult for some people.

During the late 1980s and early 1990s, activists began to reclaim the term and since then it has increasingly been used by a broad range of LGBTQIA+ people to describe their identity and politics, including non-English speakers as the term has become a common loan word in other languages. Many writers and thinkers have proposed contemporary definitions of queerness, including bell hooks, Audre Lorde, Judith Butler, Gloria Anzaldúa and José Esteban Muñoz. What they all tend to agree on is that the word can – in part – refer to gender or sexuality, but that it is also bigger and more complex than that. By critically deconstructing the notion that heterosexuality and binary gender are 'normal' and innate, queer theory challenges traditional or socially acceptable modes of being in general.

In referring to non-normative ways of being, definitions of 'queer' are often deliberately open-ended. This lack of a strict definition is useful as it allows us to better consider the multiple ways in which different identities might intersect along lines of race, class, ability, gender and sexuality, among others. Queerness celebrates those differences. It also speaks to the impact of a long history of oppression and how queers have found methods to navigate and challenge systems that were built to exclude anyone who does not fit socially dominant modes of being. Understood this way, to 'queer' something is to approach it in a way that troubles normative (especially heteronormative and cisgendered) ways of thinking, categorizing or being. Queerness, therefore, is not a passive quality but an active undertaking, that is fuelled by a unique blend of resistance, resilience, solidarity and compassion.

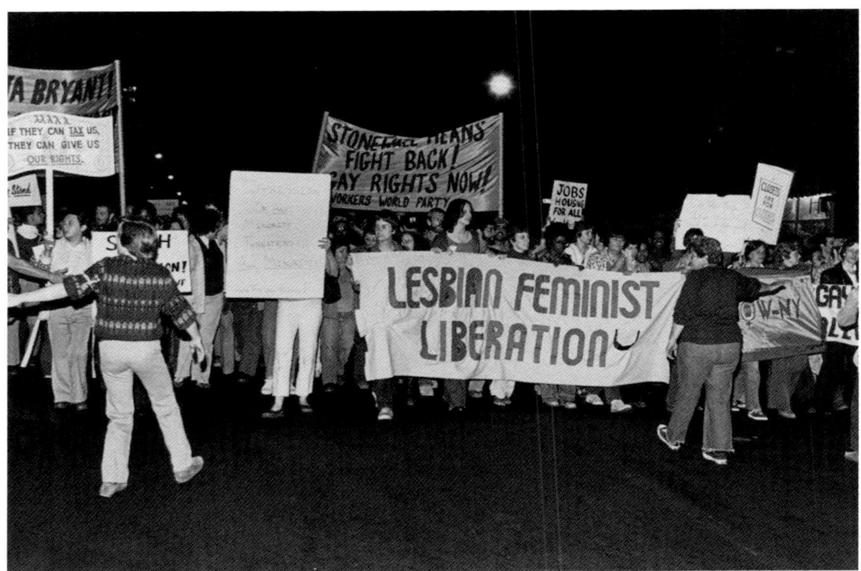

Inspired by the 1969 Stonewall Riots in New York City, which fought against discrimination of LGBTQIA+ people, gay liberation groups began leading Pride protests and parades in cities across Europe and North America. Today, Pride events in cities all around the world celebrate the creativity of the community whilst continuing to draw attention to ongoing oppression.

9 June 1977, Lesbian Feminist Liberation LGBT protesters at a gay rights march in New York City

QUEER ART HISTORY

History, and similarly art history, has overlooked or actively erased queer narratives, particularly those of women, gender non-conforming or trans people and people of colour. In recent years this has begun to shift, with more intentional efforts being made to apply a queer lens to art history, which allow us to recognize queer narratives in both historical and contemporary art.

There is a branch of art history dedicated to reassessing historical art, uncovering moments – both overt and subtle – where queerness is present. Some of these moments are more easily identified than others. For instance, asexual and aromantic perspectives can be particularly hard to find, in part because of a persistent tendency for people to focus on sexuality and romance above other forms of connection or attraction. This tendency has caused asexual theorists to extend American poet and essayist,

Yayoi Kusama
*Infinity Mirrored Room –
Phalli's Field*, 1965
Installation view, Yayoi
Kusama with *Infinity
Mirrored Room – Phalli's
Field*, Castellane Gallery,
New York, 1965

Phalli's Field reflects
Kusama's attempt to
reclaim power over her
fears. It turns repetition
and scale into a control
strategy. The piece is
made up of thousands
of stuffed fabric tubers,
grafted into phallic
shapes. Paired with the
grand mirrors, they
become hallucinatory
and infinite polka dots
and penises.

Adrienne Rich's critique of compulsory heterosexuality towards
the idea of compulsory sexuality – the assumption that everyone
experiences sexual attraction; or, likewise, romantic attraction.
In art-historical practice, this means that it is often assumed
that artwork can be understood in terms of sexual attraction
or romantic desire of the artist, thus taking any opportunity to read
sexual desire into a work – a critique which can extend to queer
theorists as well as conservative art historians. Asexual or aromantic
artists therefore rarely appear in the canon. Potential exceptions
include Japanese artist Yayoi Kusama who has said that she created
works such as *Phalli's Field* (1965; below), which feature white,
mirrored phallic forms, to conquer her own disgust and fear of sex.
Scholar Ela Przybylo has written of Kusama and American artist
Agnes Martin, that the asexual and aromantic elements of their
identities have not been understood or appropriately celebrated,
despite clues in their works. Martin has often been understood as
a closeted lesbian, and Kusama assumed as a repressed heterosexual.

Depictions of domestic interiors, meanwhile, are a compelling
example of how art can be queer in ways that may not seem
immediately obvious. For example, the early-twentieth-century
paintings by British American artist Ethel Sands of the home

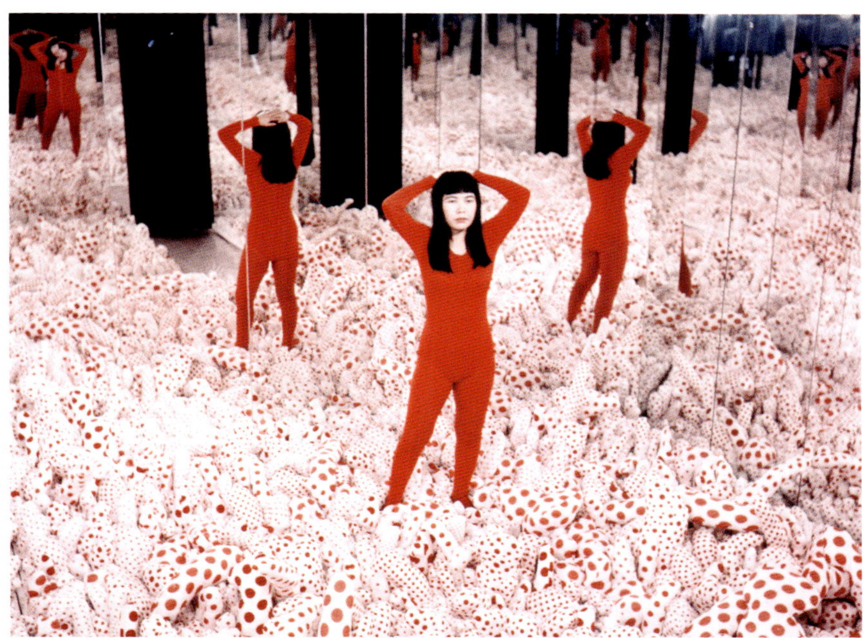

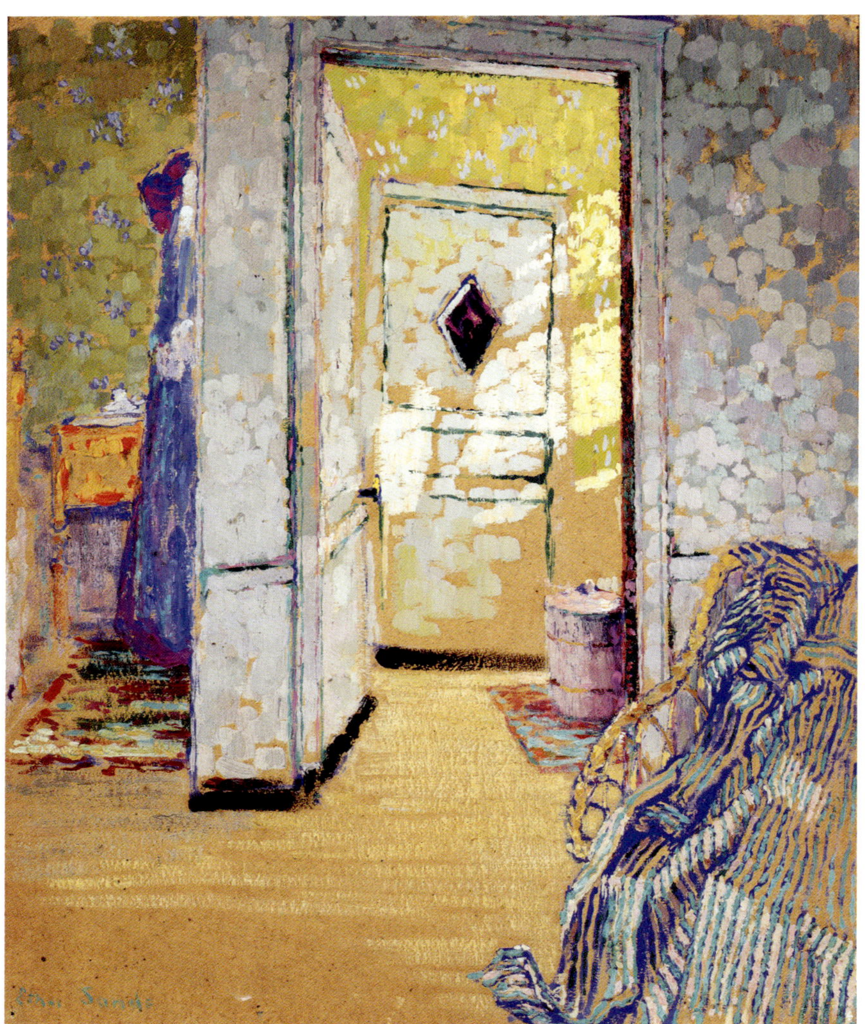

Ethel Sands
A Dressing Room,
undated
Oil on millboard
46 × 38 cm
(18⅛ × 15 in.)
Ashmolean Museum,
Oxford

A beautiful example of Ethel Sands's intimate domestic interiors and still lives that depict the home she shared with Anna 'Nan' Hope Hudson. The pair were able to create a life together due to Sands's independent wealth – a rare privilege for early-twentieth-century women. If we didn't know the background, would we read the painting as queer?

she shared with her romantic partner Anna 'Nan' Hope Hudson
(opposite). There is not necessarily anything within the paintings
themselves to indicate their queerness. However, historic accounts
of the time reveal the domestic relationship that played out in
these rooms. That information provides an opportunity to view the
work through a queer lens, to reconsider the experiences that the
paintings speak to. Almost a century later, Tammy Rae Carland's
photographic series *Lesbian Beds* (2002; below) depicts unmade
beds that, to all but the most expert queer eye, could belong to
anyone. The title, however, clearly positions them as queer.
Viewing these beds and boudoirs with some knowledge of the
people who occupied them can deepen our understanding of
the work. They become touchstones for lesbian visibility and
indicators of a life lived against the grain. In the case of Ethel Sands
or Tammy Rae Carland, the queerness in their work is discernible
largely because of historical records or the ways in which they

Tammy Rae Carland
Untitled (Lesbian Bed #13),
2002
C-print
101.6 × 76.2 cm
(40 × 30 in.)

**Tammy Rae Carland's
photographic series
depicts unmade beds
that could have recently
been occupied by anyone,
but the clue is in the
title, as well as the very
nuanced details that
may only be readable to
an experienced lesbian
eye. A cat, a sports sock,
a nightdress or, in this
instance, the suggestive
slit of a pillowcase.**

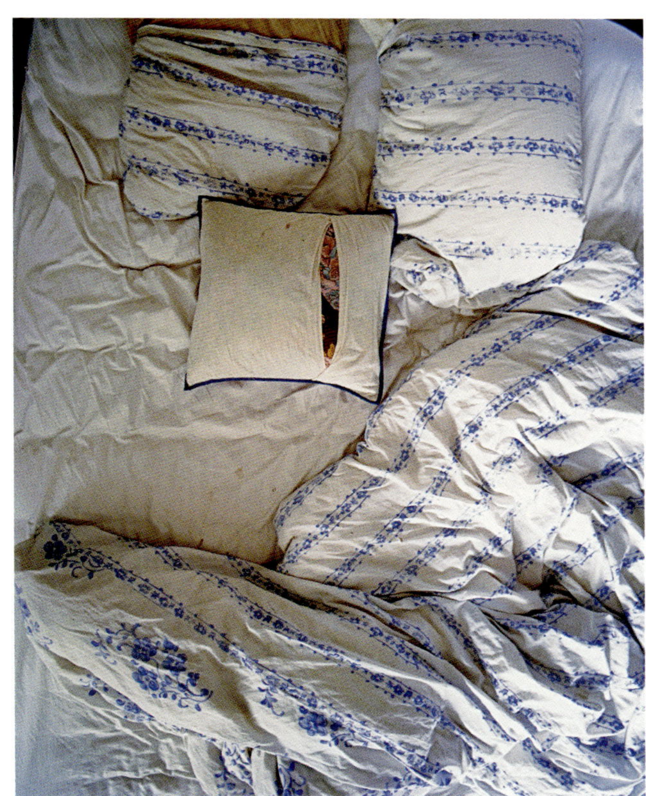

titled or spoke about their art. This raises a question: how many opportunities have been lost to recognize queerness in art, simply because it was never documented or acknowledged at the time?

Who, then, is responsible for framing an artwork as queer – the artist, the curator, the critic or the viewer? Historically, context often decides whether an artwork's queerness is seen or overlooked. This stretches as far back as ancient Egyptian joint tombs and Japanese Edo-period Shunga woodblock prints, which freely depicted same-sex erotic scenes but were often confined to private collections. Consider also Cornel Brudaşcu (below, pages 36–37), one of Romania's leading artists, who did not publicly come out as gay until later in life. It was only then that his paintings explicitly embraced homoerotic themes. Yet, critics have since retrospectively applied a queer lens to his earlier works, reading into them a queerness that may have been unconscious or coded.

The curators of a landmark exhibition of Gustave Caillebotte's work (opposite) in 2024 took a similar approach, examining the French Impressionist's numerous depictions of male subjects in a way that was open to the possibility he may have been sexually attracted to men. This interpretation was met with both enthusiasm

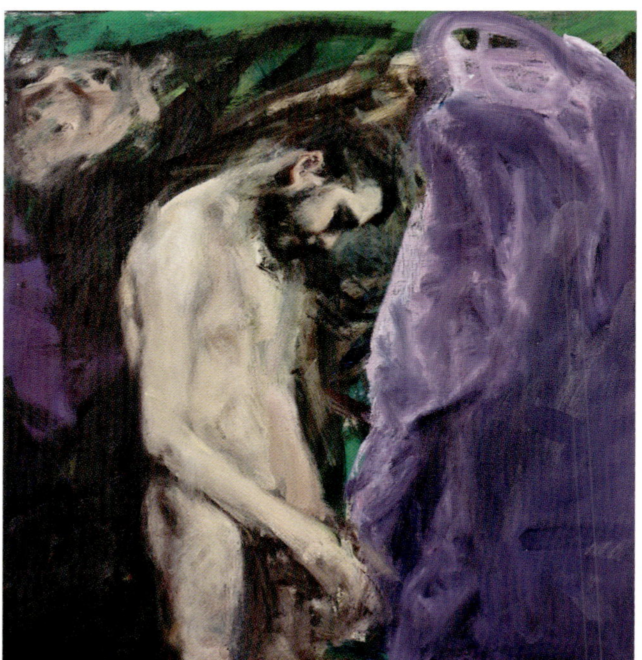

Cornel Brudaşcu
Untitled, 2019
Oil on canvas
80 × 75 cm
(31½ × 29⅝ in.)
Plan B, Cluj, Berlin

In this later work by Brudaşcu, known for his expressive figuration and exploration of male intimacy, the nude male body is painted with classical tenderness. Here, the figure is enveloped in movement and surrounded in colour, a birdlike shape in front of him. Brudaşcu depicts the figure with his hands over his genitals, drawing attention to his personal nakedness.

Gustave Caillebotte
Man at His Bath, 1884
Oil on canvas
144.8 × 114.3 cm
(57 × 45 in.)
Museum of Fine Arts,
Boston

**Caillebotte's portrayal of
a nude man in a domestic
interior was radical in that
it challenged nineteenth-
century gendered
conventions of the bather
motif. Rejecting the
heroic idealization of male
nudity in mythological
or historical scenes and
instead placing him in
a space traditionally
reserved for the female
subject, Caillebotte
opens the image to queer
readings.**

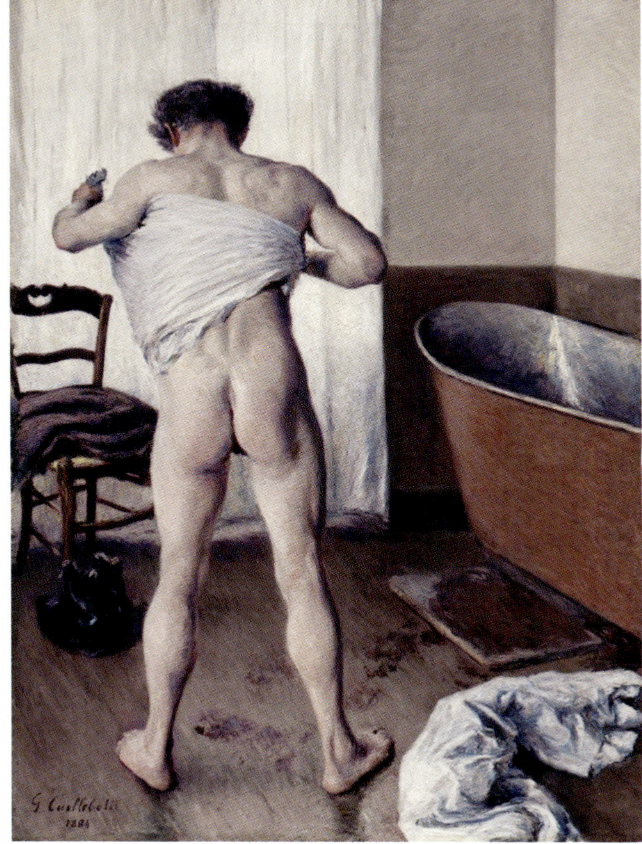

and resistance; while many celebrated the exhibition's sensitivity
to the ways in which gender and sexuality can be expressed or
hidden, some critics labelled the curators' approach inappropriate
given the lack of concrete biographical evidence. The German-
Swedish artist Lotte Laserstein (pages 54–55) created paintings
that can be – and have been – read as queer, yet discussions
of queerness have been largely absent from the art-historical
framing of her work, leading to both frustration and speculation.
Likewise, Iranian painter Bahman Mohasses often chose male
nudes and homoerotic motifs as his subject matter, and some
works featured abstracted male bodies engaging in group sex.
Despite being openly gay, the queer aspects of his visual language
went unspoken in official accounts, with some works later being
censored and even destroyed.

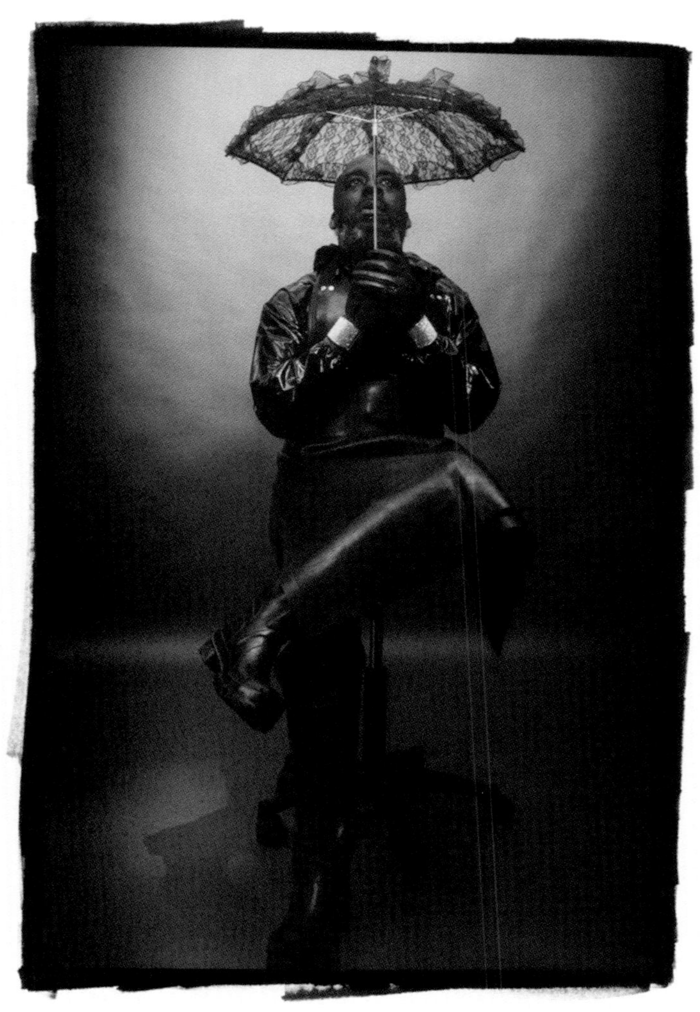

Ajamu X
Umbrella, 2023
Platinum print
61 × 50.8 cm
(24 × 20 in.)

**Commissioned by the
Autograph Gallery,
London (previously
known as the Association
of Black Photographers),
this self-portrait pays
homage to Rotimi
Fani-Kayode's *Umbrella*
(1987), a photographic
self-portrait in a similar
pose with legs crossed
and umbrella aloft.
The work reflects
Ajamu's personal
connection with Fani-
Kayode, who was the first
Black gay photographer
he encountered as a
student.**

There are many other artists who have been explicit about their identity and the queerness of their work, yet this aspect has been downplayed or deliberately omitted in mainstream discourse. In a book such as this, artists' studios or estates must approve the reproduction of their artwork for inclusion, meaning there is an element of self-identification in the framing of their art as queer, however, this isn't necessarily the case in a broader sense. Queer readings could, and should, be applied to many artworks, regardless of (our knowledge of) the artist's identity.

We are able to access queer art histories thanks to the tireless work of artists, collectors, patrons, curators and writers committed to preserving them. At a grassroots level, communities of artists have preserved the legacies of those whose work didn't receive due recognition during their lifetimes, particularly those lost to HIV/AIDS. For example, in the United Kingdom, artists such as Sunil Gupta and Ajamu X have played a crucial role in building archives and championing fellow queer artists and artists of colour since the 1980s. Meanwhile, institutions like the Leslie-Lohman Museum of Art in New York, the Museum of Sexual Diversity in São Paulo, and the Sunpride Foundation in Hong Kong have built extensive collections of LGBTQIA+ art, actively centring under-represented voices. Similarly, initiatives such as the GALA Queer Archive in Johannesburg and the ONE Archives in Los Angeles work to safeguard and amplify queer cultural histories, ensuring they are accessible to future generations. Museums such as the Frick Collection in New York and the Stedelijk Museum in Amsterdam have even been making an effort to queer their permanent collections and public displays, incorporating LGBTQIA+ perspectives into their interpretation.

Without these dedicated efforts, many of these stories – and the artists behind them – might have been lost to time

For too long, queer art history has been dominated by white, cisgender male perspectives, often at the expense of women, non-binary and trans artists, artists of colour and others from marginalized backgrounds. This book seeks to expand that narrative – presenting a broader, more inclusive history of art that reflects the vast and intersecting identities shaping queer creativity.

WHERE CAN WE FIND QUEER ART?

Queer people have always existed. Therefore, queer art has always existed, all around the world and throughout human history, regardless of the words used to describe it at the time. Attitudes towards LGBTQIA+ identity within social and political frameworks of any given time or location impact the openness with which queerness might be expressed creatively, either at the point of creation or in the display and circulation of art. When or where objects were made, therefore, tends to affect how easy examples are to find or how readable they are as queer.

Homoerotic themes are evident in numerous ancient artworks, such as the Khajuraho Temple sculptures (page 22) in northern India, which include explicit depictions of lesbian and gay sex, and the Greco-Roman Warren Cup (opposite), which depicts male-male intimacy. Medieval European art contains many references to queer love, such as the same-sex couples depicted in the *Bible moralisée* (below). Gender-variant and intersex figures also appear throughout history and across the world, from saints to allegorical characters, long before the modern era. Illuminated manuscripts from medieval Europe and Persia, for example, sometimes depict intersex figures, and the ancient Greek mythological figure of Hermaphroditus was a popular subject for artists from antiquity

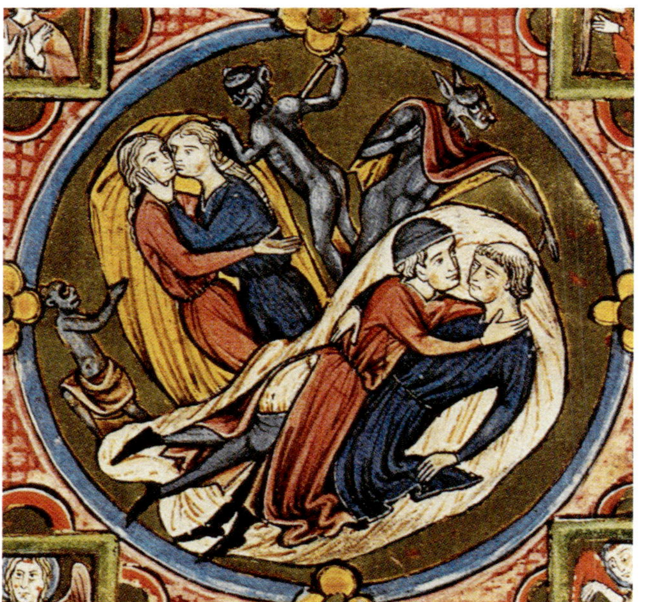

Bible moralisée (detail)
Paris, 1225–49
Austrian National Library, Vienna

The illuminated manuscripts of the medieval period were visual commentaries of biblical events. This example from the 1220s is from one of the earliest *Bibles moralisées*, which includes two depictions of two same-sex couples – one female and one male – each kissing and embracing.

The Warren Cup
Drinking-cup,
15 BCE–15 CE
Roman, Levant,
Jerusalem
Silver, chased and gilded,
height 11 cm (4⅜ in.),
diameter 11 cm (4⅜ in.)
British Museum,
London

The Warren Cup is an ancient Greco-Roman cup made of silver, decorated with male same-sex acts in relief. In ancient Rome, they had no word for 'homosexuality' but representations such as these were common in art from the period.

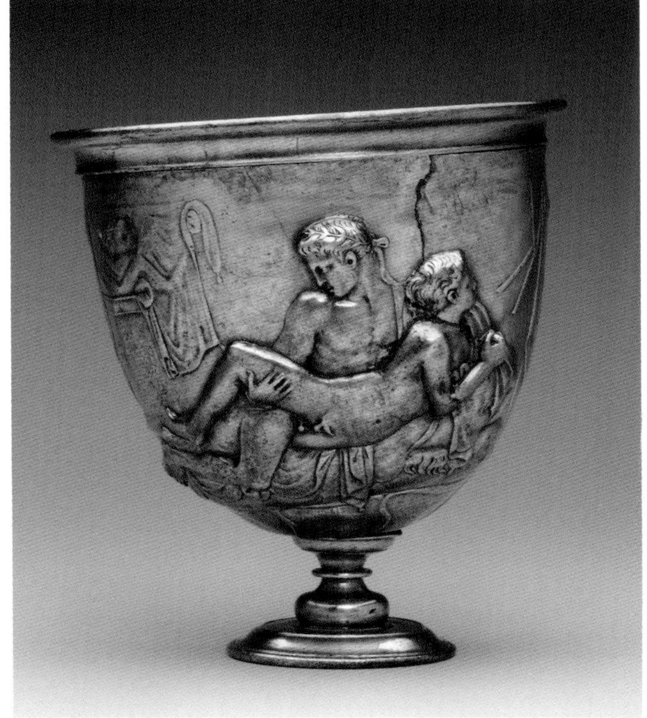

onwards, usually depicted with breasts and a penis. Christian religious legends record saints such as the Byzantine monk Marinos, who lived his entire adult life as a man, despite being raised as a girl – something only discovered by the other members of his order after he died when they were preparing his body for burial. In ancient Hindu art, the deity Ardhanarishvara – a revered patron of hijras – is the combined form of Shiva and Parvati, and is often depicted as being half male and half female.

During the Renaissance, northern Italian cities were hubs for same-sex relationships, despite the fact that they were criminalized under anti-sodomy laws, carrying the threat of imprisonment or execution. Artists such as Michelangelo and Titian alluded to homosexual love in their work. Donatello has recently been cited as the first artist from the early modern period to be known publicly as gay. His bronze *David* (c.1440s; page 23) has widely been interpreted as homoerotic, partially due to his nakedness, the effect of which is emphasized by his hat and boots – their presence making the absence of his other clothes appear more intentional.

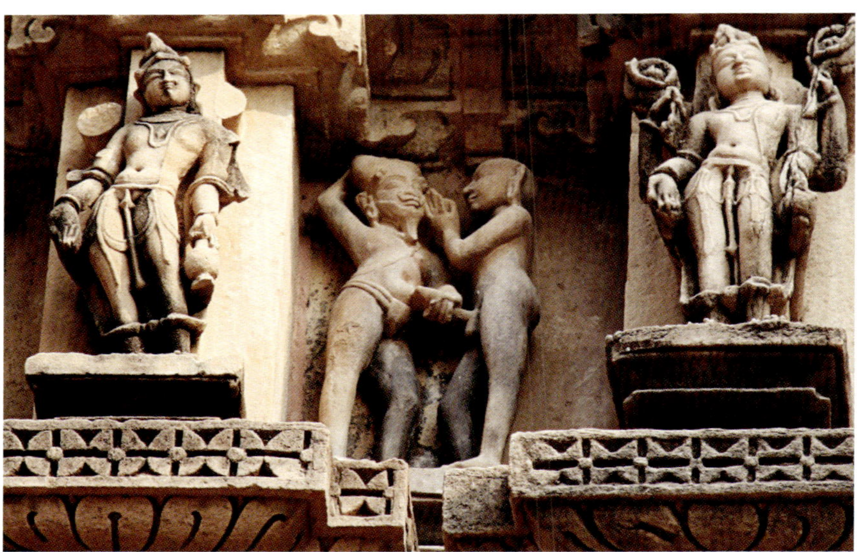

The Baroque painter Caravaggio is famous for the homoerotic themes in his work: his sensuous depictions of male bodies, a notable absence of female nudes and the fact that he never married, have caused art historians to conclude that he was likely gay, although there is no concrete biographical evidence to confirm this.

Traces of queer life appear throughout art history, and we'll find them if we look for them, but the study of art history has not always acknowledged their existence

Records of women loving women are notably scarce, in part because women's contributions to culture are less well recorded generally, but also because legal and religious systems were even less likely to specifically name same-sex desire among women than they were for men, although the punishments for lesbians could be just as severe as those for gay men. In medieval Europe, there are records of women being executed or sentenced to life imprisonment for having sex with other women. However, medieval European legal and religious texts tended to treat these acts in vague and euphemistic terms which, as the historian Edith Benkov argues, effectively 'erased the lesbian' from official documents.

Khajuraho Temples
Erotic relief details,
950–1050 CE
Sandstone
Madhya Pradesh, India

Built in the tenth century, the Khajuraho Temples are famous for their intricate stonework, which depicts a range of subjects from various areas of life, including erotic sculpting on the walls that shows people of the same sex engaging in sexual acts, most frequently women.

Donatello
David, c.1440s
Bronze, height 158 cm
(62¼ in.)
Museo Nazionale del
Bargello, Florence

**This free-standing
nude sculpture was
commissioned by
the Medici family.
Michelangelo wrote
numerous love poems
addressed to men, and
his depiction of the
biblical figure of David
as a muscular youth
is charged with erotic
energy.**

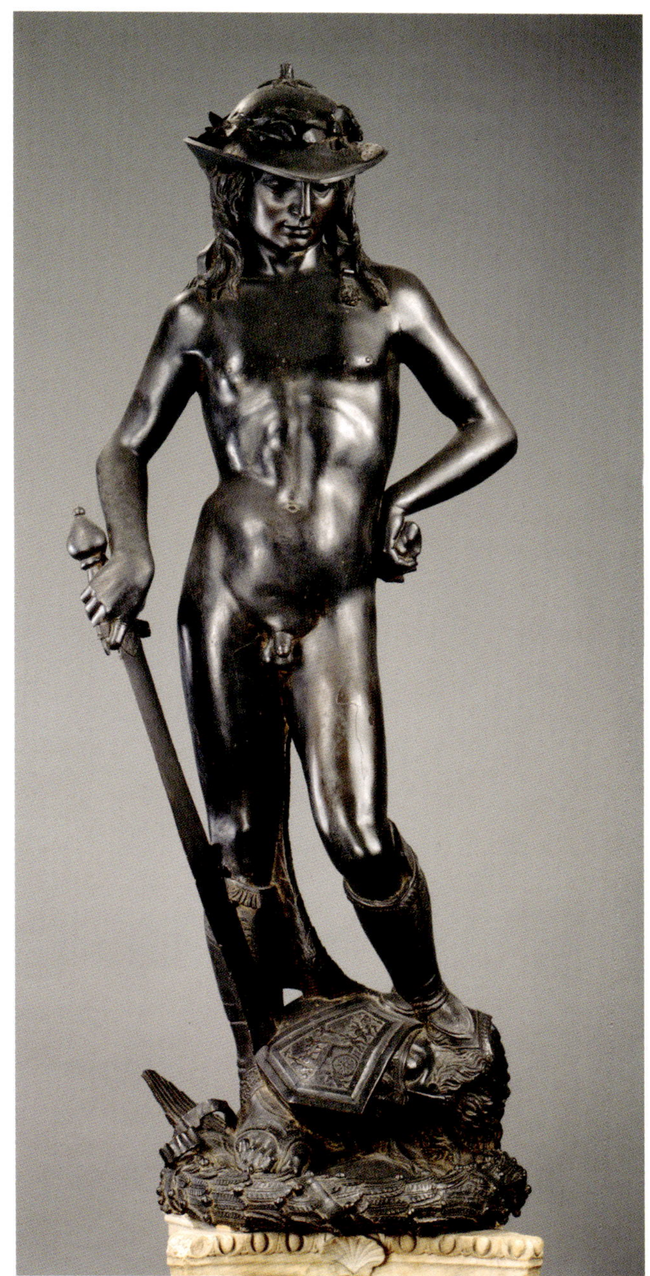

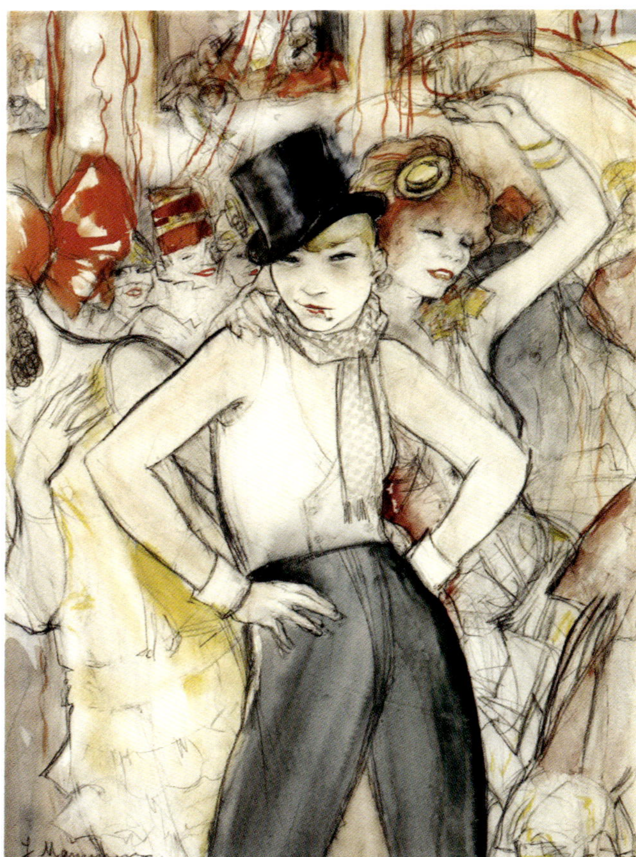

Jeanne (Johanna) Mammen
She Represents (Carnival Scene), c.1928
Watercolour and pencil on paper
42 × 30.4 cm
(16⅝ × 12 in.)
Private collection

Jeanne Mammen is famous for her illustrations of Weimar-era Berlin, particularly her portraits of women. Here she depicts a self-assured, androgynous figure enjoying a party in a lesbian bar, surrounded by feminine women.

By the late nineteenth century, homosexuality began to be considered as an identity within European and American art. The painting and photography of the time that captured details of queer life were typically set in private locations such as domestic spaces, clubs and bars. German painters Otto Dix and Jeanne Mammen depicted the drag queens and lesbians that frequented Berlin's underground night-time venues during the 1920s (above), which led to their work being condemned by the Nazis. Ongoing censorship in the early twentieth century meant that references to queerness were often heavily coded. Symbols used to identify queerness in daily life, such as peacock feathers or flowers (green carnations worn by men or violets exchanged by women), appeared in paintings. Queerness was often hidden in plain sight; Romaine Brooks, for example, presented female subjects

Gran Fury
*ACT UP, SILENCE =
DEATH*, 1987
Offset lithograph
85 × 56 cm
(33½ × 22 in.)

**The pink triangle was
a symbol used by the
Nazis to mark gay men
and trans women in
concentration camps.
The activist art collective
Gran Fury appropriated
and inverted this image
to indict inaction
during the AIDS crisis,
redefining the role of
graphic design in public
health activism in the
process.**

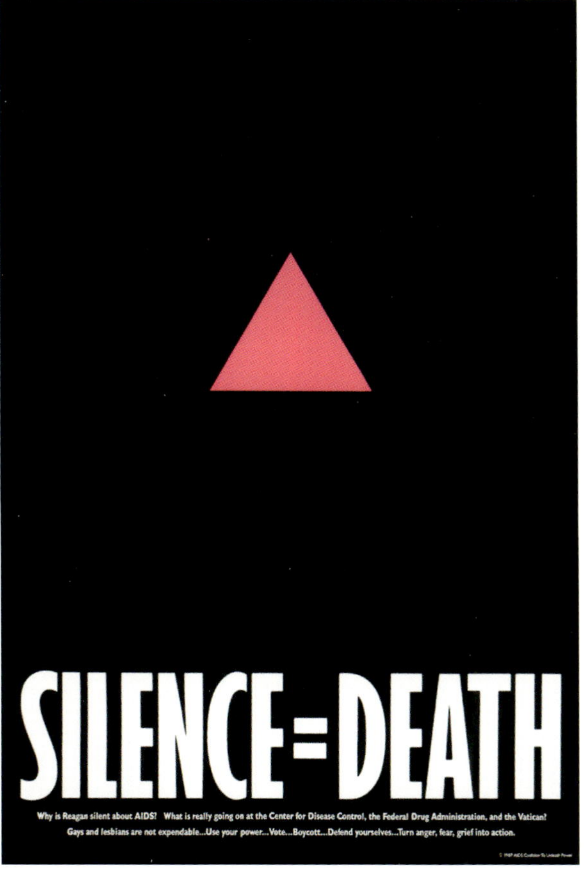

as Amazons, which allowed her to dress them in masculine attire.
These allusions to queer life would have absolutely been readable
to the experienced eyes of others within the community, and with
hindsight they are often palpable.

After the 1969 Stonewall Riots in New York City, gay liberation
groups formed across the West, and the global Pride movement
was born. As public understanding evolved, art and culture began to
more openly reflect queerness. In the 1980s and 1990s the AIDS
pandemic decimated a generation of queer people as governments
neglected to act and the media responded with vitriol. As the crisis
unfolded, the fight for freedom escalated and activism took hold
of the community. Groups such as ACT UP (AIDS Coalition to
Unleash Power) organized large acts of civil disobedience, and queer
art became increasingly politically charged. Collectives such as fierce

fierce pussy
I AM A lezzie..., 1991
Photocopy on paper
43 × 28 cm (17 × 11 in.)

fierce pussy is a queer artist collective whose work reclaims language and asserts visibility and solidarity across queer and trans identities, with a raw, zine-like aesthetic.

pussy and Gran Fury (both emerging out of ACT UP) challenged systemic oppression by bringing artwork directly into the streets, wheatpasting posters (page 25 and above), producing stickers and t-shirts, and organizing projects that intervened in public space.

-

The fact that queer life has long been censored and criminalized is reflected within art history and the art world

-

For a long time, queer art was not accepted within galleries and museums. However, there is a rich history of art that occurred outside of the cultural mainstream, flourishing in alternative spaces – from bars and clubs to zines and underground magazines.

In the mid-twentieth century, artists like Tom of Finland and Bob Mizer found ways to share their work through American beefcake magazines like *Physique Pictorial* (opposite), which in turn provided

Tom of Finland
Cover of magazine
Physique Pictorial,
Volume 7, No. 1
(Spring 1957; this was the first publication to feature the work of Tom of Finland)

First printed in 1951, *Physique Pictorial* was a pioneering magazine, which managed for the most part to avoid censorship in the United States by framing homoerotic imagery as male fitness. Although it was never explicitly framed as a gay magazine, it was the first of its kind to target a gay male audience. Tom of Finland's hypermasculine figures were used for a number of the early covers.

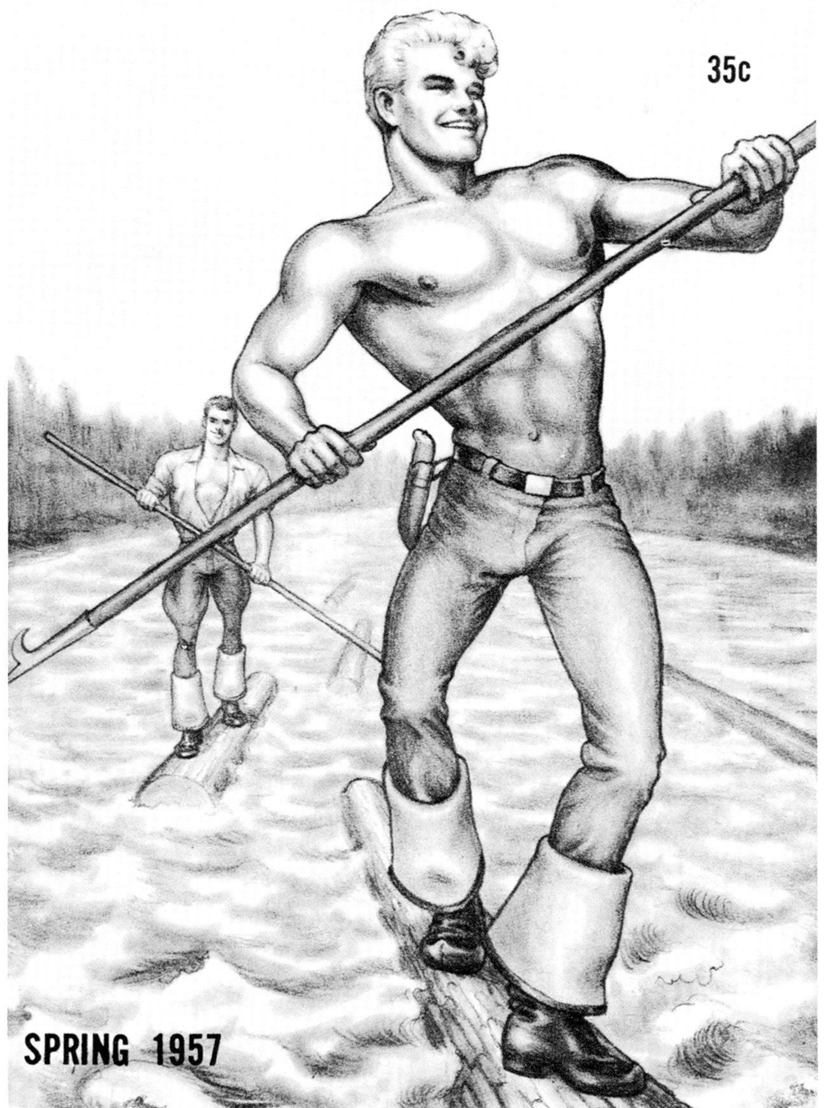

PHYSIQUE PICTORIAL
35c
SPRING 1957

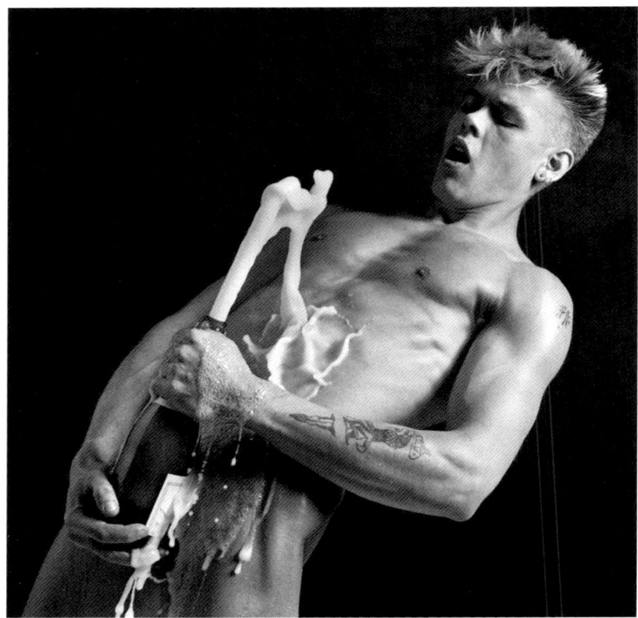

Erwin Olaf
Joy, 1985
From the *Squares* series
Gelatin silver print
37.5 × 37.5 cm
(14⅞ × 14⅞ in.)

Erwin Olaf was a gay
photographer and queer
rights activist whose
work merged camp and
eroticism, often using
staged scenes that
reference queer visual
codes and culture.

source material for many artists, including David Hockney.
Erwin Olaf's photograph *Joy* (1985; above) depicts a naked young
man spraying the contents of a phallic champagne bottle all over
his muscular, tattooed body. Appearing on postcards that were sent
all over the world at the height of the AIDS pandemic, it became a
symbol of hope and resistance within a climate of overt homophobia
and terror. Decades later, the now iconic image can be found on the
walls of some of Europe's leading art institutions.

For many people across the world, living openly as queer or
creating explicitly queer art remains difficult or dangerous.
Some artists relocate to places where they can express themselves
more freely, while others find creative, coded ways to navigate
restrictive environments. For example, photographer Slava Mogutin
(opposite), who became the first Russian to be granted political
asylum in the United States on the grounds of homophobic
persecution in 1995, or Ugandan artist Leilah Babirye (pages 72–73),
who fled to New York City in 2015 after being publicly outed by the
local media. Like so many others, these artists were forced to leave
their homes because of their commitment to queer visibility and
LGBTQIA+ rights in their art, which they have continued to tackle
from safer environments.

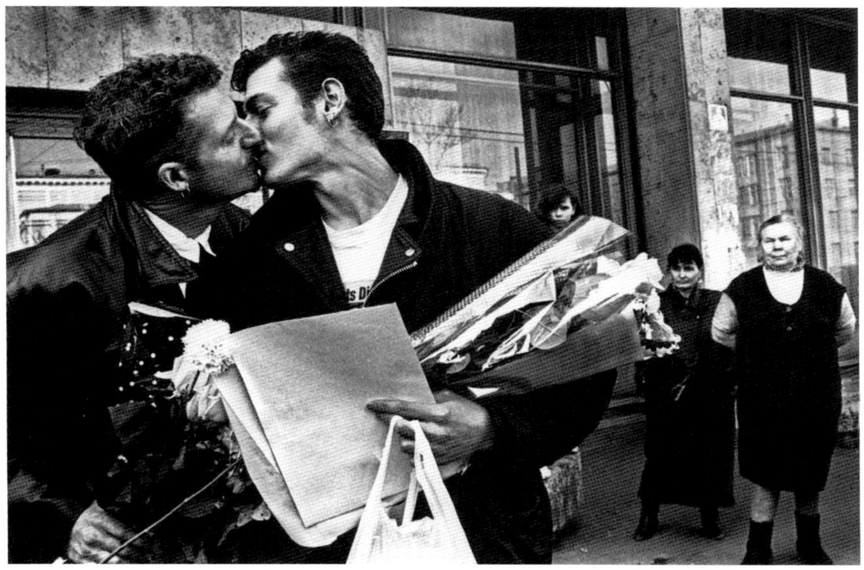

Slava Mogutin (with Robert Filippini)
Russian-American Wedding, Palace of Weddings #4, Moscow, 12 April 1994

Captured by the couple's friend Laura Ilyina, this image of Slava Mogutin with his then boyfriend, Robert Filippini, kissing in Moscow after attempting to marry each other on Mogutin's twentieth birthday, juxtaposes tender affection with the disapproval of onlookers nearby. Denied by Russian authorities, the couple faced threats of imprisonment and charges of 'hooliganism' under laws prohibiting the promotion of same-sex desire.

Queer migration is often accompanied by ongoing persecution. In places like London, Berlin and New York City – which have a long history of providing refuge for queer people – there are still serious threats being faced, particularly by those who are trans, intersex or people of colour. In 2023, the European Union Agency for Fundamental Rights reported that LGBTI people in Europe experienced significantly more violence and everyday harassment than in 2019, with trans and intersex people the most affected.

Legislative progress made in recent decades is also being unpicked, particularly regarding trans rights. In 2025, the International Lesbian, Gay, Bisexual, Trans and Intersex Association reported that while progress is still being made in terms of the decriminalization of same-sex relations globally, LGBTI people 'have been facing an unprecedented wave of attacks'. From the UK Supreme Court ruling that, for the purposes of the 2010 Equality Act, 'woman' is defined according to a person's sex assigned at birth, followed by the UK government issuing guidance suggesting that trans people should be barred from single-sex spaces; to the swathe of anti-trans legislation introduced by President Trump and state legislatures in the United States; to measures introduced in Peru establishing a prison sentence for anyone found teaching youth about sexual diversity, LGBTQIA+ rights are under threat across the world. The time and place in which art is made naturally influences how openly it can reference queer life. In more recent years, the internet has become an important tool for sharing art that may be restricted if exhibited in real life. For example, Nigerian crypto-artist Osinachi produced *Becoming Sochukwuma* (opposite) in response to the country's 2014 'Anti-Gay Law', as an NFT (Non-fungible token), which meant it could travel far and wide in the digital realm without restriction. In unsafe contexts, art remains a vital space for queer self-expression and community building.

We have chosen not to present these stories, artists and artworks chronologically primarily because queer histories resist linear narratives; they unfold across different timelines, pathways and geographies. By placing artists from diverse contexts into dialogue, we invite connections across generations and borders. In doing so, we hope to illuminate shared struggles, break down traditional canon hierarchies and highlight how queerness continually reshapes our understanding of both history and our collective future.

Osinachi
Becoming Sochukwuma,
2019
Digital artwork
40 × 50 cm
(15¾ × 19¾ in.)
Private collection

Inspired by Chimamanda Ngozi Adichie's essay 'Why can't he just be like everyone else?', written in response to a law in Nigeria which introduced prison terms of up to fourteen years for same-sex sexual activity, Osinachi imagines a queer Nigerian man embracing self-love through dance. The work was rendered in Microsoft Word and sold as an NFT on SuperRare for $80,000.

KEY READING

bell hooks, *Art on My Mind: Visual Politics*, New York:
   The New Press, 1995
Catherine Lord and Richard Meyer, *Art & Queer Culture*,
   New York: Phaidon Press, 2013

KEY ARTISTS

Ajamu X | Francis Bacon | Giovanni Bazzi | Bernice Bing |
   Romaine Brooks | Donatello | Sunil Gupta | David Hockney |
   Bob Mizer | Robert Rauschenberg | Simeon Solomon |
   Toyen (Marie Čermínová)

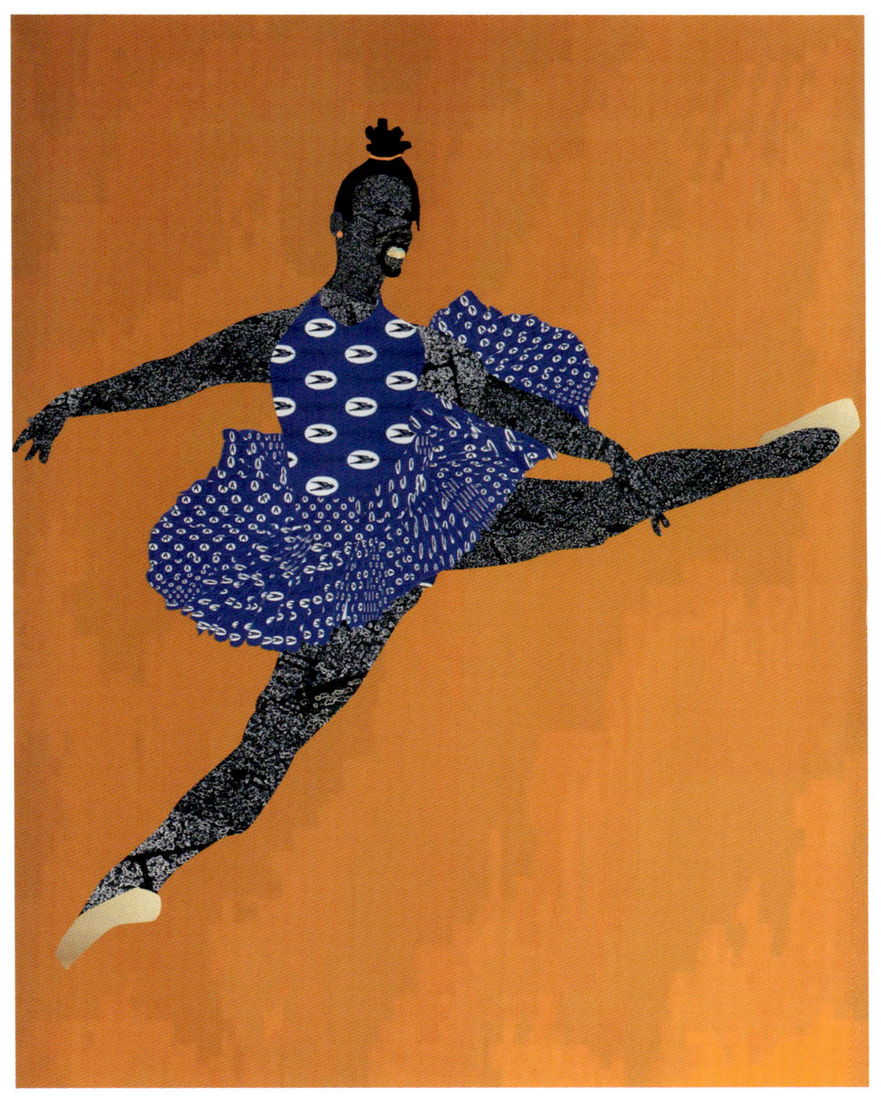

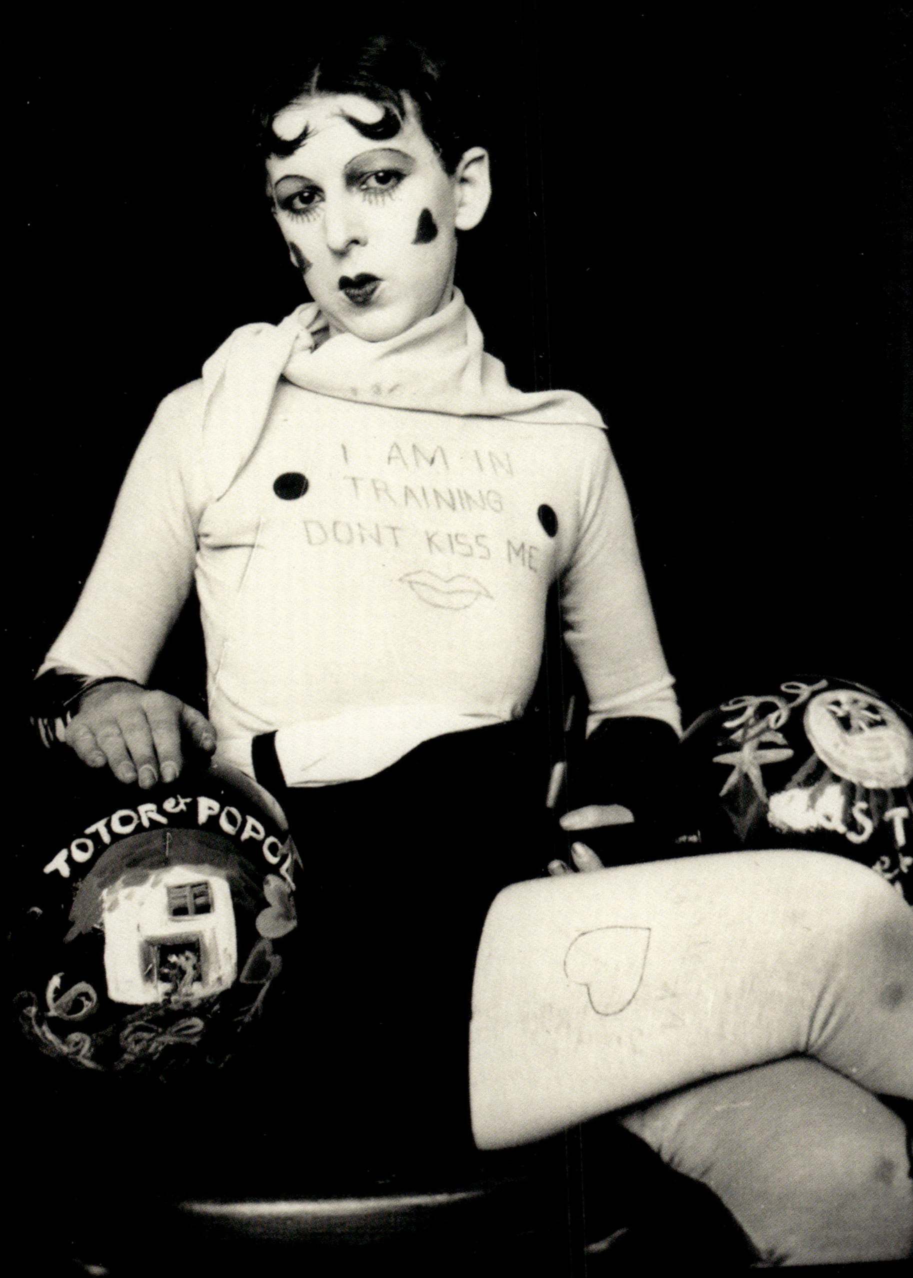
I AM IN
TRAINING
DONT KISS ME
TOTOR & POPOL

QUEER SELVES

-

Queer artists have long turned
their gaze inward

-

Queer selfhood is fluid and complex. It resists a singular or static definition, emerging through the confluence of personal histories, cultural expectations and acts of resistance. The philosopher Judith Butler famously argued that gender identity is 'not an expression of what one is, but something one does' – a continuous journey of 'becoming'. Understood this way, queer identities are always in-progress, constructed/realized through repeated acts that challenge what critic Leslie Fiedler calls the 'tyranny of the normal'.

As such, queerness is inherently intersectional – it rejects fixed categories of being, overlapping with, troubling and complicating other facets of identity such as nationality, race, culture, gender and class. Poet and theorist Audre Lorde described how these struggles are all interconnected, meaning that facing them often involves confronting multiple layers of marginalization – such as homophobia and racism – simultaneously, rather than as separate challenges. Responding to this complexity, many queer artists are drawn to themes of selfhood – not to explore a single or stable identity, but to explore, question and understand layered contradictions that shape lived experience. In doing so, their art negotiates the intersections of who they are and how they are seen.

A crucial motivation for queer self-representation is the desire to control one's own narrative. For much of modern history, queer identities have been criminalized and rejected by society, forcing people to conceal their true selves. Many artists responded by encoding their queerness in subtext or abstraction, embedding hidden meanings in symbols and visual 'codes' that were legible to queers but inconspicuous to the wider public. This covert expression affirmed queer existence under oppression, turning even the decision to conceal or reveal one's identity into an act of self-definition. At the same time, as LGBTQIA+ rights and representations of queer people have improved, many artists have faced the pressure of being defined solely by their queerness – flattening their complexity as individuals.

Queer people, histories and communities have long had their stories shaped by others – whether through media stereotypes, pathologizing medical narratives or societal forces that silence or marginalize them. Self-representation in art serves as a powerful corrective to these external impositions. Since queer identity is inherently self-invented, artworks often function not merely as reflections but as acts of construction. In asserting their visibility on their own terms, queer individuals engage in a deeply political and personal process. Unlike the prescribed 'life scripts' inherited by cisgender and heterosexual individuals, such as the nuclear family and the sort of career trajectory required to support one, queer people often create their own definitions of kinship and selfhood. This process enables a way of living beyond normative structures, charting a path that aligns with Jack Halberstam's concept of 'queer time', departing from a linear model that goes from milestone to milestone – adolescence, marriage, reproduction, retirement – and embracing instead alternative rhythms and spaces, often found in nocturnal worlds such as the nightclub and other non-normative experiences.

Queer aesthetics often turn beauty itself into a site of resistance. Mainstream standards of beauty have long been defined by a colonial, cis, patriarchal and heteronormative framework that favours white, slim, able-bodied, cisgender and heterosexual norms. Any deviation from this ideal is often marked as ugly or deviant. Queer artists have often deliberately highlighted or reinvented forms of beauty that have been marginalized – whether through androgyny, camp or other avant-garde art forms, which make clear the political dimensions of aesthetics.

For many LGBTQIA+ artists, artistic practice becomes a space for self-exploration and empowerment. Self-portraiture, for example, offers a means of articulating identity in one's own terms – shaping how the 'self' is seen, understood and remembered. Rather than allowing identities to be defined by stereotypes or by others, queer artists are able to present themselves and their stories on their own terms.

This chapter explores queer self-representation as multifaceted, contradictory and transformative – a continual reimagining of what it means to be self-defined in a world that seeks to impose rigid categories.

KEY READING

Judith Butler, *Gender Trouble: Feminism and the Subversion of Identity*, New York: Routledge, 1990

Audre Lorde, *Sister Outsider: Essays and Speeches*, Freedom, CA: Crossing Press, 1984

KEY ARTISTS

Ron Athey | Rosa Bonheur | Lola Flash | Martine Gutierrez | Marie Høeg | Roni Horn | Ghada Khunji | Greer Lankton | Ma Liuming | Robert Mapplethorpe | Christina Quarles | Gray Wielebinski

CORNEL BRUDAŞCU
ROMANIA, b.1937

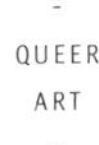

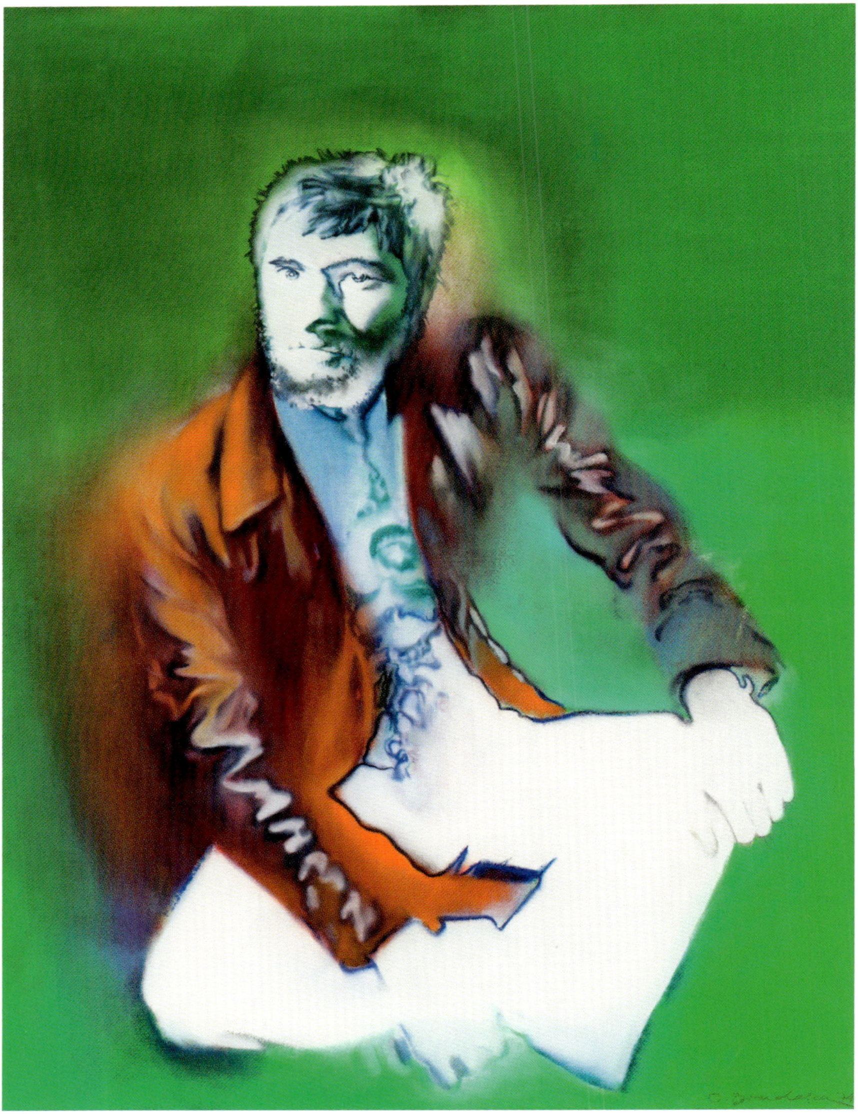

Cornel Brudaşcu
Portrait (Ion Munteanu),
1970
Oil on canvas
120 × 91 cm
(47¼ × 35⅞ in.)
Mircea Pinte
Collection, Cluj

**Portrait (Ion Munteanu)
is dedicated to a friend
and colleague who
took his own life at
a young age. Here,
Brudaşcu pays tribute
to an artist he admired
greatly, capturing his
unconventional character
and freezing him in what
Brudaşcu has called 'an
eternal youth beyond
death'.**

Cornel Brudaşcu is a Romanian painter, celebrated as one of the country's leading artists of the twentieth century. Although he began painting in the 1960s, it was not until after the turn of the century that his work began to receive international recognition. Brudaşcu studied at the Institute of Fine Arts Ion Andreescu in the Transylvanian city of Cluj-Napoca where he still lives and works. He is widely considered to be a forerunner and mentor of the Cluj School, a group of younger painters known for a style of loose figuration that responds to post-communist life.

In 2015 Brudaşcu was included in Tate Modern's exhibition 'The World Goes Pop', which directly aligned him with the Pop Art movement. His large portraits of fellow artists and Western pop icons are painted with bold colours and flat surfaces reminiscent of leading Pop artists such as David Hockney and Andy Warhol. Painting from his own collection of solarized photographs and magazines, Brudaşcu combines photorealist figuration with hazy dreamlike edges, creating his own distinct style of Pop Art, for which he is now well known.

Since the Romanian Revolution in 1989, Brudaşcu's paintings have shifted away from his characteristic Pop Art portraits. Adopting a looser, more expressive style of brushwork, his later paintings often depict male nudes and homoerotic scenes. This shift in his work coincided with him becoming more open about his sexuality, as he began publicly identifying as gay later in life. The gestural paintings from this period possess a frenetic energy, speaking to his own journey towards self-acceptance and openness, having lived for most of his adult life under the dictatorship of the Socialist Republic of Romania.

KEY WORKS

Composition, 1970, Museum of Art, Cluj-Napoca, Romania
Guitarist, 1970, Museum of Visual Arts, Galaţi, Romania

KEY FACTS

Brudaşcu had limited access to international popular culture in communist Romania. However he was able to borrow imported Western magazines from a friend, such as the German *Popcorn*.

Brudaşcu has exhibited alongside his former student and close friend Alin Bozbiciu, a leading young painter from the last wave of the Cluj School, in shows that include portraits they have painted of each other.

CLAUDE CAHUN
FRANCE, 1894–1954

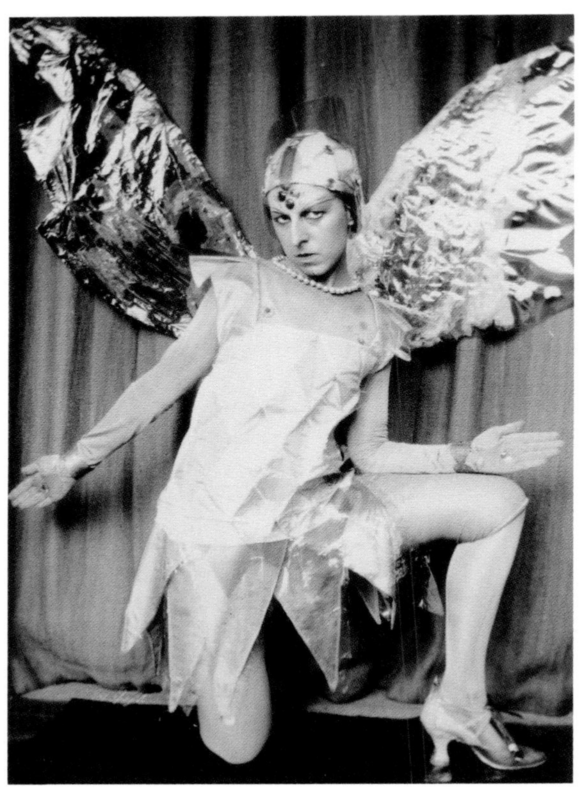

Artist, writer and resistor Claude Cahun challenged societal norms
through groundbreaking photography, sculpture, poetry, essays
and activism. Born in Nantes, France, Cahun's artistic identity
was intertwined with their lifelong romantic and creative partner,
Marcel Moore. Cahun met Moore when they were teenagers, and
the pair became inseparable collaborators, both adopting alliterative
pseudonyms and living their artistic lives together in radical defiance
of convention. Cahun's photographs were taken in private, often
with Marcel behind the camera. They were highly personal, intimate
acts of self-fashioning; not intended for public viewing.

**Claude Cahun and
Marcel Moore**
Untitled (Claude Cahun in
Le Mystère d'Adam), 1929
Gelatin silver print
10 × 7.6 cm (4 × 3 in.)

**Created for a
performance of the
medieval play *Le Mystère
d'Adam*, this staged self-
portrait presents Cahun
costumed in metallic
wings and theatrical
makeup. Cahun merges
futuristic, angelic and
androgynous motifs,
destabilizing ideas of
fixed identities. This
is just one example
of the artist's lifelong
exploration of gender
as masquerade and
resistance.**

Across their body of work, Cahun explored identity as a performative and mutable construct, even describing themself as having multiple 'faces' and many 'masks'. In their photography, they presented themself as variously gendered – sometimes genderless – personas. Doll, bodybuilder, angel, aviator: each photograph blurred the line between artifice and sincerity. To Cahun, selfhood was not fixed or innate, but something to be played with and redefined.

Cahun was also a prolific writer. Their 'anti-memoir', *Aveux non avenus (Disavowals or Cancelled Confessions)* published in 1930, is a hybrid work, presenting photomontages made in collaboration with Moore alongside text. It is an early example of queer experimental autobiography, interlacing surrealist reflections on selfhood, artifice and performance among their personal narratives.

Politically, Cahun's work goes hand in hand with their resistance to fascism following the Nazi invasion of Jersey, where they had settled with Moore to avoid anti-Semitic violence. As a Jewish artist and committed anti-fascist, Cahun helped craft subversive propaganda using German-language poetry, illustration and collage. Together the pair created humorous 'paper bullets' which they clandestinely distributed amongst the occupying soldiers, surreptitiously placing them in their pockets or leaving them crumpled on car seats to be found later. Arrested and sentenced to death in 1940, Cahun and Moore survived to see liberation. Cahun died in 1954 in Jersey and was buried in St Brelade's Church cemetery, where they were joined by Moore twenty years later.

Cahun's work was largely forgotten after the Second World War until it was rediscovered in the late 1980s.

KEY WORKS

I am in Training Don't Kiss Me, 1927
Self Portrait as Elle in Barbe Bleu, 1929

KEY FACTS

Around 1914 Cahun adopted the gender-neutral pseudonym 'Claude', along with their grandmother's surname, although they continued to use their given name in private.

Cahun and Moore were both members of the *Association des Écrivains et Artistes Révolutionnaires* (Association of Revolutionary Writers and Artists) alongside Surrealists such as Man Ray and André Breton.

LEONOR FINI
ARGENTINA, 1907–96

Leonor Fini moved fluidly between artistic and personal identities.
Born in Buenos Aires to an Argentine father and an Italian
mother, she was raised in Italy by her mother, who fled to prevent
her oppressive father from taking custody. Fini's mother began
disguising her as a boy in public to protect her from repeated kidnap
attempts by her father, and she grew up with a strong distrust of
patriarchal authority.

Fini moved to Paris in the 1930s and began moving in Surrealist
circles, and though she exhibited with them, she rejected an official
invitation to join the group due to the misogyny she perceived from
their leader, André Breton. She resisted the movement's ideal of
the passive female muse, declaring: 'I have always refused the male
dictate. I have painted women not as they are seen but as they
see themselves.'

A prolific artist who worked over seven decades, her work is
populated by sphinxes, masked figures and dominant, otherworldly
women – part of what she called her 'theatre of desire'. Fini
frequently painted intimate groupings of female subjects and
women sharing erotic moments, which she described as the
'feminine experience'. Her paintings often blurred the boundaries of
humans, animals and mythic forms, reflecting identity and presence
as fluid and transformative. She was close to figures like Leonora
Carrington and Remedios Varo, who, like her, used surrealism to
explore femininity, sexuality and transformation beyond the male
gaze. She sometimes included men in her paintings, though they
usually appear passive and often androgynous.

Fini was openly bisexual, surrounding herself with lovers of all
genders. She rejected the term 'lesbian', alongside marriage and
monogamy, living for much of her life in a ménage à trois with
two male partners. Her aversion to labels extended to her artistic
identity: she lived entirely on her terms, slipping between roles as
painter, writer, designer and performer.

Leonor Fini
*La Leçon de Botanique
(The Botany Lesson)*, 1974
Oil on canvas
120 × 120 cm
(47¼ × 47¼ in.)
Private collection

**This is a late work that
distills Leonor Fini's
preoccupation with
gender, power and
metamorphosis. The
botanical setting suggests
fertility, natural cycles
and transformation,
echoing earlier works
where androgynous
figures exist in lush,
dreamlike landscapes.**

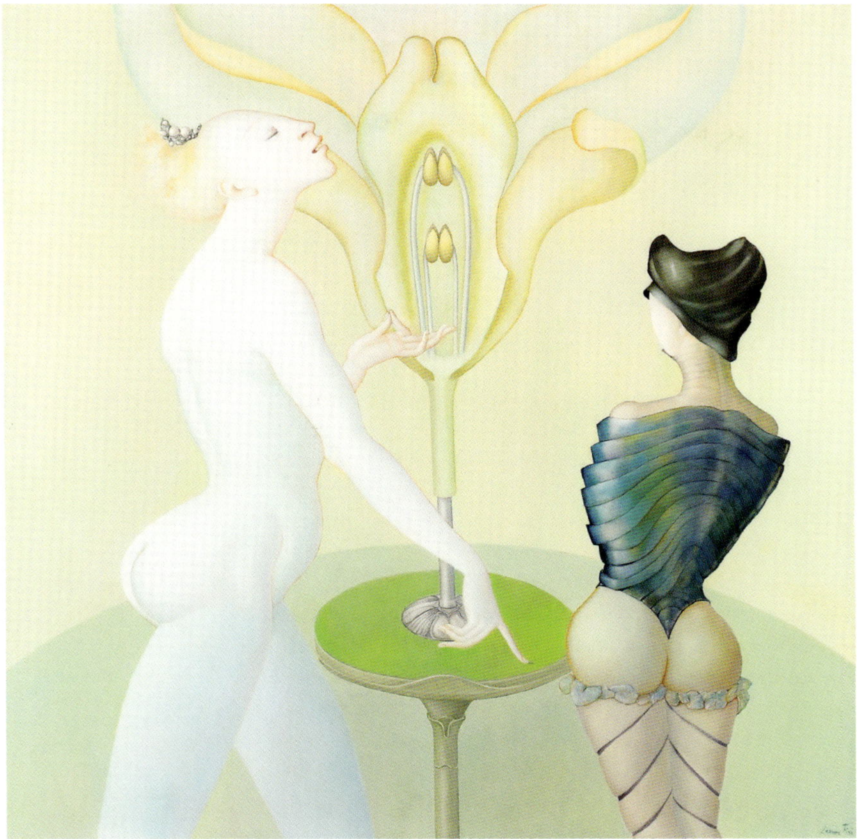

KEY WORKS

Two Women, 1939, Nationalgalerie, Berlin, Germany
Little Guardian Sphinx, 1943–4, Tate, London, UK

KEY FACTS

Later in life, Fini was part of several Surrealist exhibitions,
    including 'Fantastic Art, Dada, Surrealism' (1937) at the
    Museum of Modern Art, New York.
Fini curated an exhibition of Surrealist furniture that opened
    at her friend Leo Castelli's Paris gallery on the eve of the
    Second World War.

GLUCK
UNITED KINGDOM, 1895–1978

Gluck was a painter who rejected the constraints of traditional artistic, societal and gender boundaries. Born into a wealthy Jewish family in London, Gluck pursued artistic training at St John's Wood School of Art.

After art school, Gluck joined the artist colony at Lamorna, Cornwall, where they bought a studio. The small seaside village drew a community of queer artists, including British artists Marlow Moss and Ithell Colquhoun, who lived openly alongside one another. In Lamorna, Gluck began cutting their hair short, wearing sharply tailored suits and smoking a pipe – stylistic choices which would have been understood at the time as radical 'cross-dressing'. Gluck also adopted their singular, genderless name, and began refusing all titles, writing on the back of publicity prints, 'please return in good condition to Gluck, no prefix, suffix or quotes.' They stuck to this adamantly, despite the friction it caused in the art world: when an art society of which Gluck was vice-president used 'Miss Gluck' on their letterhead, they resigned.

Gluck's work, which predominantly consisted of portraits, floral paintings and rural landscapes, was marked by distinctive clarity and depth, created through meticulous layering of paint. Their self-portraits powerfully assert the trailblazing ways in which they presented their gender. In 1932, they designed and patented the 'Gluck Frame', which was three tiers high and coloured to match the architecture of the room – a design that would soon become a staple feature of Modernist and Art Deco interiors, as well as art galleries across the world.

The wealth of Gluck's family, who financed their career, made it possible for them to live a life of relative autonomy that was otherwise unattainable to many queer people of their era. However, their defiance of gender norms and life lived freely have made them an inspirational figure for the LGBTQIA+ community.

Gluck
Medallion (YouWe), 1936
Oil on canvas
30.5 × 35.6 cm
(12 × 14 in.)
Private collection

One of Gluck's most intimate and celebrated works, *Medallion (YouWe)* immortalizes Gluck's relationship with philanthropist, playwright and artist Nesta Obermer. Created to commemorate the couple's exchange of rings in lieu of marriage, the painting captures a moment of shared devotion: the two figures with heads touching in quiet unity. Gluck referred to the piece as the 'YouWe' picture.

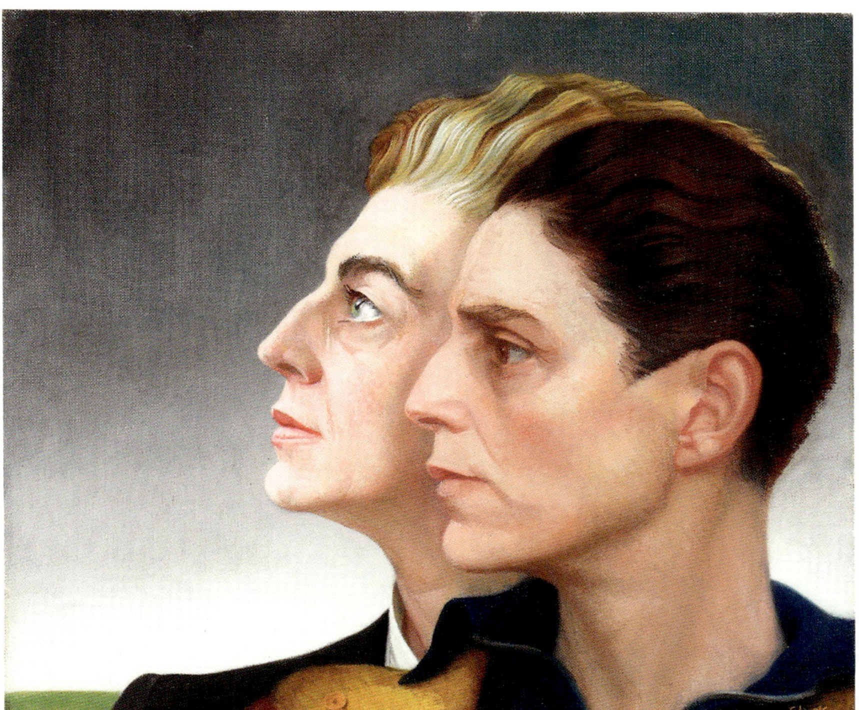

KEY WORKS

Flora's Cloak, 1923, Tate, London, UK
Gluck, 1942, National Portrait Gallery, London, UK

KEY FACTS

In 1923, artist Romaine Brooks painted a portrait of Gluck titled
  Peter (A Young English Girl).
Gluck's painting *Medallion (YouWe)* later became the cover
  image for the paperback *The Well of Loneliness* by Radclyffe
  Hall, a novel that was banned for its open depiction of
  lesbian relationships.

REN HANG
CHINA, 1987–2017

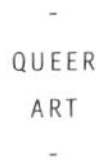

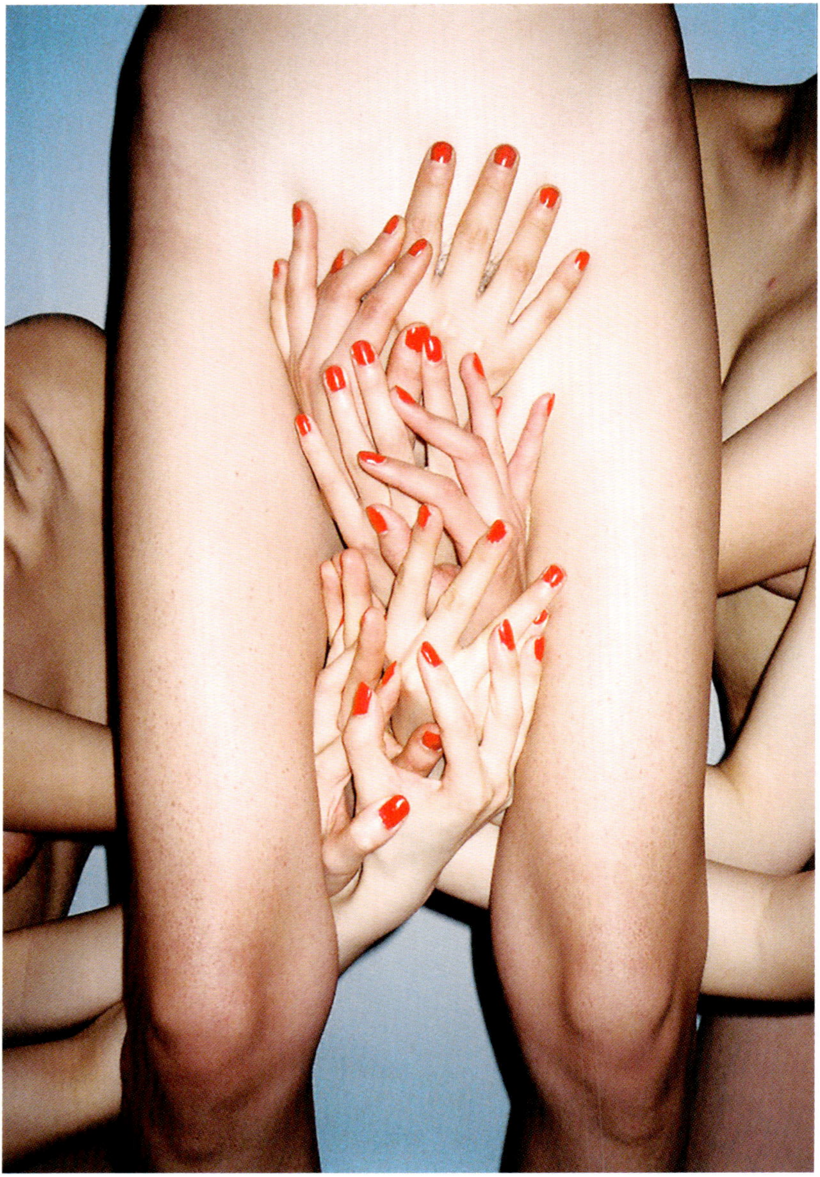

Ren Hang
Untitled, 2015
Chromogenic print

**Hang's images, shot
on a Minolta X-700
– a simple point-and-
shoot film camera
– are recognizable
for their harsh colour
saturation, evoking a
sense of intimacy and
vulnerability in a country
where queer expression
has been censored.**

Ren Hang was a Chinese photographer and poet whose work captured the tension between beauty, eroticism and defiance in an era of increasing state censorship. He shot to stardom in the early 2010s, amassing a cult following.

Born in Changchun, China, he initially studied advertising before turning to photography. His images – stark, surreal compositions of naked bodies – challenged conservative attitudes towards nudity, sexuality and queer desire in China. His approach was playful yet provocative, creating a deeply intimate and radical body of work. Alongside his photography, he wrote poetry that shared the same surreal and deeply personal sensibility.

Hang's distinctive aesthetic was minimalist and high-contrast, often defined by the harsh directness of a single flash. His compositions stripped away shadows, creating an unfiltered sense of immediacy that felt raw, instinctive and sexually provocative. When asked how to describe his work, he said he preferred to call it 'pornographic' rather than 'erotic', and unlike the carefully staged homoeroticism of artists such as the photographer Robert Mapplethorpe, Hang's images retain a spontaneity that feels blunt, visceral and unapologetic. His visual language also resists a hypermasculinity that often dominates queer male representation.

Though he insisted his work was not overtly political, Hang acknowledged that Chinese politics wanted to interfere with his art. His depictions of same-sex intimacy and gender fluidity stood in quiet defiance of a country where LGBTQIA+ rights remain precarious. 'Are we all ashamed of the bodies we own?' he once asked, 'We should be proud of them – or at least recognize them and value them – recognize and value our own existence.'

Hang struggled with depression, which he wrote about intimately in his blog, and, at the age of twenty-nine, he took his own life. His work continues to inspire a new generation of Chinese photographers, such as Lin Zhipeng (aka No.223) and Fish Zhang.

KEY WORKS
Untitled, 2011
Untitled, 2013

KEY FACTS
In 2012 Ai Weiwei named Ren Hang, who was just twenty-four, among China's top four emerging photographers.
Hang was self-taught. He first picked up a camera the day before leaving for university.

K8 HARDY
UNITED STATES, b.1977

Born in Fort Worth, Texas, K8 Hardy is a New York City-based
multidisciplinary artist working with performance, fashion
and photography. Influenced by DIY punk aesthetics, fashion
subcultures and feminist art traditions, K8 Hardy challenges
commercialized notions of femininity and queerness. The *Position
Series* (2007–12), Hardy's most celebrated body of work,
deconstructs the conventions of fashion photography, interrogating
the politics of the gaze. The series consists of self-portraits in
which Hardy – often wearing unexpected outfits, striking an
exaggerated pose – engages with the camera in ways that disrupt
passive consumption. The images have a deliberately unpolished,
lo-fi quality, which rejects the airbrushed perfection of mainstream
fashion photography. Hardy fractures that visual language, using the
formal qualities of editorial photography against itself.

Hardy's process is deeply intuitive and performative, rooted in
improvisation and play. She often sources clothing from thrift stores
or assembles makeshift outfits on the spot, embracing imperfection
and spontaneity. 'I don't think about it as styling,' Hardy has said,
'I think about it as costuming, constructing a persona, shifting
identities.' This fluid approach challenges not only the rigidity of
fashion industry norms but also the broader societal expectations
around gender, identity and self-presentation, emphasizing
transformation over fixed identity.

Beginning in 2007 – the same year the iPhone arrived on the
market – the *Position Series* foreshadows the impact of smartphones
on the ways in which we create and share images. Hardy's tongue-
in-cheek self-portraits serve as a critical reflection on the rise of
social media and dating apps, particularly the effect these platforms
have had on the ways we present ourselves, curate our identities and
perform for digital audiences. As Hardy herself puts it, 'Persona is
a reaction to patriarchy ... Authenticity is slippery.' Hardy's work
exposes and dismantles rigid societal expectations, using fashion as
a medium to subvert imposed identities and assert the freedom to
exist beyond prescribed norms.

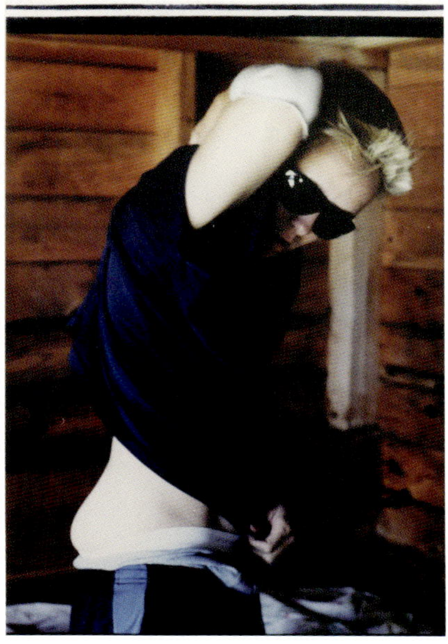 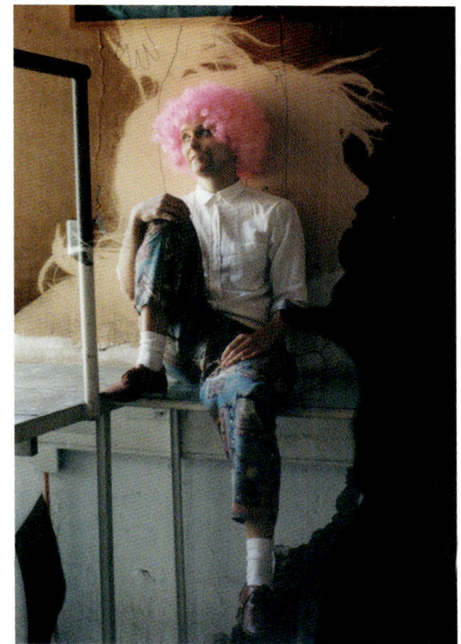

K8 Hardy
Position Series, 2007–12
Chromogenic colour
prints
76.2 × 50.8 cm
(30 × 20 in.)

**Blurring fashion and
performance, Hardy's
portraits present the
artist (or occasionally
her sister) as a rotating
cast of personas – some
playful, some provocative
– all challenging fixed
identity. Drawing on
popular archetypes and
artifice, the images
reflect on the ways we
perform and curate
ourselves for the
camera, questioning
how identities are
constructed, styled
and consumed.**

KEY WORKS

Position Series #20, 2009
Outfitumentary, 2016

KEY FACTS

K8 Hardy is a founding member of the feminist genderqueer
artist collective LTTR (a mutable acronym that has stood
for many different things, from 'Lesbians to the Rescue' to
'Lacan Teaches to Repeat'). During the 2000s, the collective
produced events, screenings, performances and a zine-
inspired journal dedicated to 'highlighting the work of radical
communities whose goals are sustainable change, queer
pleasure and critical feminist productivity'.

In 2012, Hardy's work was included in the Whitney Biennial,
where she presented *Untitled Runway Show*, a live performance
featuring models in improvised outfits made from reworked
thrifted clothing.

HANNAH HÖCH
GERMANY, 1889–1978

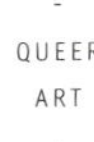

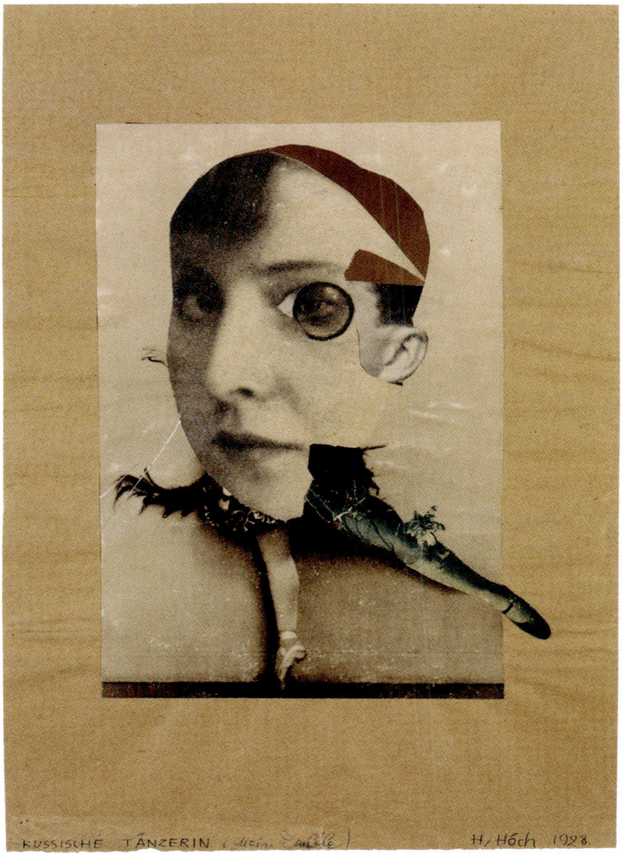

Radical collage artist and feminist Hannah Höch was a defining
(if often lesser-known) figure of Berlin Dada. Born in Gotha,
Germany, she trained at the Berlin School of Applied Arts, where
she studied glass design and graphic arts before turning to collage –
a medium she would revolutionize.

Höch's works were created by splicing images from journals
and magazines, deconstructing and challenging dominant images
of femininity, nationalism, gender roles and power with a wit that

still resonates today. She believed handicrafts were important but overlooked because of their feminine associations, and therefore deliberately embraced them as a means of reclaiming undervalued forms of creative expression.

From 1917, Höch was a vital member of the Berlin Dadaist circle – a group known for their passionate rejection of traditional art forms following the First World War. As the only woman in the Berlin group, she was often sidelined and criticized by the other members, including her then partner Raoul Hausmann, who later refused to acknowledge her part in the movement. Her contributions were at one point described by Hans Richter as simply 'the sandwiches, beer and coffee'.

Höch was unconventional for the time in that she wore masculine clothes and had relationships with both men and women. After leaving Hausmann and the rest of the Berlin Dadaists, she moved to the Netherlands, where she began a nine-year partnership with Dutch writer and linguist Matilda (Til) Brugman. The couple never labelled themselves as 'lesbians', which was a term beginning to be used more widely in the 1920s, but instead referred to their 'private love relationship'. Höch explored the cultural archetype of the *Neue Frau* – the 'new woman', focusing on patriarchal contexts in which this new woman was expected to exist.

Höch pioneered the media of 'photomontage' – the practice of assembling collages from mass-produced materials, printed matter and photographs: a radical turn away from the dominant media of painting or sculpture. Photomontage pushed the boundaries of what was considered 'legitimate' art, inviting questions of value and authorship, while appropriating fragments of popular culture. By incorporating fragmented and coded elements, Höch queers the very act of portraiture, refusing singularity.

Hannah Höch
Russische Tänzerin – Mein Double (Russian Dancer – My Double), 1928
Photomontage
30.5 × 22.3 cm
(12⅛ × 8⅞ in.)
Herzog Anton Ulrich Museum, Brunswick

This self-portrait illustrates Höch's ability to experiment with identity through collage. The composition presents a hybridized figure – part woman, part mechanical construction, wearing a monocle. In the early twentieth century, the monocle was worn by lesbians as a symbol of their sexuality – a trope alluded to by the famed Parisian lesbian bar of the 1920s and 1930s, Le Monocle.

KEY WORKS

Dompteuse, 1930, Kunsthaus Zürich, Switzerland
Der Schöne Po, 1959, private collection

KEY FACTS

Höch's planned 1932 exhibition at Bauhaus Dessau was cancelled as part of the Nazi campaign against 'degenerate art'.
The landmark 1968 exhibition 'Dada, Surrealism and their Heritage' (Museum of Modern Art, New York) acknowledged Höch as a key Dadaist pioneer.

EIKOH HOSOE
JAPAN, 1933–2024

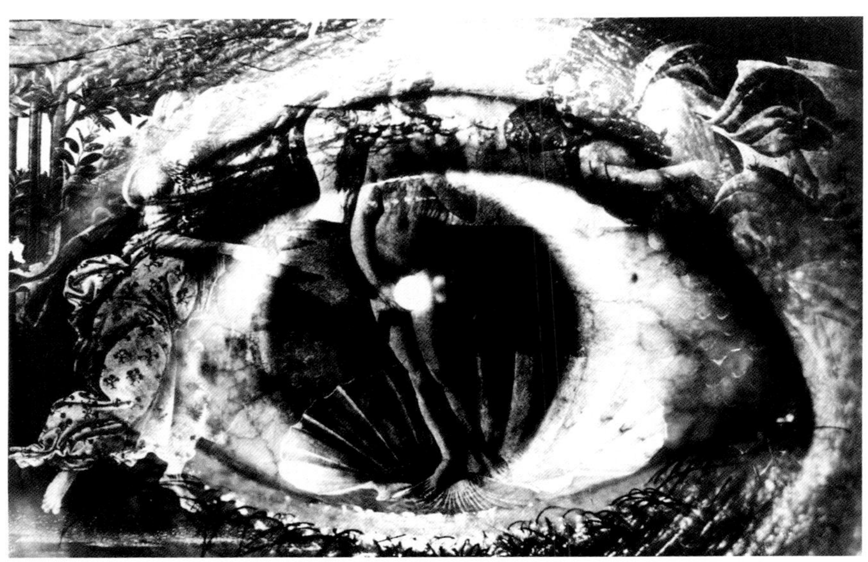

Eikoh Hosoe was one of Japan's most significant photographers, renowned for his surreal, psychologically charged aesthetic that explored the intersections of performance, eroticism and identity. His work engaged with queerness through an encoded visual language, alluding to homosexuality rather than depicting it overtly.

Born in 1933, Hosoe spent his early years in Japan, which was devastated by the Second World War. He later pursued photography, winning the top prize in the student section of the Fuji Film Contest in 1951 while studying at Tokyo College of Photography, before becoming a freelance photographer.

Emerging in the late 1950s, Hosoe was instrumental in pushing Japanese photography beyond tradition, embracing an avant-garde approach. His collaborations with cultural figures – including Tatsumi Hijikata, a pioneer of the radical Japanese dance-theatre form Butoh – cemented his reputation as a provocateur, exploring themes of desire, death and transformation through his lens.

Like so many of his generation, Hosoe's life was irrevocably changed by the bombings of Nagasaki and Hiroshima in 1945 when he was twelve years old, and his work often explored personal and collective histories, usually evoking imprints of memory or loss rather than documenting literal events. In his *Kamaitachi* series (1965–8) for example, named after mythical kamaitachi earth spirits and created in collaboration with Tatsumi Hijikata, Hosoe used myth, dreamlike imagery and performance to explore his childhood evacuation to rural Yonezawa during the war. The works do not recreate exact memories or specific scenes. Rather, they are products of fleeting memory and fabulation – filling in the gaps left by trauma both emotionally and historically; using folklore, performance and poetic reconstructions to explore what remains traumatic and unspeakable in many historical accounts.

His later series, *Embrace* (1971), pushed his work into more tender and intimate territory, featuring stylized pairings of ambiguously gendered bodies. Another 1971 series depicts the doll-maker and performer Simon Yotsuya dressed as a female doll, posing in various locations around Tokyo.

Eikoh Hosoe
Ordeal by Roses #19, 1961
Gelatin silver print

Ordeal by Roses **was a collaboration between Hosoe and the author Yukio Mishima. The series presents a naked Mishima in theatrically staged compositions that allude to the writer's homosexuality, which caused controversy in the United States and Japan. Some images in the series capture Mishima performing erotic fantasies for the camera whilst others, like #19, pay homage to his love of Renaissance paintings.**

KEY WORKS

Man and Woman, 1960
Embrace, 1970

KEY FACTS

In 1960, Hosoe co-founded the Jazzu Eiga Jikken-shitsu (Jazz Film Laboratory) alongside Shuji Terayama, Shintaro Ishihara and others – a multidisciplinary collective producing intense and expressive works.

Beyond his photographic practice, Eikoh Hosoe was an active member of artist collectives and played a vital role in fostering Japan's photographic community. In 1995, he was appointed director of the Kiyosato Museum of Photographic Arts, Hokuto, where he worked to preserve and promote the legacy of Japanese photography.

BHUPEN KHAKHAR
INDIA, 1934–2003

Bhupen Khakhar is celebrated internationally as a central figure within modern Indian art. His brightly coloured paintings depict elaborate scenes that reflect the social and spiritual intricacies of life in his home country.

The Mumbai-born artist moved to Baroda to study art criticism in 1962, which is where he was introduced to the art world. Following his mother's death in 1980, Khakhar started 'coming out' in his painting by incorporating more overt references to same-sex desire. This move in his work followed time spent in England in the late 1970s, where he experienced the gay rights movement and connected with openly queer British Pop artists. The openness with which he dealt with his sexuality in his work during this period made him a pioneer in gay visibility in India, where gay rights activism didn't begin to take shape until the late 1980s.

A typical composition within Khakhar's paintings situates one, two or three large figures in the foreground against a rich landscape filled with details from urban life. In a play with perspective inspired by European painters such as Henri Rousseau and Paul Gauguin, smaller figures occupy architectural structures as they engage in daily tasks and ritual. The dynamic settings reveal shifting concerns within Indian society – details relating to religion, war, politics and industry loom in the background. The larger figures often articulate personal elements from the artist's own life, which he spoke openly about being unable to conceal in his art. One such painting is *Yayati* (1987), in which an elderly male figure engages in an intimate moment with a younger winged male figure.

Khakhar's paintings weave together personal and collective identity, merging queer selfhood with broader themes of Indian society. Frequently described as confessional, his work illuminates private desires and vulnerabilities through vivid, diaristic imagery. Yet Khakhar did not isolate queerness as solely private or marginal. His paintings situate queer experience within the fabric of daily life. In *Two Men in Benares* (1982), an openly homosexual encounter is neither hidden nor separated from the spiritual and social life of the city. Khakhar's work offers a bold reimagining of visibility within an Indian societal context.

Bhupen Khakhar
Yayati, 1987
Oil on canvas
91 × 122 cm
(35⅞ × 48⅛ in.)
Private collection

The story of king Yayati, who exchanged his age with his son after being cursed to become old and impotent, comes from the Indian epic poem the Mahabharata. By referencing the ancient story in a tender expression of same-sex love, based on Khakhar and his partner at the time, the painting subverts the moral framework that pits the pursuit of worldly desires against spiritual fulfillment.

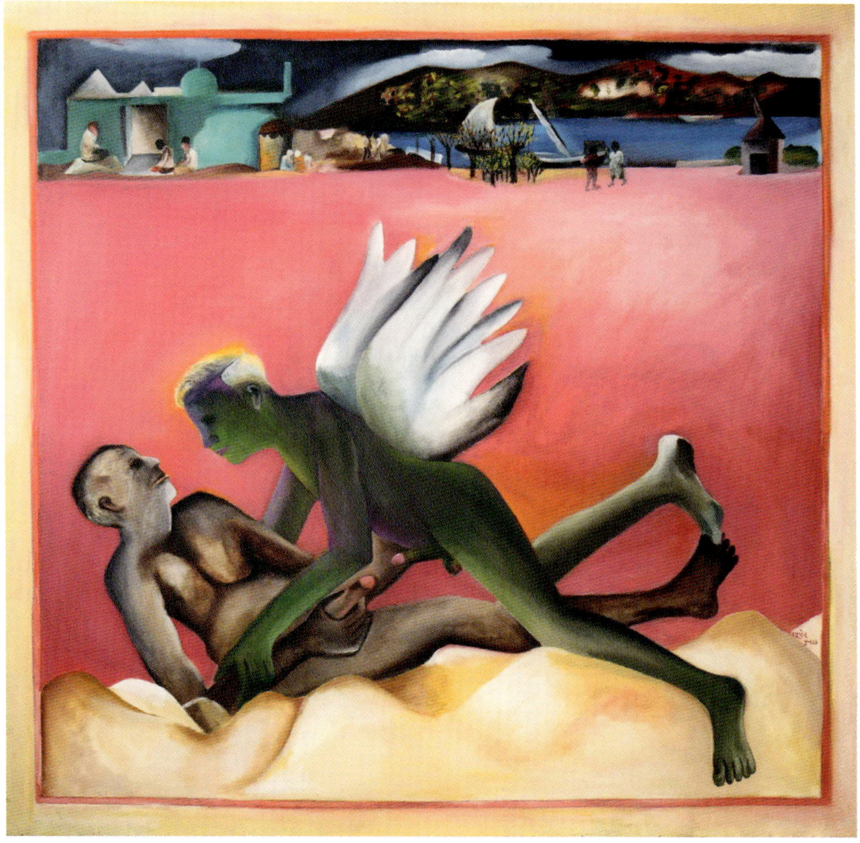

KEY WORKS

You Can't Please All, 1981, Tate, London
Two Men in Benares, 1982, private collection

KEY FACTS

Before achieving fame as an artist, Khakhar was a self-taught
painter who had initially qualified and worked as a chartered
accountant.

Khakhar is associated with a group of artists known as the Baroda
Group, who championed narrative figuration within painting.

LOTTE LASERSTEIN
GERMANY, 1898–1993

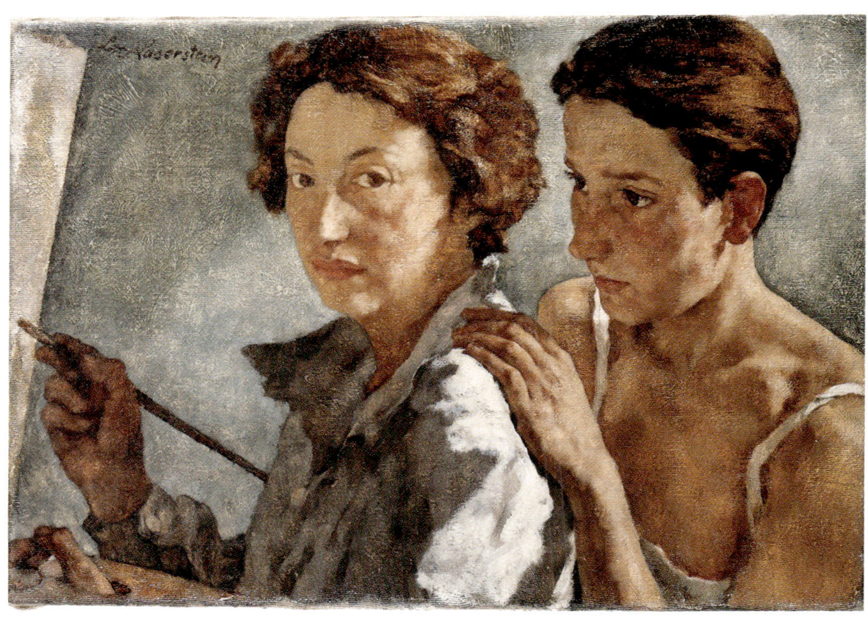

Lotte Laserstein was a trailblazing German-Swedish painter whose intimate portraits captured the complexities of identity in the interwar period. Born in East Prussia, she first studied at a private art school in Berlin run by her aunt, before gaining admission to the prestigious Berlin Academy of Fine Arts as one of the first women to study there. By the late 1920s, she had established herself within the city's progressive art scene. She set up her own studio, funding it through painting lessons, and presented her first solo exhibition in 1930 at Gurlitt's Gallery, Berlin, to critical praise.

Laserstein's career was cut short by the rise of the Nazi regime, which classified her as 'three-quarters Jewish'. This barred her from pursuing professional opportunities and, in 1937, she was forced to abandon her studio. She fled to Sweden, leaving behind much of her early work and artistic momentum. Laserstein would remain in Sweden for the rest of her life, where she garnered widespread respect as a portraitist. Celebrated for her technical mastery

Lotte Laserstein
*Ich und mein Modell
(I and my Model)*,
1929–30
Oil on canvas
49.5 × 69.5 cm
(19½ × 27⅞ in.)
The Bute Collection
at Mount Stuart,
Isle of Bute

Painted in Berlin during the culturally vibrant Weimar Republic, *I and My Model* captures the intimate, layered relationship between Lotte Laserstein and Traute Rose. They are presented together with a quiet intimacy that differs from many conventional artist-muse relationships. Neither figure is reduced to an object, instead suggesting mutual regard and the potential blurring of personal and professional boundaries.

and psychological depth, Laserstein's work is deeply sensitive to her subjects, often exploring scenes of isolated women and leisure activities. Her female subjects are often marked by their androgynous dress – countering prevailing conventions of the time.

Throughout the late 1920s and early 1930s, Laserstein frequently painted her close friend and muse, the athlete, photographer and tennis coach Traute Rose. As an independent, androgynous and socially emancipated woman, Rose embodied the figure of the *Neue Frau* – the 'new woman' of Weimar Berlin.

Laserstein's sexuality remains unconfirmed. However, it is important to recognize the potential for queerness within these works. Art history has long accepted the possibility of heterosexual dynamics between male artists and their female sitters without definitive proof, and same-sex intimacy should be afforded the same imaginative space. The coding of Laserstein's portraits of Rose invites a reading that acknowledges the potential for queer affection, charged with desire – vitally challenging the assumption that historical figures were heterosexual unless explicitly stated otherwise.

Laserstein's work often engaged with her own identity as a woman navigating both the male-dominated art world and a rapidly changing society. There is little surviving documentation from the period to contextualize Laserstein's sexuality, and no known writings in which she addresses it directly. The same-sex intimacy and androgyny in her work subvert heteronormative expectations, speaking to both the possibility and subtlety of coded queer expression.

KEY WORKS

Self Portrait with a Cat, 1928, Leicester Museum and Art Gallery, Leicester, UK

Morning Toilette, 1930, National Museum of Women in the Arts, Washington, DC, USA

KEY FACTS

Laserstein was among the first women to study at the Berlin Academy of Fine Arts, where she won the Academy's gold medal.

Laserstein's legacy was revived when the Neue Nationalgalerie in Berlin acquired *Abend über Potsdam* (Evening over Potsdam) in 2010, reintroducing the public to her work.

AGNES MARTIN
CANADA, 1912–2004

Canadian-born American painter Agnes Martin is known for her subtle, hand-drawn grid works and restrained use of colour. Martin moved to the United States in 1931 and found success in New York, where she was part of the bohemian artist community at Coenties Slip, later described by art historian Jonathan Katz as 'one of America's only largely queer artistic enclaves'.

Her large-scale artworks, ruled with pencil lines and painted with gentle washes, are deeply spiritual. Inspired by Zen Buddhism, Taoism and Christian mysticism, the repetitive, rhythmic nature of her paintings evokes a meditative state and space for contemplation, holding remarkable depth in its simplicity. Martin considered herself an Abstract Expressionist, but her muted tones and highly restricted palette, often limited to a single colour, also align with the aesthetics of Minimalism. In this way, her works could be understood as queer refusal – a rebuttal of narrative, normative subjectivity and spectacle – an articulation of queer selfhood through both atmosphere and absence, distilling emotion into space and line. By being devoid of figuration or obvious narration, they resist the demand for visibility that is often placed on queer artists.

During her life, Martin talked explicitly about her aversion to sex and distaste for romance, leading some queer historians to believe that she was possibly asexual and aromantic, as well as a lesbian. This does not necessarily mean, however, that she never had sex or romantic relationships. Indeed, more recent art-historical accounts suggest that Martin had relationships with several women, including the sculptor Chryssa Vardea and her gallerist Betty Parsons.

In any case, navigating her identity within the rigid heteronormativity of the time is believed to have aggravated her lifelong struggles with schizophrenia and to have contributed to a psychotic breakdown in 1962. In 1967, at the height of her artistic recognition, she abruptly left New York in a pickup truck and fled to New Mexico, where she would not paint again for many years.

Martin resumed painting in 1973, choosing solidarity over conformity and famously declaring that she worked with her 'back to the world'. In New Mexico, she lived simply, surrounded by nature and the quiet companionship of close female friends.

Agnes Martin
Words, 1961
Ink and graphite on paper mounted on canvas
61 × 61 cm
(24 × 24 in.)
Private collection

This work consists of a cruciform grid of triangles set against a plane of trembling horizontal lines. Throughout her career, Martin believed in art's ability to express experience that is 'wordless and silent' – a philosophy reflected in the title of this painting.

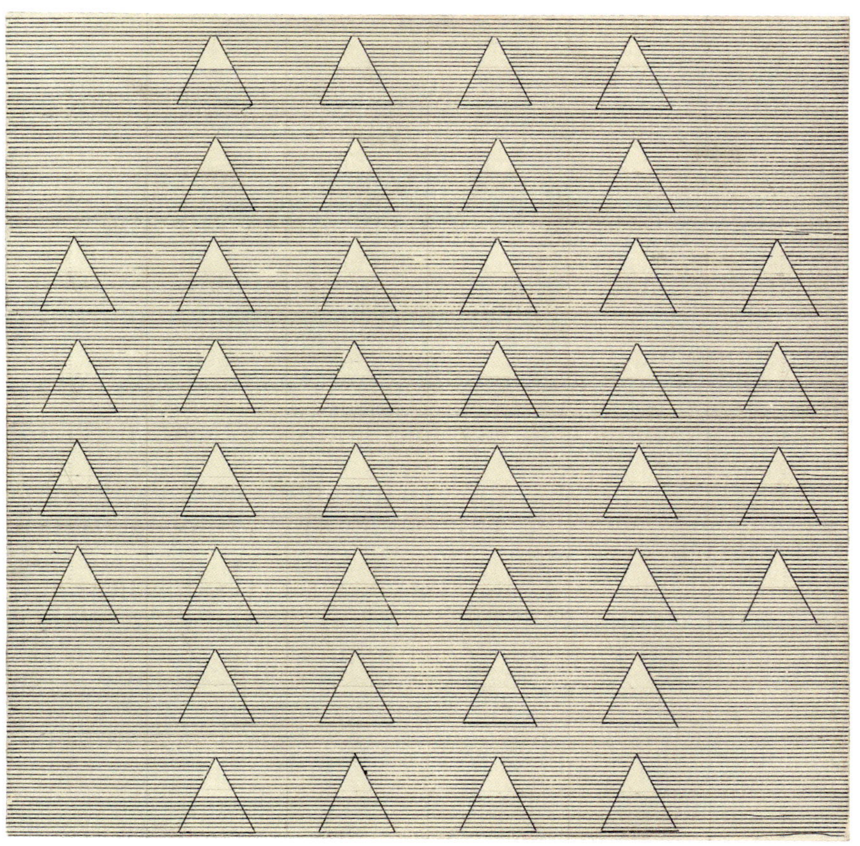

KEY WORKS

Friendship, 1963, Museum of Modern Art, New York, USA
The Islands I–XII, 1979, Whitney Museum of American Art,
  New York, USA

KEY FACTS

Martin considered her work an expression of the inner self,
  stating 'My paintings are not about what is seen. They are
  about what is known forever in the mind.'
In 1998, Martin was awarded the National Medal of Arts by
  President Bill Clinton.

JOSÉ PÉREZ OCAÑA
SPAIN, 1947–83

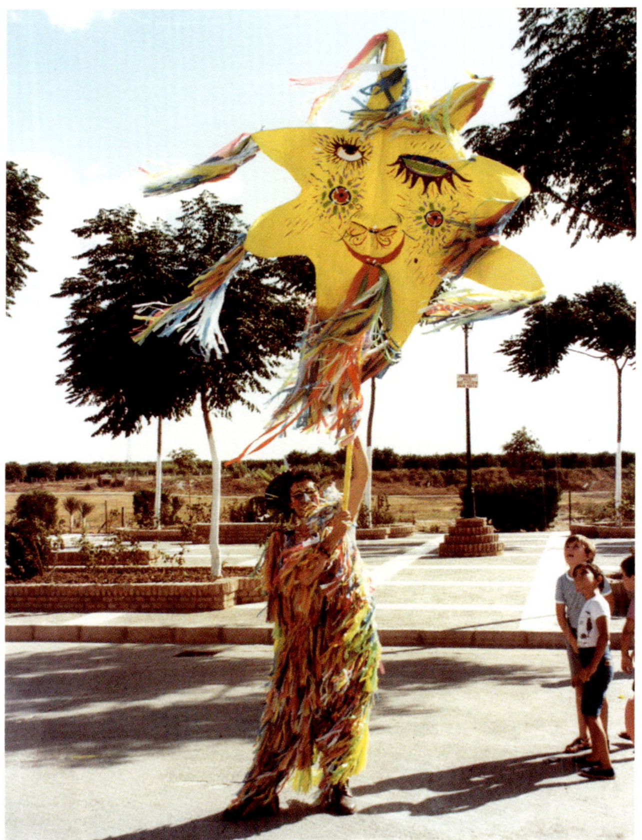

José Pérez Ocaña
Ocaña dressed as the sun in the Plaza de la Alameda, before the start of the children's festival parade during the 11th Youth Week. Photographed by José Manuel González Blanco. Cantillana, 23 August 1983

Tragically, Ocaña died from hepatitis in 1983 following an accident during a public performance in Cantillana, the very town where he had repeatedly faced hostility and homophobia from locals. His final parade was characteristically flamboyant, with Ocaña dressed spectacularly as the sun, adorned with strips of colourful tissue paper and tassels.

José Pérez Ocaña – commonly known as Ocaña – was a Spanish drag queen, artist, actor and activist. His vibrant presence became symbolic of queer visibility and political defiance during the Francoist dictatorship and transitional regime that followed, making him an iconic figure in Spain's 1970s countercultural movement.

Born in Cantillana, Spain, Ocaña lived openly as a gay man in a climate of intense social conservatism. In 1971, he moved to Barcelona, quickly establishing himself as a provocative and bold presence on Las Ramblas – a series of pedestrian boulevards known for street performers and market stalls). Here, Ocaña was

celebrated for his drag performances, in which he walked
Las Ramblas in handmade costumes, actively engaging passers-by
through direct interaction as part protest, part performance.

Inspired by folk art, religion and communal pageantry, Ocaña's
performances frequently involved camping and queering traditional
Holy Week parades in spontaneous 'happenings'. Instead of religious
statues, he carried papier-mâché angels and other figures, leading
sensational processions through Barcelona with a carnivalesque
spirit. Alongside his performances, Ocaña maintained a prolific
studio practice that included elements of painting, sculpture and
photography. His paintings – which were frequently executed on
found materials – depict saints, martyrs and androgynous figures
in a bright, naive style whilst his sculptures reimagine sacred forms
in a playful yet subversive way, contributing to his broader project
of queering traditional Spanish cultural symbols.

Perhaps best known for his disruptive and scandalous actions,
Ocaña provocatively appeared at significant cultural events. Notable
among these were the International Anarchist Days at Parc Güell
in 1977 – where his explicit performances, including nudity and
fellatio, caused outrage – and his spontaneous striptease at the
Canet Rock music festival the same year.

Despite his influential role within queer and artistic communities,
the sensationalism surrounding his life has often overshadowed
his work as an artist, with recognition beyond his performance art
beginning to emerge only recently. Ocaña described how he was
often asked if he was a transvestite, to which he would respond:
'I am not a transvestite, I am a theatre and my stage is the Rambla.'

KEY WORKS

Sin título (La vieja) (Untitled [The Old Woman]), 1974,
Museo Nacional Centro de Arte Reina Sofía, Madrid, Spain
Untitled (The One), 1975, Museo Nacional Centro de Arte Reina
Sofía, Madrid, Spain

KEY FACTS

Ocaña participated in Spain's first Gay Pride parade in 1977,
where he was disparaged by gay activists uncomfortable with
his gender nonconformity.
In 1979, Ocaña performed *Der Engel, der in der Qual singt* (The
Angel Who Sings in Agony) in Berlin. The performance featured
Ocaña speaking with a cardboard cutout of Marilyn Monroe.

(Overleaf)
José Pérez Ocaña
Mi velatorio o
Premonición (My Wake
or Premonition), 1982
Oil on canvas
190 × 300 cm
(74⅞ × 118⅛ in.)
Centro de Interpretación
de la Obra de Ocaña,
Cantillana, Sevilla

Ocaña's paintings are as
exuberant and dynamic
as his performances. *Mi*
velatorio o Premonición
is one of his best-known
works, partly because
of its large scale. The
painting stages the
artist's own death at
a wake with Ocaña
depicted in attire
reminiscent of an altar
boy, surrounded by
friends and lovers.

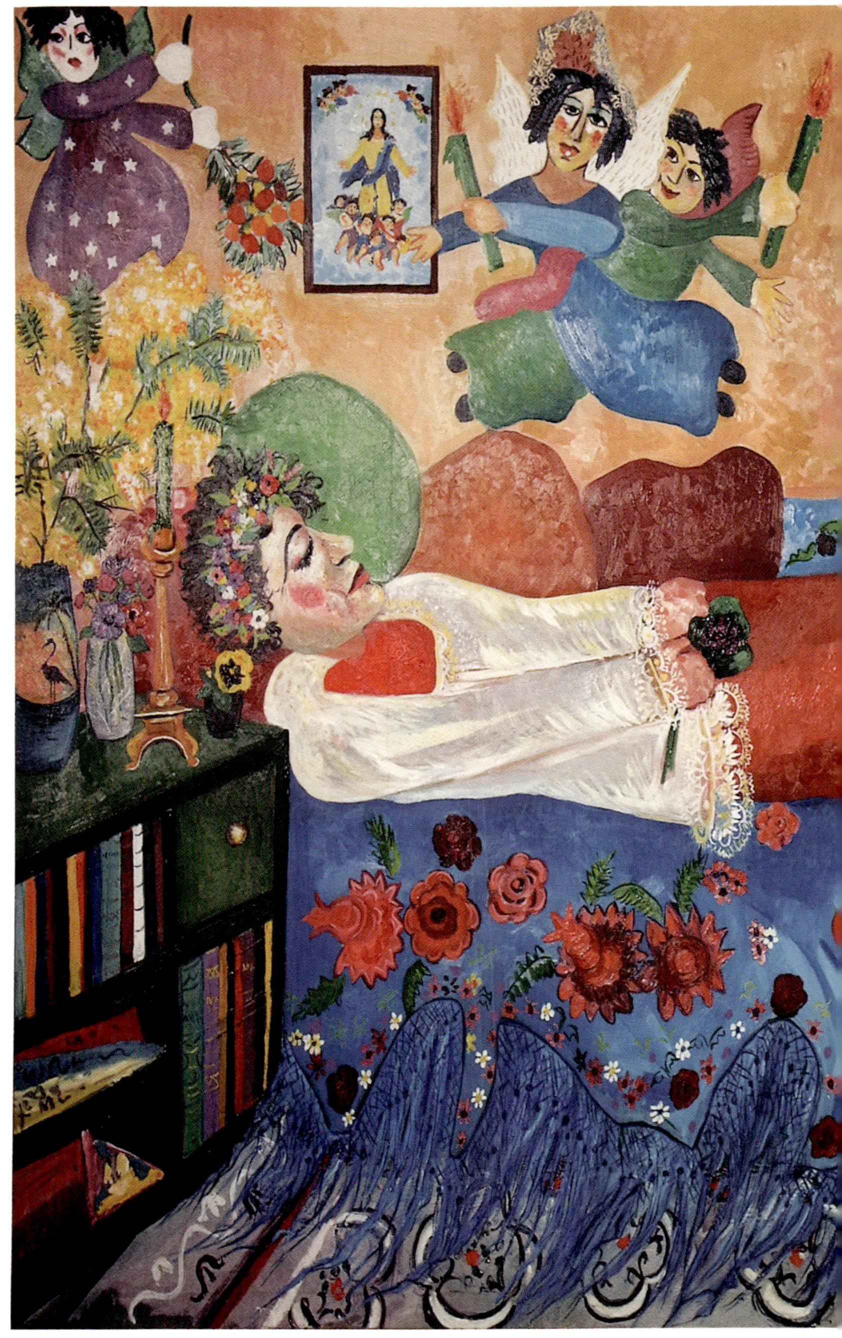

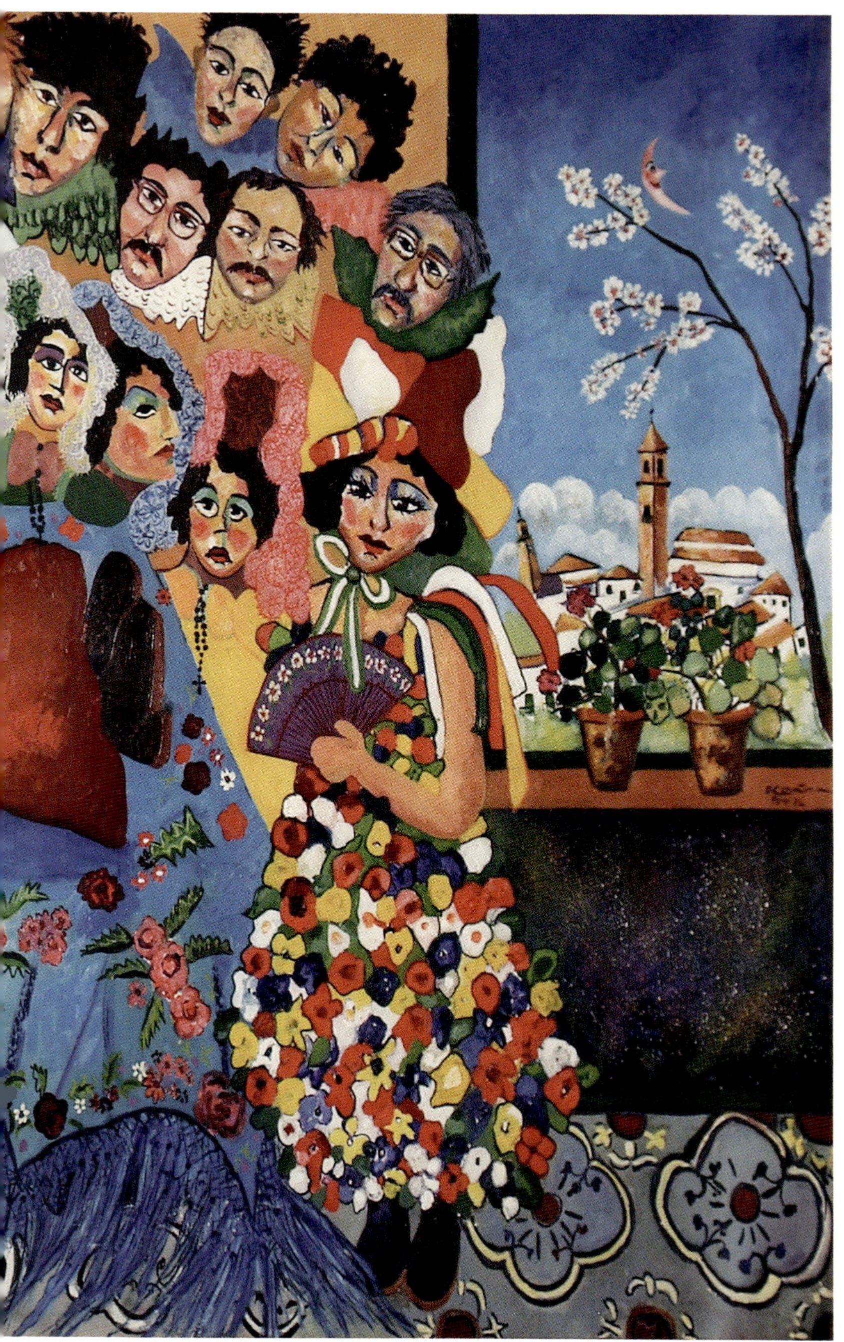

CATHERINE OPIE
UNITED STATES, b.1961

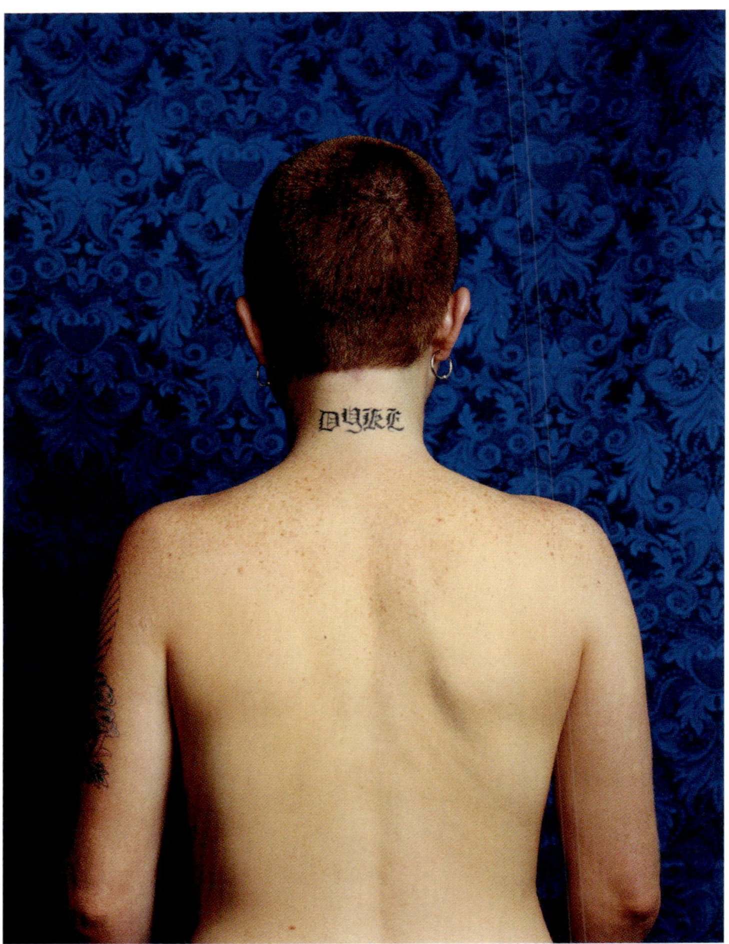

Catherine Opie is an American photographer known for her portraits and landscapes that explore queer community and subcultures in relation to mainstream narratives of American identity. Her work foregrounds the reality of lived experience for the queer community she is a part of, as well as other under-represented identities. She is best known for her images of the leather dyke scene in San Francisco, which emerged in the 1990s.

Catherine Opie
Dyke, 1993
Chromogenic print
101.6 × 76.2 cm
(40 × 30 in.)

In *Dyke*, as in her self-portraits, Opie utilizes a rich fabric background which speaks directly to the sixteenth-century paintings of Hans Holbein. Whereas Holbein used artefacts in his portraits to describe what his royal subjects did, Opie points out that here, 'the artifact is … not within the things surrounding the portrait,' it's on the body: 'Dyke is the subject. *Dyke* is the title.'

In her *Portraits* series (1993–7), Opie photographed friends from the queer scene against block-colour backgrounds. Through formal poses and lighting, she imbues the studio portraits with the qualities of historical painting and early twentieth-century documentary photography. The staged nature of these works speaks to the concept of identity-as-performance, yet there is still a strong air of sincerity surrounding each subject – suggesting that performance and authenticity are not opposites. Since the 1990s, Opie has become a much-celebrated figure within the global LGBTQIA+ community.

Working in clearly defined series, Opie devotes several years to each body of work. Whether black-and-white images of empty freeways or mini-malls, domestic scenes occupied by herself and her lesbian friends or portraits of young surfers, each series presents a deep and thoughtful observation that merges the documentary with the personal. Whatever Opie's subject, there is always a political subtext to the work, which often concerns the intrinsic link between identity and space, examining the ways these are shaped by socio-political context. Her work is deeply rooted in American culture, critically exploring various manifestations and interpretations of national identity, community and belonging, resulting in an expansive view of what it means to live in America.

KEY WORKS

Self Portrait/Cutting, 1993
Self Portrait/Nursing, 2004

KEY FACTS

Opie's work featured heavily in the 2000s US television drama *The L Word*, including in the opening credits and several fictional exhibitions – she even made a guest appearance as herself. The show played a key role in the development of contemporary lesbian culture, especially in America, and Opie's inclusion solidified her as an icon within the culture.

In 2022, Opie photographed trans actor Elliot Page for the front cover of his memoir *Pageboy*. The red background and Page's seated position atop a high stool reference a 1993 portrait of Opie's friend and long-time subject, Pig Pen.

ERICA RUTHERFORD
UNITED KINGDOM, 1923–2008

Erica Rutherford was a painter, printmaker and writer. Her work explored identity as a process of becoming, as an inward-facing longing for a self that is still emerging. Rutherford's paintings speak powerfully to experiences of potential and future identities, capturing a tension against outward societal expectations. The Edinburgh-born artist studied in London and went on to settle in Prince Edward Island, Canada, where she became an influential art educator within a close-knit community.

The art that Rutherford produced during the late 1960s and early 1970s reflects key developments in her gender identity journey. By the late 1960s, then living in Canada and in her forties, Rutherford began drawing confidence from resources like pamphlets exploring transsexualism produced by the Erickson Educational Foundation and started experimenting with femininity in her clothing as well as considering gender-affirming surgery.

Discovering that women's fashion accommodated a range of body types, Rutherford found garments she could wear with ease – opting for more unisex styles in daily life and dressing in women's clothing at home. In her faceless self-portraits from this period, such as *The Green Chair* (1974), she depicted herself in the outfits she preferred. These works of Pop Art are private visions of the woman she hoped to become in public, capturing queer identity as something self-fashioned and creatively imagined. By painting herself in these clothes, Rutherford explored and affirmed her emerging self, presenting queerness as an uncharted space of possibility and becoming.

Painted from photographs she took of herself, the series of paintings captures the internal conflict her new wardrobe presented – moving between fascination, secrecy, unease and satisfaction. In her 1993 autobiography, *Nine Lives*, she wrote, 'To other people, my art emanates serene confidence and affirmation of the positive joys of life, but I arrived at it from tortured doubts, and regard the results as imperfect sketches. Still, these imperfect sketches have provided me with a justification for a life that, fraught as it was with entanglements and frustrations, would have otherwise reduced me to despair.'

Erica Rutherford
Red Stockings, 1970
Gouache on paper
70.7 × 58.4 cm
(27⅞ × 23 in.)
National Portrait Gallery,
London

Red Stockings is a faceless self-portrait, in which the artist reclines on a bed boldly revealing bright red stockings worn with black shiny boots, mini skirt and a flowing shawl, capturing a moment of private experimentation with gender expression that is likely familiar to many trans people.

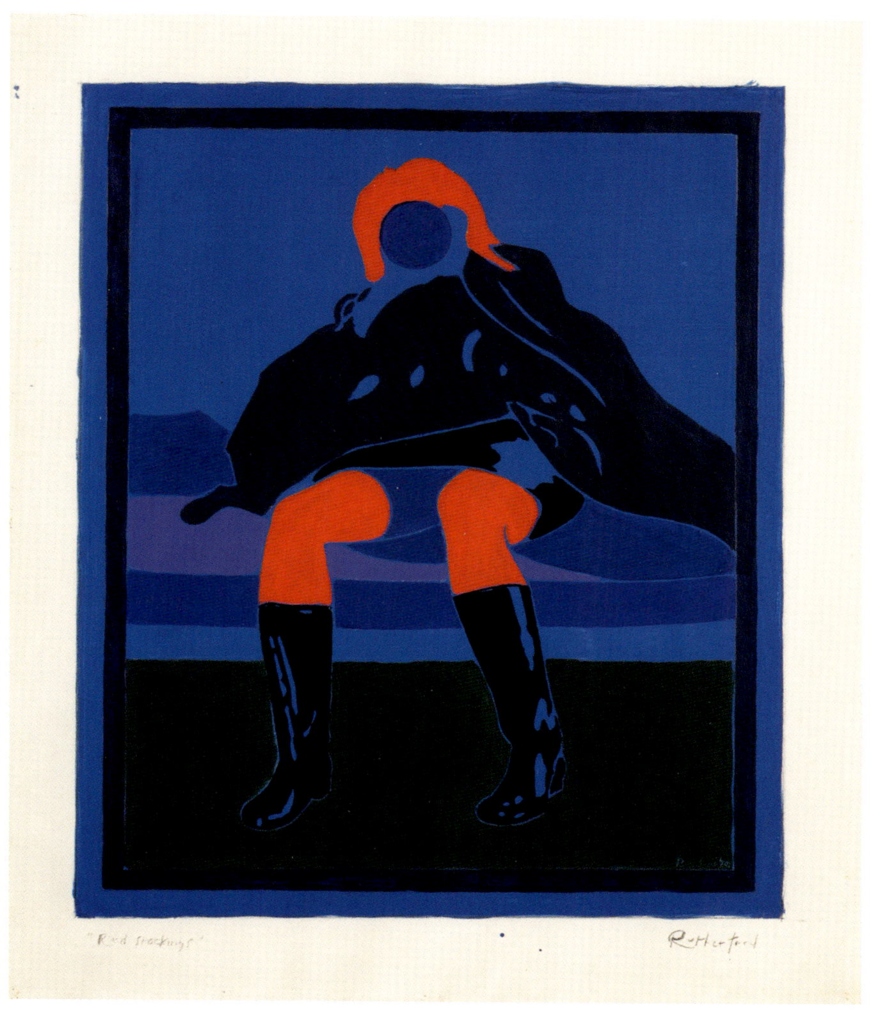

KEY WORKS

The Coat (The Mirror), 1970, National Gallery of Ottawa, Canada
The Bed, 1973, Tate, London, UK

KEY FACTS

Rutherford became the first artist from Prince Edward Island
 to have work featured at the Venice Biennale, in 2024.
She is recognized as one of the first openly transgender artists
 in Britain.

ANDY WARHOL
UNITED STATES, 1928–87

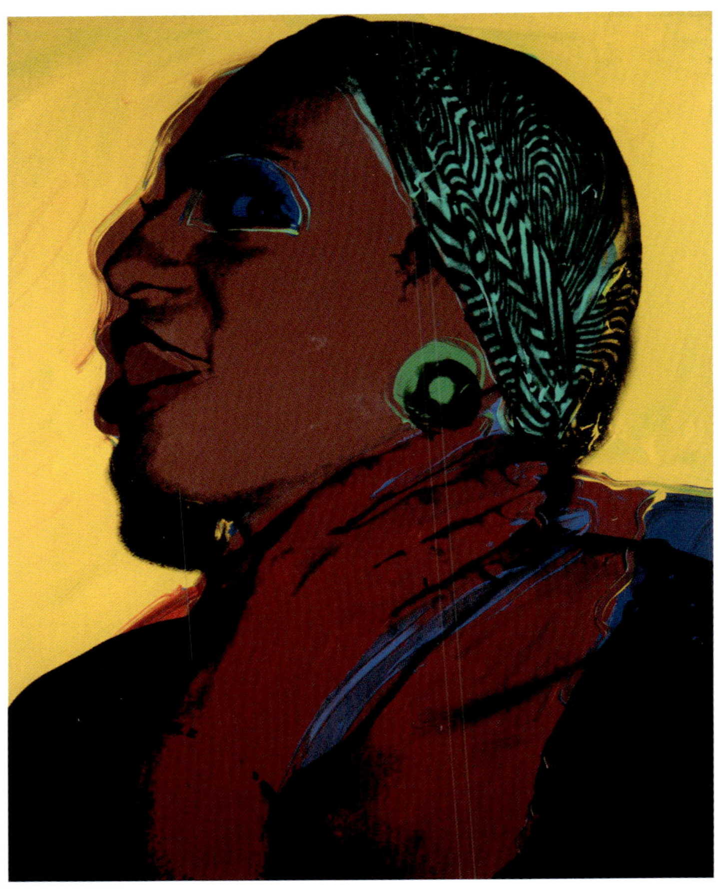

Andy Warhol was a leading figure in the Pop Art movement, known for his mass-produced, celebrity-driven imagery. Born Andrew Warhola to a Slovakian working-class family in Pittsburgh, Warhol's work engaged with themes of performance and the fluidity of identity – concerns central to his personal life and creative circles – and featured many queer subjects. As an openly gay artist working in post-war America, Warhol navigated a world where homosexuality was still criminalized.

Warhol's series *Ladies and Gentlemen* features over 250 portraits of Black and Latinx drag queens and trans women from New York's ballroom and nightlife scenes. Rather than the household names featured in Warhol's earlier portraits, these were unknown figures who tended to be marginalized within society. One of the central figures in the series is Wilhelmina Ross, a performer at the Gilded Grape, a popular gay nightclub in 1970s New York.

Warhol studied commercial art at Carnegie Mellon University (then the Carnegie Institute of Technology) before moving to New York in 1949. By the 1960s, Warhol had become a central figure in the avant-garde scene and founded The Factory, his now-iconic studio space that became a hub for artists, musicians, drag queens and underground celebrities.

Throughout the 1950s, he was a hugely successful illustrator, winning multiple awards and working with clients such as *The New York Times*. Warhol's most notable artistic medium was silkscreen printing – a commercial process he began using in 1962 to create mass-produced images. The 1960s saw his exploration of portraits of celebrities, such as Elizabeth Taylor, Elvis Presley and Marilyn Monroe. In the 1980s, he collaborated with younger artists such as Keith Haring (pages 156–57) and Jean-Michel Basquiat, with whom he produced more than 150 collaborative canvases.

Warhol's engagement with queer identity ran throughout his practice – from his early male erotic drawings to films such as *Flesh* (1968) and *Women in Revolt* (1971), which cast trans women like Candy Darling and Holly Woodlawn, as well as the more gender-fluid drag artist Jackie Curtis. He embraced artifice, repetition and celebrity as queer strategies that foregrounded, rather than concealed, meaning. Warhol's subversion of gender norms and mainstream aesthetics continues to shape contemporary art. He is now considered one of the most influential artists of the twentieth century – an icon whose work challenged the boundaries of identity, fame and representation with a distinctly queer sensibility.

KEY WORKS

Flesh, 1968

Small Acetate (Self-Portrait in Drag), 1980, Andy Warhol Foundation for the Visual Arts, New York, USA

KEY FACTS

Warhol's first international retrospective, held at Stockholm's Moderna Museet in early 1968, gained notoriety for the exhibition brochure's statement: 'In the future everybody will be world-famous for fifteen minutes.' This phrase, widely attributed to Warhol, made its debut in this show.

The Andy Warhol Museum opened in Warhol's hometown of Pittsburgh on 13 May 1994.

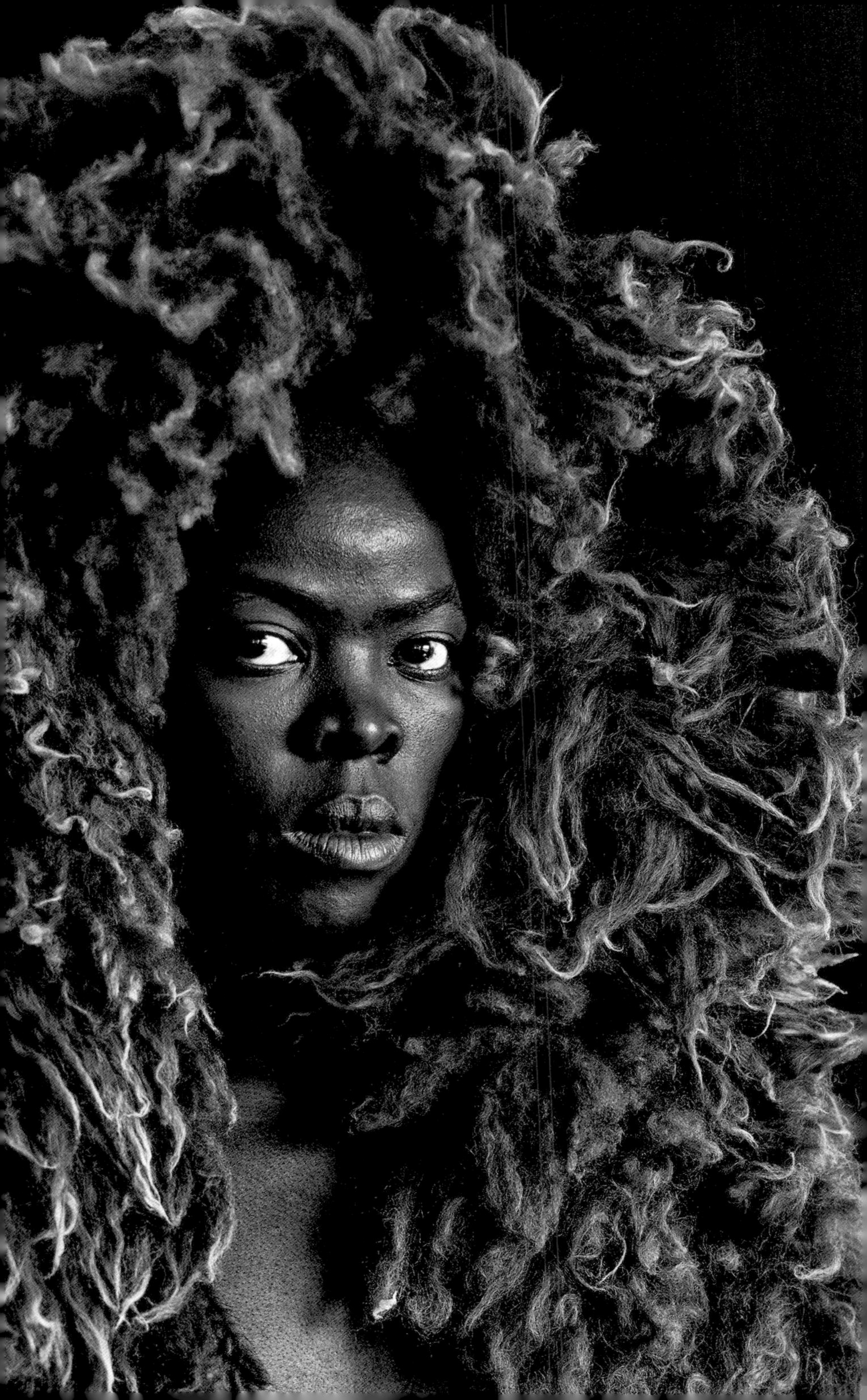

RESILIENT
HISTORIES

For many LGBTQIA+ artists, creating art
is a form of historical activism

Queer histories are, by necessity, narratives of resilience – stories shaped by survival but also by creativity and defiance. Dominant cultural institutions have long silenced queer voices, sometimes erasing their histories altogether. In response, many LGBTQIA+ artists have become activist historians, engaging with hidden or erased histories.

This erasure is not a passive oversight, but a tool used to delegitimize historic and contemporary queer identities. By suggesting the absence of a queer past, these narratives imply that queerness has no rightful place in the present. As a result, queer artists have often sought to preserve letters, photographs and other archival materials. Others go further, constructing new narratives and filling the gaps in history left by censorship and criminalization. For generations, queer communities have thrived underground – in private salons, secret bars and through coded letters. An absence in traditional archives does not signify the non-existence of queer people; it reflects the prejudice and secrecy that pushed these lives out of public view.

In reclaiming these narratives, queer artists have worked to construct archives, repurposing oppressive imagery and embedding personal, cultural and political narratives within their work. This act can be understood as a form of *disidentification* – a survival strategy written about at length by the theorist José Esteban Muñoz, who explored the ways in which queer individuals engage with culture in layered ways, rethinking and re-encoding the dominant meaning of cultural texts or objects in a way that 'both exposes the encoded message's universalizing and exclusionary machinations and recircuits its workings to account for, include, and empower minority identities and identifications'. As French philosopher Michel Foucault argued, the control of historical narratives is a form of power itself. What is recorded and remembered is deeply political, and never neutral.

Art becomes a way to challenge that power. Many have turned to fiction, fragments and speculation to bridge what the archive omits – piecing together letters, photographs and oral histories to fill in gaps. Scholar Saidiya Hartman calls this 'critical fabulation' – giving new life to voices silenced by the record. Traditional methods of historical recording are often not equipped to capture lives that appear only as fragments, misrepresentations or absences. In re-imagining these stories, queer artists practise a form of radical imagination, envisioning a past (and, by extension, a future) in which queer lives are visible, valued and connected across time.

Creating these archives and representations of historical queer figures – real and imagined – can be an act of mourning as much as preservation. When official records are silent due to neglect, systemic erasure under patriarchal or colonial regimes; or in cases where so many lives have been lost that community knowledge has been prevented from being passed from one generation to the next, artists and historians fill in the gap. These acts generate a shared knowledge of existence, which also serves to acknowledge the loss the community has suffered.

Through resistance, reinvention and radical imagination, queer artists have ensured that their histories are not only remembered – but impossible to ignore.

KEY READING

Michel Foucault, *The History of Sexuality, Volume One: The Will to Knowledge*, London: Penguin Classics, 2020

Saidiya Hartman, 'Venus in Two Acts', Durham, NC: *Small Axe*, 1 June 2008, 12 (2), 1–14

José Esteban Muñoz, *Disidentifications: Queers of Color and the Performance of Politics*, Minneapolis: University of Minnesota Press, 1999

KEY ARTISTS

Jess T. Dugan | Tom of Finland | Hilary Harkness | Derek Jarman | Glenn Ligon | Kent Monkman | Kawira Mwirichia | Hannah Quinlan and Rosie Hastings | Athi-Patra Ruga | Ebun Sodipo | Maud Sulter| Wu Tsang

LEILAH BABIRYE
UGANDA, b.1985

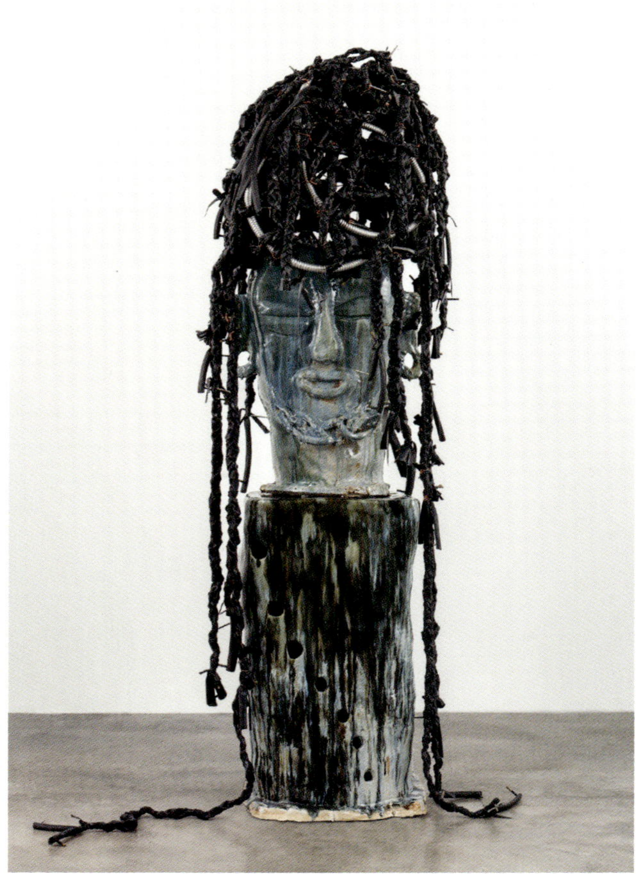

Leilah Babirye is a multidisciplinary artist whose practice reclaims queerness through sculpture, drawing and assemblage. Working with found and discarded materials, Babirye transforms everyday objects – such as bike chains, scrap metal and tyres – into powerful representations of queer strength, beauty and resilience. Her work reimagines queer kinship by creating alternative ancestral lineages rooted in Uganda's cultural traditions.

Leilah Babirye
*Namasole Wannyana,
Mother of King Kimera
from the Kuchu Royal
Family of Buganda*, 2021
Ceramic, wire, metal
electrical conduit, bicycle
tyre inner tubes and
found objects. Overall
dimensions (in two parts):
273 × 84 × 84 cm
(107½ × 33⅛ × 33⅛ in.)
Stephen Friedman
Gallery, London and
New York

**'Kuchu' is Ugandan slang
for a gay person. Sculpted
from discarded materials
such as metal scraps,
bicycle chains and burned
wood, Babirye's regal
sculpture – here named
after a Buganda princess
– helps form part of
Babirye's imagined
Kuchu lineage.**

Born and raised in Kampala, Babirye left Uganda in 2015
after being publicly outed in a local newspaper, amid a rise in
violent anti-LGBTQIA+ sentiment and legislation. She sought
asylum in New York City, where she continues to live and work.
Her sculptures – often monumental in scale – are deeply informed
by the structure of the clan system of the Buganda Kingdom, which
traditionally recognizes lineage through totems associated with
particular kin groupings. Babirye uses this framework to construct
queer ancestral figures, positioning LGBTQIA+ people as rightful
inheritors and creators of a powerful cultural legacy.

Her figures often take the form of stylized heads and masks,
echoing the visual language of traditional African sculpture
while inserting contemporary queer identities into its canon.
These sculptures honour ancestors – real or imagined – whose
queerness was erased or denied. In doing so, Babirye builds a
symbolic archive of queer presence, community and survival.

The artist's use of discarded materials is also a pointed cultural
reference. In Luganda, the word *abasiyazi* – a derogatory term for
gay people – derives from sugarcane waste, something seen as
valueless and thrown away. By transforming salvaged objects into
regal, dignified forms, Babirye challenges the logic of disposability
and reclaims what society deems worthless. Her practice becomes
an act of resistance: a declaration that queer lives are not only
valuable but central to our collective history.

As Uganda continues to pass laws that endanger queer citizens
– including the 2023 Anti-Homosexuality Act – Babirye's work
stands as both testimony and protest. Her sculptures give form to
chosen families, to exiled ancestors and to futures where queerness
is visible, venerated and free.

KEY WORKS

Kinsambwe from the Kuchu Lungfish Clan, 2022, Whitney Museum
of American Art, New York, USA
Nakimbugwe from the Kuchu Royal Family of Buganda, 2024,
de Young Museum, San Francisco, USA

KEY FACTS

Inspired early in her art education by Henry Moore's skeletal
forms, Babirye began collecting and drawing animal bones.
Babirye learned woodwork from street artisans rather than at
school and, like them, works without preparatory sketches.

JOAN E. BIREN (JEB)
UNITED STATES, b.1944

Joan E. Biren, widely known as JEB, is a pioneering American feminist photographer, filmmaker and activist. JEB's work has provided an unparalleled visual record of lesbian lives and histories. Her journey as an artist began in 1971 with a borrowed camera and a personal photograph – a self-portrait kissing her lover, Sharon Devey, which she made in response to never having seen an image of a lesbian kiss. Starting at a time when lesbian representation was scarce, she made it her mission to document the lives of LGBTQIA+ individuals. She stated, 'Wherever lesbians gathered, where I could take pictures, I would be there.'

JEB's work is deeply rooted in activism. In the early 1970s, she co-founded the Furies Collective, a radical lesbian feminist separatist group based in Washington, DC. The collective sought to dismantle patriarchal structures and build a self-sufficient community of women, publishing *The Furies*, a newspaper that examined politics, sexuality and feminist theory.

In 1979, she self-published *Eye to Eye: Portraits of Lesbians*. The groundbreaking collection of black-and-white portraits depicts lesbians in their homes, workplaces and communities. She spent months travelling across America to find women willing to appear in her book, each subject risking losing their children, families, jobs or homes by coming out as lesbian. JEB's next book, *Making a Way: Lesbians Out Front* (1987), presented scenes from everyday lesbian life accompanied by brief descriptions of each woman. The book features over one hundred lesbians, from poets and filmmakers, to politicians and physicians, each 'making ways to live and love as they choose'.

JEB's commitment to representation extends beyond her photography. From 1979 to 1985, she developed and toured *Lesbian Images in Photography: 1850–the Present*, fondly known as the 'Dyke Show'. This grassroots, ever-evolving slide presentation explored historical photographs by figures such as Berenice Abbott and Alice Austen (pages 108–9) alongside contemporary work by herself and peers like Tee Corinne (pages 110–11) and Cathy Cade.

JEB (Joan E. Biren)
Priscilla and Regina, Brooklyn, New York, 1979
Silver gelatin print

JEB took this photograph in 1979 to include in her book *Eye to Eye: Portraits of Lesbians*. The image is particularly significant because it offers an affirming portrayal of Black lesbian intimacy, representations of which were almost entirely absent from art, the media and public discourse at the time.

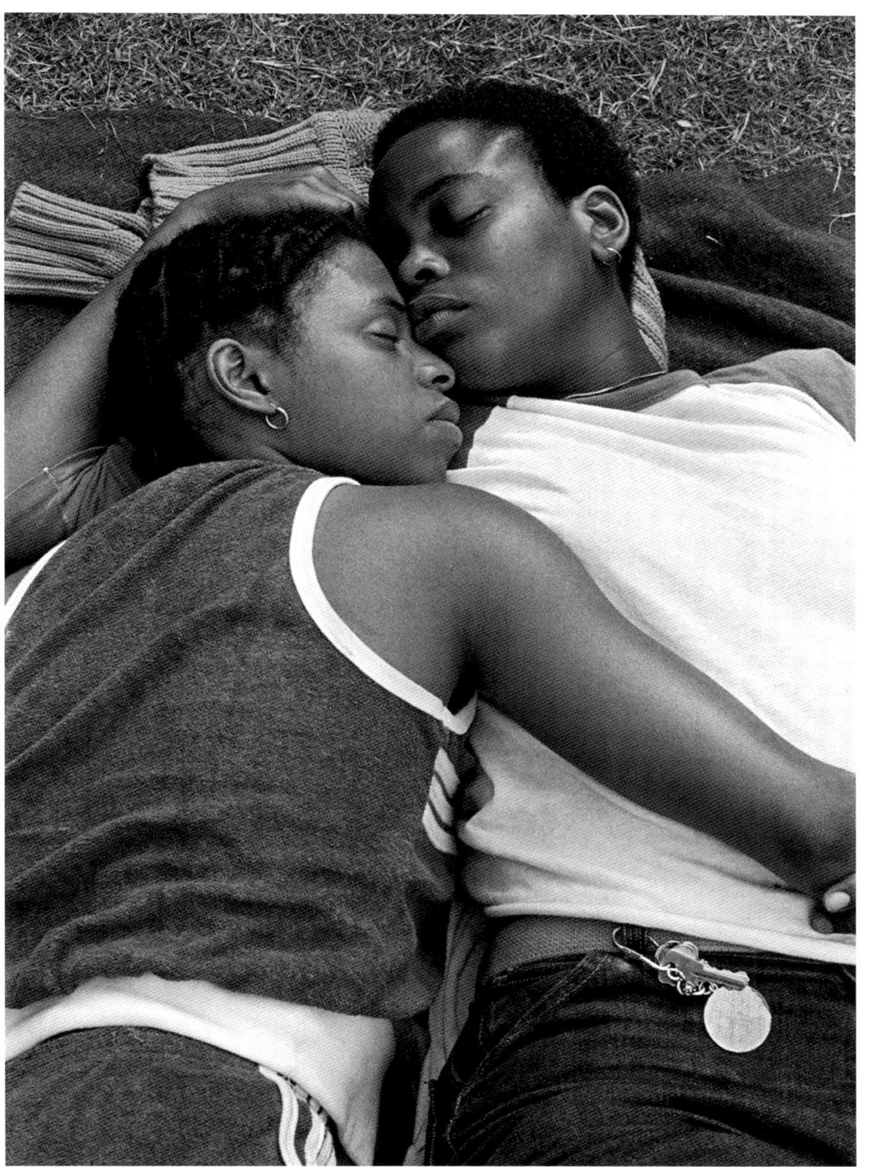

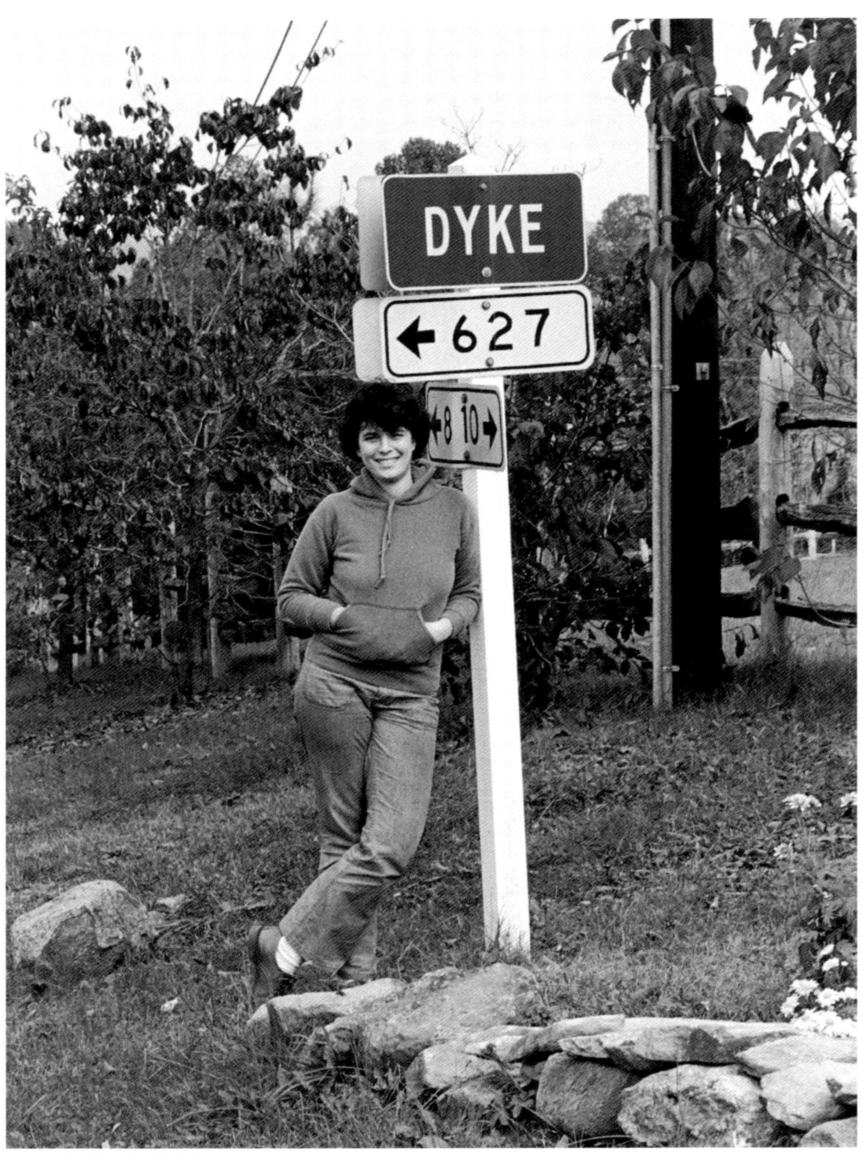
DYKE
← 627
← 8 10 →

JEB (Joan E. Biren)
Dyke, Virginia, 1975
Silver gelatin print

During the 1970s, JEB travelled across America finding lesbians who were willing to be photographed for her as she created an early archive of lesbian visibility. Here she poses for a self-portrait as she leans against the signpost for an aptly named community in Greene County, Virginia.

Structured into six chapters, the slideshow, which JEB presented and narrated live, spanned more than 300 images over two-and-a-half hours. Carting the archive around in her VW Microbus, JEB presented it more than eighty times in over sixty locations including colleges, lesbian bars, feminist bookshops and community centres. In 2023, at the age of seventy-eight, JEB presented *The Dyke Show* live for the final time at the Leslie-Lohman Museum of Art in New York City. Although she'll never present the work live again, a recording of her final presentation exists for future presentations.

By the 1990s, JEB shifted her focus to filmmaking, continuing her commitment to documenting LGBTQIA+ lives. Her films, including *For Love and For Life* (1990), *A Simple Matter of Justice* (1993) and the award-winning *No Secret Anymore: The Times of Del Martin & Phyllis Lyon* (2003), chronicle key moments in queer history and the lives of activists who paved the way for future generations.

KEY WORKS

Self-portrait with Sharon, 1970
Kady and Pagan in their Cabin, Monticello, NY, 1978

KEY FACTS

In 2021, forty years after *Eye to Eye: Portraits of Lesbians* was self-published by JEB, the book was reprinted by Anthology, featuring new essays from the photographer Lola Flash and former soccer player Lori Lindsey.

JEB's archive, housed at Smith College in Massachusetts, USA, encompasses approximately 64,400 images – one of the most comprehensive studies of the lesbian movement to date.

PAUL CADMUS
UNITED STATES, 1904–99

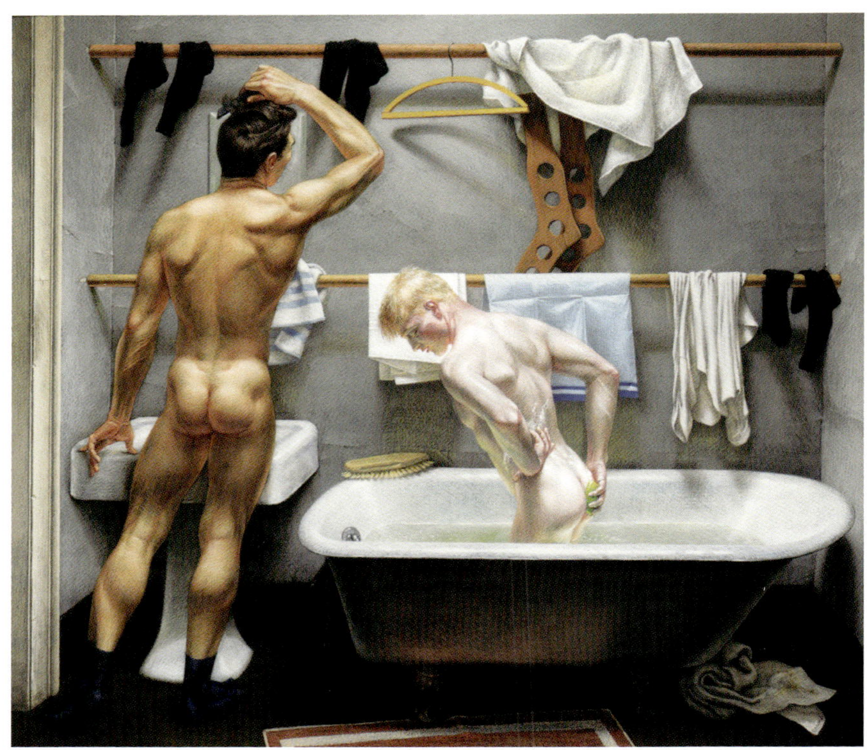

Paul Cadmus was a classically trained painter and printmaker. Born
in New York City, Cadmus imbued his works with incisive critiques
of American society, often exposing hypocrisies surrounding
sexuality, class and morality.

Some of Cadmus's works capture scenes of quiet queerness
– the subtleties of queer desire in public. Many were homoerotically
charged and bold at a time when queerness was hidden. *The Fleet's In!*
(1934) remains one of Cadmus's most infamous works. Commissioned
by the US Navy under the New Deal's Public Works of Art Project
(where the Government commissioned artists to depict optimistic

Paul Cadmus
The Bath, 1951
Tempera on
composition board
36.4 × 41.4 cm
(14⅜ × 16⅜ in.)
Whitney Museum of
American Art, New York

**The Bath encapsulates
a moment of domestic
intimacy that is charged
with sensuality. Both
male nudes are painted
with anatomical detail
and clarity, cleaning
themselves in the
bathroom – an act of
erotic attention and
routine.**

visions of America during a time of economic desperation), the painting depicts a chaotic, bawdy scene of sailors on shore leave. Revelling in a haze of debauchery, they mingle with women and men in an exuberant display of homoeroticism and hedonism. The figures capture a palpable tension between discipline and indulgence with tightly stretched uniforms, intertwined arms and fleeting glances.

The painting scandalized its patrons, leading to the US Navy removing it from public display, and was one of the earliest known cases of censorship of a gay artist in the United States. Official objections at the time focused on the depiction of public drunkenness and solicitation, but the real 'offence' lay in its queer subtext. For example, one of the women has an Adam's apple, meanwhile the blond 'pansy' figure's red tie, a subtle signal of availability, and his gesture of offering a cigarette to another male sailor underscore these themes.

Cadmus faced censorship throughout his career, fuelled by a defiant honesty. Beneath the satire, a deep care for his subjects is evident – each figure is rendered with painstaking individuality, their bodies and postures conveying nuance and complexity. His works capture the choreography of queer desire, playing out in public space. Despite living during a time when queerness was forced underground, his paintings are homoerotically charged and bold, and often feature his muse and partner, Jon Anderson.

KEY WORKS

Greenwich Cafeteria, 1934, Museum of Modern Art,
　New York, USA
Gilding the Acrobats, 1935, Metropolitan Museum of Art,
　New York, USA

KEY FACTS

Cadmus studied at the National Academy of Design in New York
　City from the age of fifteen, receiving a medal for excellence
　and discipline before beginning to exhibit his work and publish
　illustrations.
Despite his talent, Cadmus was not a prolific artist. He painted
　using egg tempera – a time-consuming medium – which meant
　that he only produced one or two works per year.

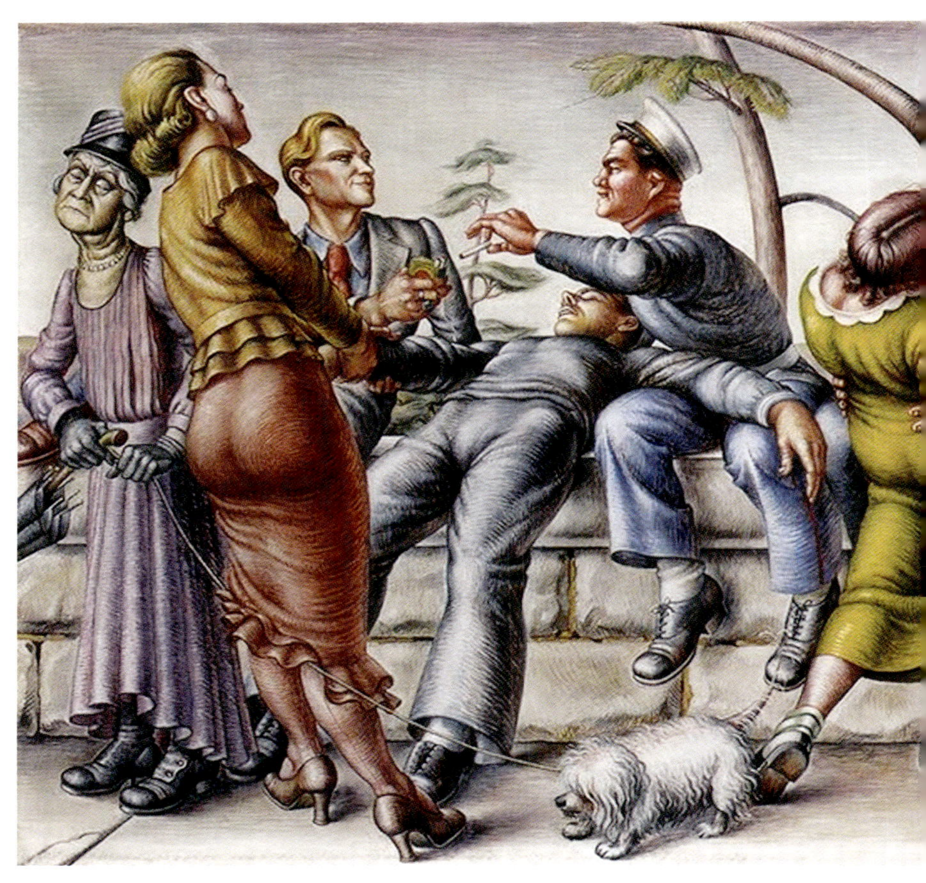

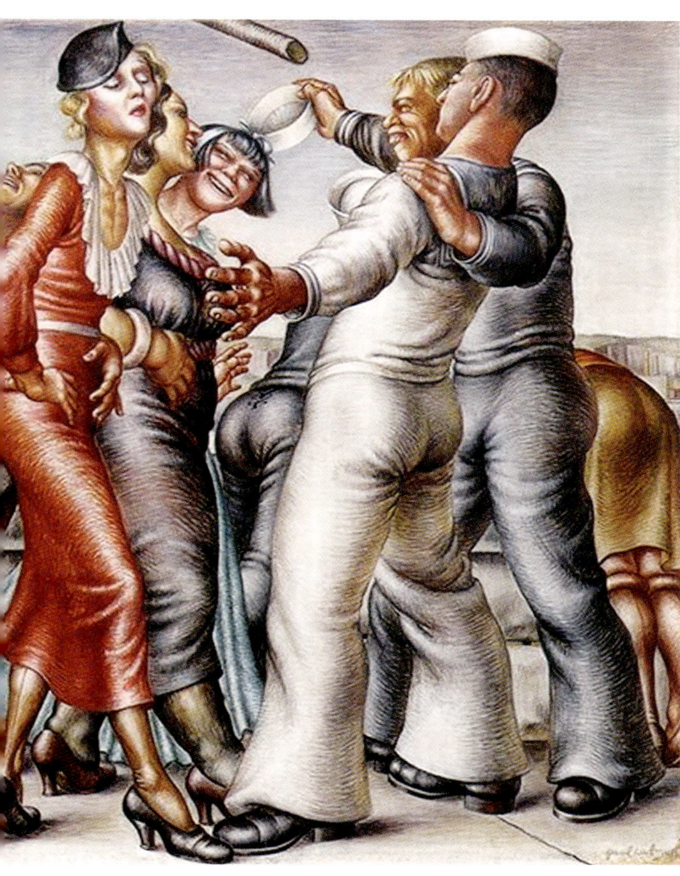

Paul Cadmus
The Fleet's In!, 1934
Tempera on canvas
94 × 170.2 cm
(37 × 67 in.)
Navy Art Collection,
USA

The Fleet's In scandalized audiences in 1934. References to homosexuality, such as sailor's genitals depicted in close proximity, as they either embrace women or, just as pointedly, reject them, led to the work being removed from public display.

ROTIMI FANI-KAYODE
NIGERIA, 1955–89

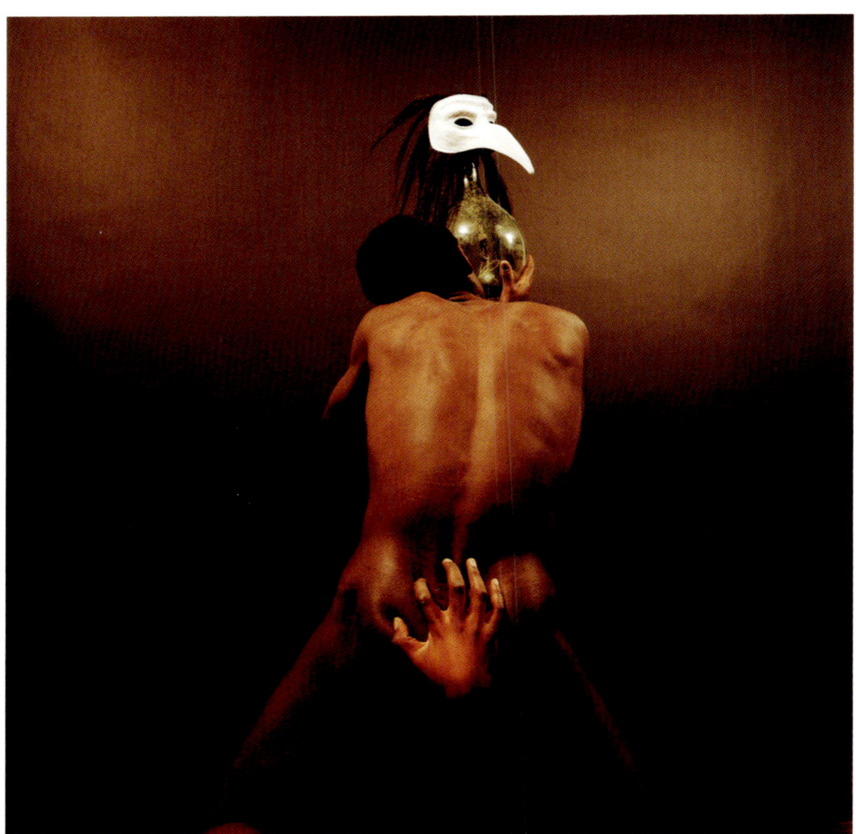

Rotimi Fani-Kayode was a Nigerian photographer, celebrated as one
of the most significant artists of the 1980s, despite a tragically brief
six-year career.

Born in Lagos, Fani-Kayode was taken by his family to Brighton,
England, to escape the civil war in Nigeria when he was eleven.
At twenty-one, he relocated to the United States, where he earned
his MFA from the Pratt Institute and became acquainted with
photographer Robert Mapplethorpe. He later returned to England
to pursue his artistic career.

Rotimi Fani-Kayode
*Every Moment Counts
(Ecstatic Antibodies),*
1987–8

**Rotimi Fani-Kayode's
powerful late work
explores spirituality and
eroticism, using these
lenses to confront illness,
sexuality and race. This
staged photographic
work, which was created
during the AIDS crisis
and the final year of the
artist's life, works to
reclaim the Black queer
body as a site of resilience
and desire.**

Fani-Kayode's photographic work explored histories of colonialism, experiences of racism and the tensions between his queer identity and his Yoruba heritage. Drawing from the religious practices of his parents, he blended Yoruba iconography with Western artistic traditions. His references to Yoruba iconography are often ironic signifiers of African culture and belief – exposing the contrived construction of 'otherness' in the West. In many of his images, Fani-Kayode incorporated erotic symbolism, such as references to Esu, a trickster and messenger deity, who is often depicted with an erect penis. Fani-Kayode has said that his allusions to Esu represent the fluidity of sexuality, implying the possibility of being 'led astray' by divine forces.

Central to Fani-Kayode's work were themes of religious eroticism, queer Black desire and the notion of sexuality as a healing force. His stylized photographs present Black male bodies as sites of erotic devotion, often adorned with fetishistic elements, ceremonial objects and traditional African attire. He primarily depicted Black men, frequently using his own body as a subject, positioning himself at the intersection of race, sexuality and spirituality. Fani-Kayode's practice profoundly engages with personal and collective histories through challenging exploitative mythologies and colonial narratives that have been projected onto Black bodies as objectification. By investigating and re-mythologizing the past, he counters historical narratives constructed by colonial powers, such as the designation of African art as 'primitive', or as of purely anthropological interest.

Rotimi Fani-Kayode passed away from AIDS-related complications in 1989, at the age of thirty-four.

KEY WORKS

Umbrella, 1987
Snap Shot, 1987

KEY FACTS

Fani-Kayode frequently collaborated with his partner, Alex Hirst, whom he lived with in London. Hirst died of AIDS in 1992.

In 1988, Fani-Kayode co-founded the Association of Black Photographers alongside Sunil Gupta, Ingrid Pollard and others. He also served as the association's first chair.

MAGGI HAMBLING
UNITED KINGDOM, b.1945

Maggi Hambling is one of Britain's most distinctive and formidable artistic voices. She is a painter and sculptor whose work is charged with emotional immediacy, queer sensibility and a lifelong, devotional relationship with the sea. Hambling describes herself as 'lesbionic' – her own playful, forthright term.

Her practice was profoundly shaped by her education under artists Cedric Morris and Arthur Lett-Haines at the East Anglian School of Painting and Drawing, which became known for its unorthodox teaching and the freedom it offered young queer artists. Morris and Lett-Haines's insistence on the truth of observation, unconventional approach to life and art, and unapologetic queerness played a decisive role in shaping both Hambling's artistic practice and sense of identity. This influence can still be seen in her work, which values emotional candour above polite restraint and shows a demonstrable commitment to close looking.

Growing up on the Suffolk coast, Hambling would often begin days sketching from life on the beach. These early drawings served as the basis for paintings and sculptures that explore the presence of the sea, including her ongoing *Wall of Water* paintings, which she began in 2010. First exhibited at the National Gallery, London, in 2015, this series has since become iconic within British art.

Hambling's relationship with literature – and with Oscar Wilde in particular – has been equally formative. Wilde's writing, full of wit and moral defiance, became a touchstone for her and she has painted his likeness repeatedly throughout her career. Her public sculpture *A Conversation with Oscar Wilde* (1998), located near Charing Cross Station in London, is one of her most recognized works. Hambling's public art commissions also include *Scallop* (2003), a tribute to the queer composer Benjamin Britten located on Aldeburgh beach, and *A Sculpture for Mary Wollstonecraft* (2020), which provoked public debate for its nude depiction of the feminist pioneer.

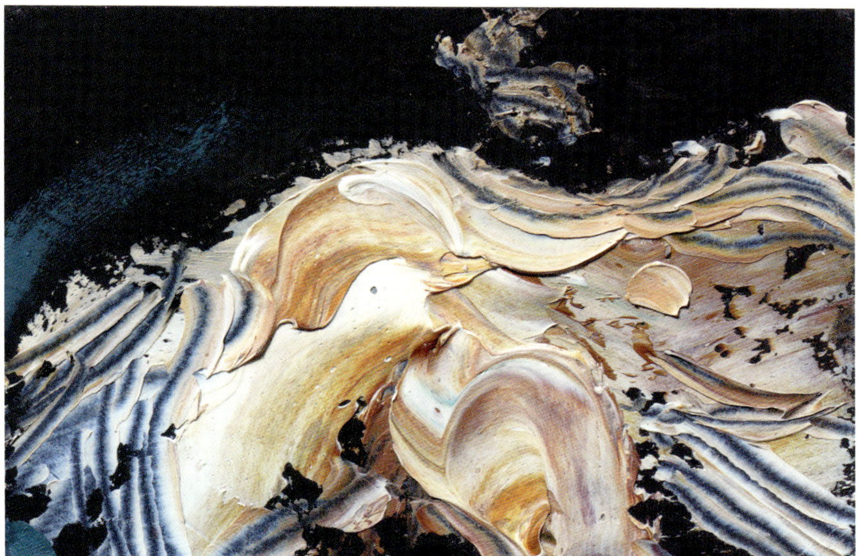

Maggi Hambling
Naked Night, 2020
Oil on board
9.5 × 14.2 cm
(3¾ × 5⅝ in.)
Pallant House Gallery,
Chichester, UK

Hambling has remarked that the breaking of a wave carries the same physical charge as an orgasm. It is a comparison that points to the bodily energy embedded in her sea paintings, evoked here in the title *Naked Night*.

Hambling's recent installation, *Time* (2025), offers an intimate reflection on her forty-year relationship with her late partner, Tory Lawrence. Forty turbulent small-scale *Nightwaves* sit alongside a central portrait, *Tory, October 2024*, which Hambling has said 'painted itself' – reflecting on love, loss and time.

KEY WORKS

A Conversation with Oscar Wilde, 1998, public work, Westminster, London, UK

Wall of Water IX, 2012, Metropolitan Museum of Art, New York, USA

KEY FACTS

Rarely seen without a cigarette in hand, Hambling was a key part of the campaign against the 2007 UK smoking ban.

In 1980, Hambling became the very first Artist-in-Residence at London's National Gallery.

HARMONY HAMMOND
UNITED STATES, b.1944

Harmony Hammond is a groundbreaking feminist artist, theorist and writer whose work has pushed the boundaries of artistic practice and political discourse for over five decades. Born and raised in Chicago, she moved to New York in 1969 and now lives and works in New Mexico. Her artistic journey has been defined by an unwavering commitment to challenging conventions, foregrounding lesbian identity in art at a time when it was largely invisible in mainstream discourse.

Hammond's work has always existed at the intersection of the personal and political. Like many feminists of the 1970s, she rejected traditional painting in favour of materials historically associated with women's creativity and domestic labour – fabric, weaving and other found materials. In 1973, the same year she came out as a lesbian, she created *Floor Pieces*, a series of hand-braided circular rugs made from scraps of fabric collected in New York's Garment District. Thickly painted in acrylic, these works defy categorization as either functional objects or paintings. By hybridizing craft-based techniques with painterly and sculptural traditions, Hammond dismantles the gendered hierarchies of media upheld by art history, which has relegated 'domestic' or 'feminine' arts to the margins. The size and placement of the *Floor Pieces* force viewers to navigate them with care and engage with them from different perspectives. Hammond challenges the passive experience of viewing art in a gallery, as well as disrupting heteronormative assumptions often embedded in domestic spaces.

Hammond's approach to materiality – incorporating unconventional materials such as leaves, hair, leather, straw and roots – is deeply symbolic. These organic, tactile materials carry communal and personal histories – evoking ideas of the body and the land, relating to themes of survival, care, loss, regeneration and identity. By repurposing these materials often dismissed, Hammond is reclaiming them as carriers of experience.

In addition to her artistic practice, Hammond has made a significant impact as an art historian and theorist. In 2000, she published her book *Lesbian Art in America*. Through her writing and curatorial work, Hammond has ensured that lesbian artists, their aesthetics and their politics have a lasting presence within feminist and contemporary art history.

Harmony Hammond
What Have You Done With Our Desire?, 1997
Mixed media in three parts
Approx. 256.5 × 261.6 cm (101 × 103 in.)
Alexander Gray Associates, New York

The title of this work is a direct quote from lesbian feminist philosopher Monique Wittig's 1979 essay 'Paradigm'. Wittig argues that attempting to erase queer desire is an act of violence, asking of heterosexual society: 'What have you done with our desire?... What do you want to do with our desire? Make it fit in? Lobotomies, forced therapy. Force it to practice heterosexuality...'

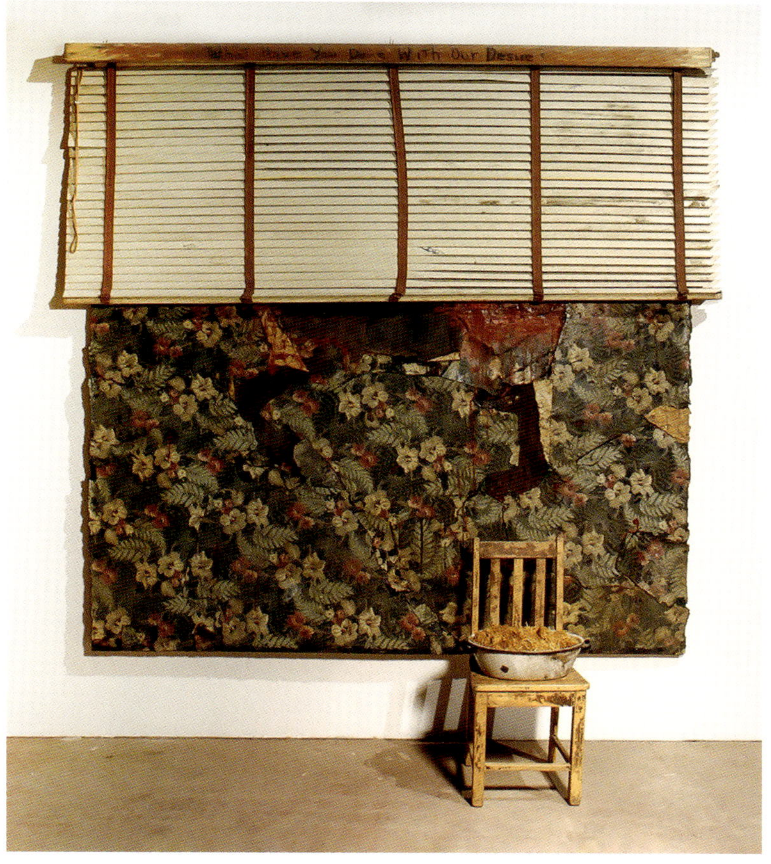

KEY WORKS

The Meeting of Passion and Intellect, 1981, National Museum
   of Women in the Arts, Washington, DC, USA
Lesbian Dreams, 1992, Minneapolis Institute of Art, USA

KEY FACTS

In the 1970s, Hammond co-founded A.I.R. Gallery, the first
   women's cooperative gallery in the United States, and the
   quarterly *Heresies: A Feminist Publication on Art and Politics*,
   which dedicated an issue to lesbian art.
Hammond curated the notable exhibitions 'A Lesbian Show'
   (1978) and 'Out West' (1999), which both asserted the
   importance of lesbian perspectives in contemporary art.

ISAAC JULIEN
UNITED KINGDOM, b.1960

Isaac Julien is a British installation artist and filmmaker whose vital interventions into contemporary art centre Black and queer perspectives. He is a pioneer of New Queer Cinema, a movement of the late 1980s and 1990s that called into question the boundaries that normative assumptions imposed onto the aesthetics of film. Julien is celebrated for his unique style of moving-image work and his innovative multi-screen installations.

Julien's distinctive visual language is both serenely poetic and deeply political. Born in London in 1960 to parents from the Caribbean island of St Lucia, he witnessed first-hand the racism and police brutality of Britain in the 1970s and 1980s.

An activist undercurrent runs throughout his work, challenging ideas around race, gender and sexuality. Through powerful storytelling, Julien reframes the archive through a postcolonial, and often queer, lens. Critical fabulation is a core principle of much of his work. The practice of 'fabulation' (weaving historical fact with fictional, imaginative storytelling) addresses gaps in the archive where histories are shaped by absence. Julien uses such gaps as springboards for reinvention. By fusing fiction with history, Julien is able to repair the archive and put absence to a productive use.

Julien's 1989 film *Looking for Langston* tells the story of the deceased Harlem Renaissance poet Langston Hughes. Rejecting the constraints of historical record, the film revolves around an imagined queer environment in which Hughes *may* have moved – filling a gap that Julien felt was missing. Made at the height of the AIDS pandemic, it remains a seminal exploration of Black, queer desire and is widely considered to be a cult classic. Celebrated internationally for his radical work, Julien continues to inspire future generations of artists who share his passion for advocating for freedom in their work.

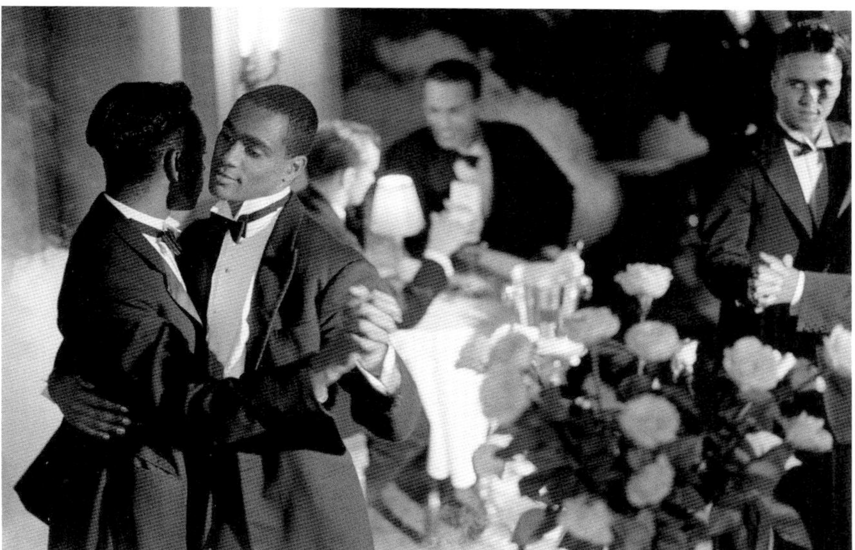

Isaac Julien
'Pas de Deux with
Roses', (*Looking for
Langston* Vintage Series)
1989/2016
Ilford classic silver gelatin
fine art paper, mounted
on aluminum and framed
Framed dimensions
58.1 × 74.5 cm
(22⅞ × 29⅜ in.)

Looking for Langston
recreates the private world
of Langston Hughes, an
important figure in the
Harlem Renaissance.
Set in a speakeasy
inspired by the Cotton
Club, the film is made
up of archival footage
including scenes of black
men dancing together.
These are spliced with
Robert Mapplethorpe's
photography,
accompanied by the
poetry of Hughes,
Richard Bruce Nugent,
James Baldwin and Essex
Hemphill.

KEY WORKS

Three, 1999
Lessons of the Hour, 2019

KEY FACTS

While a student at Central Saint Martins, London, Julien
co-founded the Sankofa Film and Video Collective in 1983,
which fostered Black independent filmmaking in Britain.
In 2022, Julien was knighted by Queen Elizabeth II for his
services to diversity and inclusion in art.

YUKI KIHARA
SĀMOA, b.1975

Yuki Kihara is an interdisciplinary Sāmoan-Japanese artist whose work interrogates colonial histories, gender identity and the politics of representation. A 'fa'afafine' – Sāmoa's third of four culturally recognized gender categories – Kihara foregrounds Indigenous knowledge systems in her art. Born in Sāmoa, Kihara later moved to Aotearoa New Zealand when she was fifteen. Kihara works across photography, video, performance and installation, often blending these art forms to critique historical narratives that have marginalized Pacific and queer identities.

Fa'afafine and other gender-diverse figures have historically been excluded from dominant art histories, often framed through an anthropological lens. Kihara's work resists this erasure, positioning fa'afafine identities as integral to both contemporary Indigenous and queer discourse. In one of Sāmoa's origin stories, the first humans

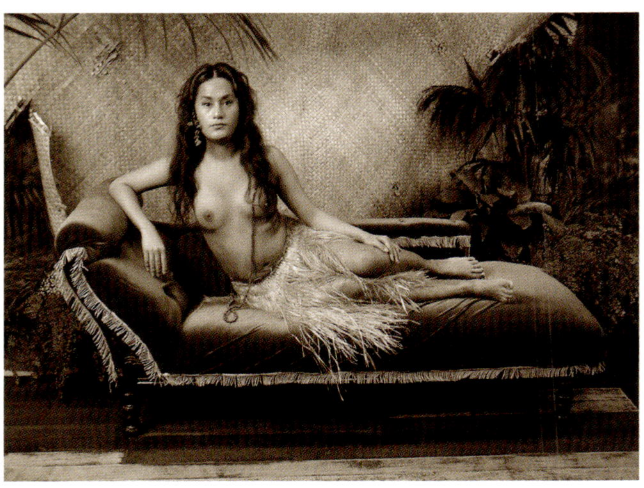
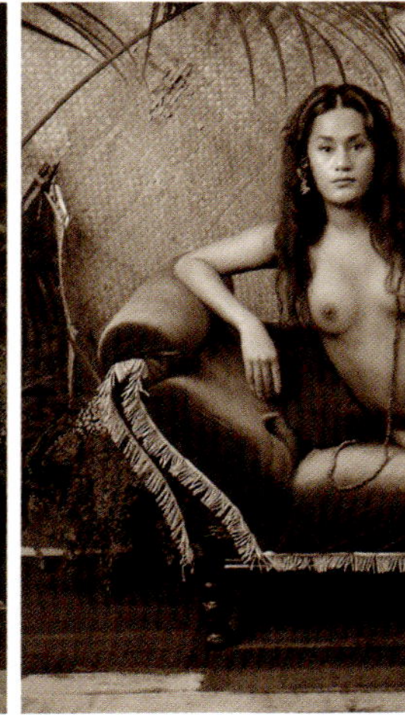

Yuki Kihara
*Fa'afafine: In the Manner
of a Woman*, 2004–5
Triptych, C-print,
each 60 × 80 cm
(23⅝ × 31½ in.)

**Kihara's triptych
subverts the colonial
gaze of nineteenth-
century ethnographic
photography, reclaiming
the presence of fa'afafine
in history. The images
immediately seem similar
to each other; however,
there are subtle changes.
In the second panel,
Kihara wears only a
necklace, and in the third
her penis is 'untucked'
and revealed, asserting
the embodiment of
fa'afafine identity beyond
colonial boundaries.**

were a male couple, Sāfa and Pili, until one was transformed into
a woman by the gods. The story reflects a culture in which gender
diversity is divinely sanctioned, and gestures to a pre-colonial
worldview in which gender is not rigidly tied to biological sex but
relational, and embedded in social and spiritual life. Colonialism
disrupted these frameworks, instead imposing a Western binary.

In 2022, Kihara became the first Pasifika and fa'afafine artist
to represent Aotearoa New Zealand at the Venice Biennale with
Paradise Camp, a project reimagining Paul Gauguin's colonial-era
Tahitian paintings through a queer Pacific lens. Kihara worked
with a group of Sāmoan fa'afafine models to stage photographs
that mirrored and subverted Gauguin's images – an act of visual
reclamation that challenges the deep-seated fetishization and
racism in Gaugin's works that regularly depicted women as
exoticized and passive.

One key image draws on Édouard Manet's *Olympia* (1863),
a painting already radical in its own time for confronting the viewer
with a self-aware, sexually autonomous female subject. Kihara's
version references both Manet and Gauguin's interpretations of
Olympia, situating fa'afafine identity within this lineage of contested
representation. Through this deliberate citation, Kihara inserts
fa'afafine subjects into a longer lineage of art-historical critique
as active agents rather than curiosities. In doing so, she purposely
unpicks the dominance of whiteness and heteronormativity that
often shapes the creative industries – resisting the inherited
frameworks of who gets to be seen and how.

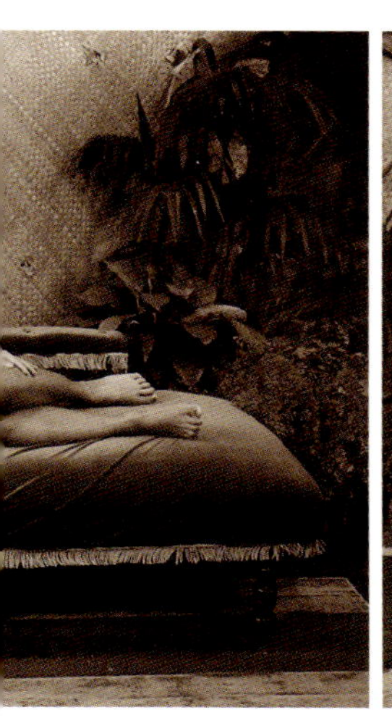
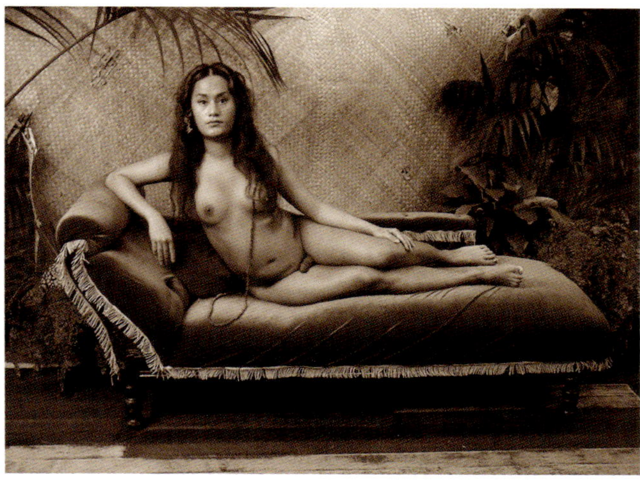

KEY WORKS

Tama Samoa ma teine Samoa: A man and a woman of Samoa,
  2004–5, Museum of New Zealand Te Papa Tongarewa
A Song About Sāmoa – Vasa (Ocean), 2019, National Museums
  Scotland

KEY FACTS

In 2008, Kihara's work was the subject of a solo exhibition at
  the Metropolitan Museum of Art in New York – the first time
  ever that a New Zealander and a Pacific Islander artist held
  a solo show at the Met.
In 2022, Kihara presented *Paradise Camp* at the Venice Biennale
  for the Aotearoa New Zealand Pavilion, making her the first
  person of Pacific descent to be presented by the country at
  the show.

Yuki Kihara
Darwin Drag, 2025
Video still, single channel
digital video, full HD,
sound, 6 min 15 sec

**In this video work,
Kihara prosthetically
transforms herself into
Charles Darwin in order
to decolonize and queer
natural history. The piece
reflects on omissions
regarding the variety of
sex traits catalogued in
On the Origin of Species,
exploring fish species
that exhibit sequential
hermaphroditism or
deviate from the binary
female-male reproductive
model.**

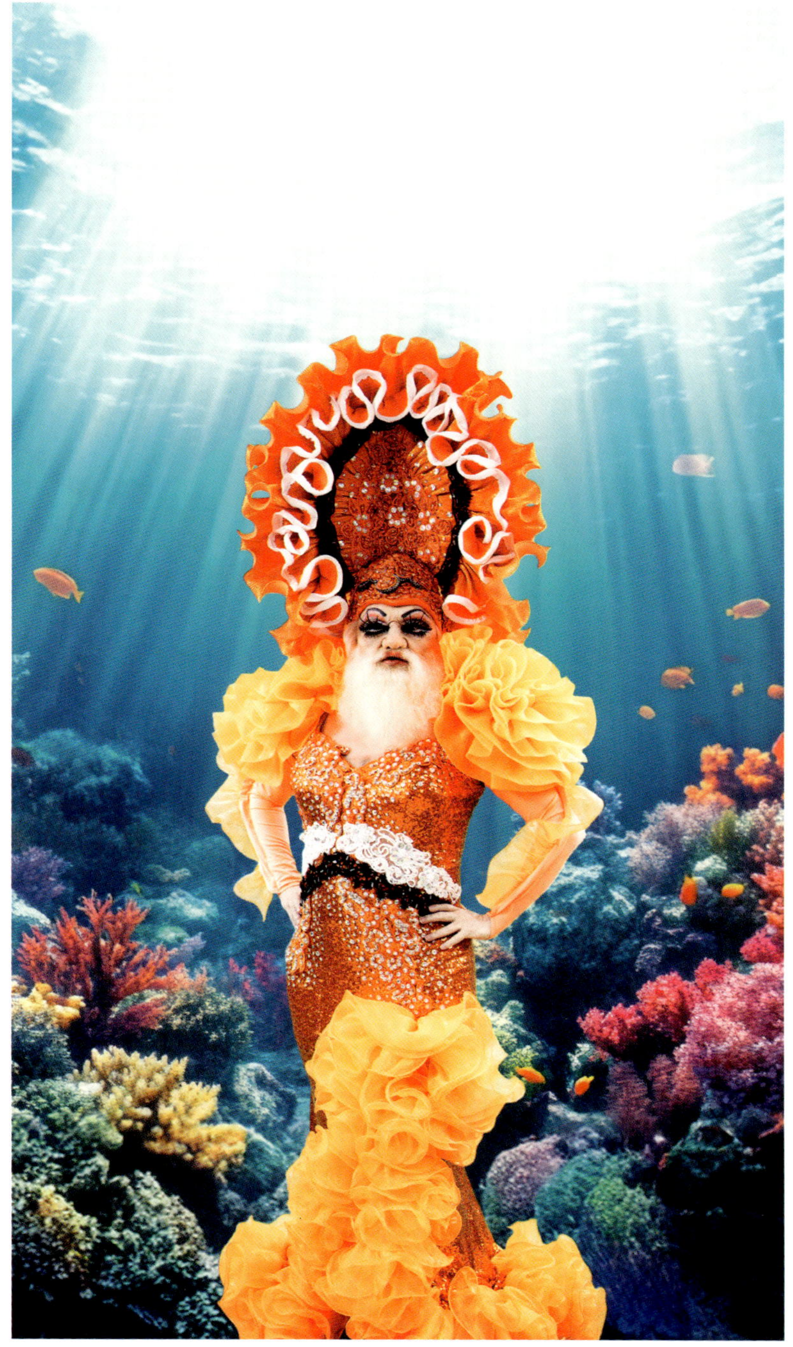

JULIE MEHRETU
ETHIOPIA, b.1970

Julie Mehretu is an Ethiopian-American painter whose large-scale, abstract artworks explore energies of social upheaval. She was born four years before the Ethiopian revolution, and her family fled Ethiopia in 1977 while the country was ruled by a military junta. Mehretu settled in Michigan when she was seven, and this early experience of displacement influenced her interest in geography and migration.

Working in drawing, painting and printmaking, she earned a BA from Kalamazoo College in 1992, an MFA from the Rhode Island School of Design in 1997, and has since received numerous awards and grants, including a MacArthur Fellowship in 2005 and a Medal of Arts from the US State Department in 2015.

Mehretu's work is recognizable for its layered abstraction – referencing history, geography and architecture. Whether working on paper, canvas or with printmaking techniques, drawing is always central to their work. She has described drawing as an 'activist gesture', an intuitive and personal process representative of individual agency and culture. Mehretu's artworks are physically large. *Mural*, commissioned in 2007 for the lobby of Goldman Sachs's New York office, measures 24 × 7 metres (80 × 23 feet) – a tennis-court sized piece which draws upon the history of capitalism, alluding to vast networks of exchange and appropriation by layering images of trade networks and drawings of financial institutions beneath abstract gestural markings.

Often beginning with found imagery (such as news photographs of protests related to conflict), she overlays each with distinctive calligraphic marks. The final works are turbulent and dynamic, incorporating geometric colour and frantic marks that draw influence from urban landscapes, building plans and aerial maps with no fixed locations. In her *Retopistics* works, she used imagery from the 2014 Ferguson uprising and the Syrian War. Mehretu's practice responds to global conflict and socio-political changes explored through an aesthetic that leaves space for possibility and growth.

Queerness is integral to Mehretu's worldview. In a 2015 interview for *The Cut*, she said that 'being queer, being a woman, being Black, being partially East African' all inform who she is, although she is wary of being reduced to a single identity category, and rejects labels such as 'queer artist' or 'Black artist'.

Julie Mehretu
Your hands are like two shovels, digging in me (sphinx), 2021–2
Ink and acrylic on canvas
243.8 × 304.8 cm
(96 × 120 in.)
Tate, London

In this large-scale work, Mehretu layers gestural marks and fields of colour to evoke a sense of fractured time and place. The title's poetic urgency points to intimacy and rupture, echoing Mehretu's sustained engagement with abstraction as a language of diasporic identity and political unrest.

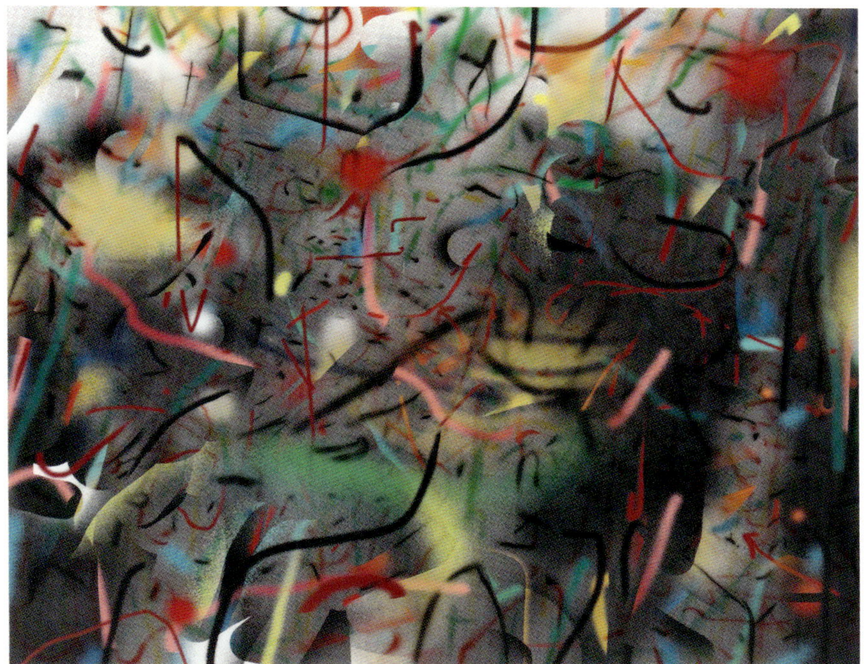

Mehretu speaks of a more expansive, fluid understanding of queerness as a method: a commitment to complexity, multiplicity and resistance to hierarchy. Her works embody a radical inclusivity – layering histories, ideas and perspectives without hierarchy.

KEY WORKS

Mural, 2009–10, Goldman Sachs, New York City, USA
Of Other Planes of There, 2018–19, Whitney Museum of American
 Art, New York, USA

KEY FACTS

In 2017, alongside Adam Pendleton, Rashid Johnson and Ellen
 Gallagher, Mehretu acquired Nina Simone's childhood home
 to preserve Simone's legacy as an artist and activist.
In 2023, Mehretu set a new auction record for an African artist
 after her 2001 painting *Untitled* sold for £9.32 million.

ZANELE MUHOLI
SOUTH AFRICA, b.1972

Zanele Muholi is a visual activist and photographer whose work focuses on Black LGBTQIA+ lives, using their work to document and challenge the systemic violence and erasure faced by queer Black communities – particularly in post-apartheid South Africa.

Born in Umlazi, a township near Durban, during the apartheid regime – a system of racial segregation enforced under white minority rule – Muholi's work is deeply rooted in politics, power and social justice. They studied Advanced Photography at Market Photo Workshop in Johannesburg before earning an MFA in Documentary Media at Ryerson University, Toronto, in 2009.

Between 2002 and 2006, Muholi created *Only Half the Picture*, their first photographic series, documenting survivors of hate crimes across South Africa's townships. This project was part of their work with the Forum for the Empowerment of Women (FEW), which they co-founded in 2002.

Many of Muholi's works are staged in public locations with historical significance. This includes beaches once segregated under apartheid, or Constitution Hill, the seat of South Africa's Constitutional Court. In occupying these spaces, Muholi challenges exclusions of Black queer and trans people, asserting their presence in sites of national memory.

One of Muholi's most significant ongoing projects, *Faces and Phases* (2006–present), consists of over 600 black-and-white portraits of Black LGBTQIA+ lives. The title reflects both presence (faces) and the evolving, complex nature of identity (phases). Muholi's participants meet the viewer's gaze directly, reclaiming space in a visual landscape that has historically erased them. Their approach is collaborative – Muholi refers to those they photograph as 'participants' rather than 'subjects', emphasizing agency and self-representation. Many participants are invited by the artist to contribute to exhibitions and discussions, further reinforcing their visibility and voice. The project is a living archive for the future – commemorating and preserving the lives of Black lesbian, trans and gender non-conforming people.

Zanele Muholi
*Somnyama Ngonyama II,
Oslo*, 2015
Gelatin silver print
50 × 43.6 cm
(19¾ × 17¼ in.)

Somnyama Ngonyama,
which means 'hail
the dark lioness', is a
series of self-portraits,
which Muholi says are
responses to their daily
experience living as a
Black queer person.
Some are responses to
personal experiences,
such as being harassed in
a hotel. Some reference
historical violence. Some
are responses to reports
of hate crimes they saw
in the news.

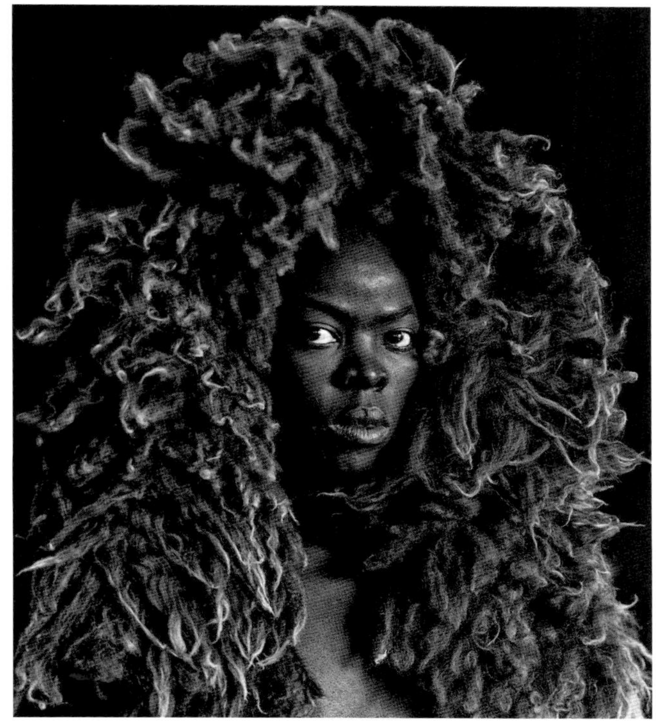

KEY WORKS

Nosipho 'Brown' Solundwana, Parktown, Johnannesburg, 2007
Sunday Francis Mdlankomo, Vosloorus, Johannesburg, 2011

KEY FACTS

In 2006, Muholi co-founded Inkanyiso, a non-profit platform and
media organization dedicated to queer storytelling, media and
advocacy.

In 2012, Muholi's apartment was broken into in a seemingly
deliberate attack: thieves ignored valuables and instead
stole over twenty external hard drives containing five years
of Muholi's photographs documenting Black lesbian lives.
Muholi believes the burglary was a hate crime intended to
silence their LGBTQIA+ advocacy.

HÉLIO OITICICA
BRAZIL, 1937–80

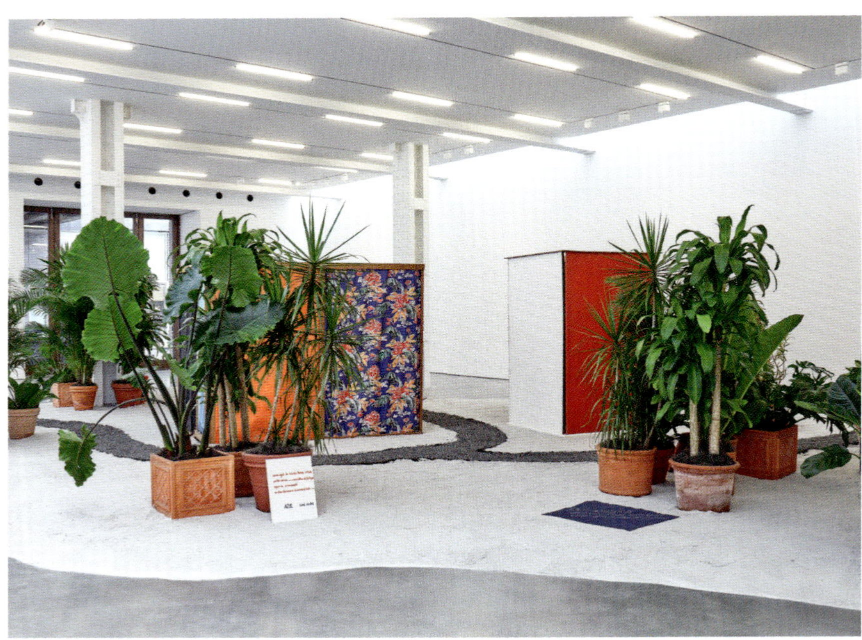

A radical, countercultural figure, activist and underground hero,
Hélio Oiticica is regarded as one of Brazil's most influential artists of
the twentieth century. Oiticica's multidisciplinary practice spanned
sculpture, performance, painting, avant-garde filmmaking and
participatory art, consistently challenging the boundaries between
art, politics and lived experience.

Born in Rio de Janeiro, Oiticica began his career in geometric
abstraction, originally working with the Rio-based Grupo Frente
before becoming a leading proponent of Neo-Concretism, alongside
artists such as Lygia Clark and Lygia Pape. Together, the Brazilian
art movement rejected current 'purist' Concrete Art, in favour of
more colour and sensuality in their choice of media. By the 1960s,
Oiticica's work had evolved into the production of socially engaged,

participatory pieces, which sought to dissolve the divide between art and life. He coined the term 'ambient art' to describe his immersive installations, which prioritized interaction and experience over traditional, formal aesthetics.

Oiticica's commitment to participatory art can be understood as an act of disrupting normative modes of engaging with and classifying art, and in doing so rejecting rigid systems. His work is profoundly queer in its resistance to categorization and in its dissolution of boundaries – between subject and object, life and art, improvisation and structure.

Between 1970 and 1978, Oiticica lived in New York's East Village, where he immersed himself in underground queer and countercultural movements, including the disco-era drug scene, and his work was heavily influenced by his time there. His 1971 Super 8 film *Gay Pride Parade* remains one of his most explicitly queer works. Capturing a moment of unapologetic queer visibility during one of New York's early post-Stonewall Pride marches, the film reflects his belief in art as a lived experience, framing joy and resistance as inseparable.

Oiticica's engagement with queerness was deeply personal and politically charged. When he returned to Brazil, he was confronted about his homosexuality. Brazil was still under a US-backed military dictatorship, which persecuted dissidents, censored artists and violently repressed queer communities. His defiance of artistic norms, state control and heteronormativity positioned him as a powerfully subversive force.

Helio Oiticica
Tropicália, Penetrables PN 2 'Purity is a myth' and PN 3 'Imagetical', 1966–7
Wooden structures, fabric, plastic, carpet, wire mesh, tulle, patchouli, sandalwood, television, sand, gravel, plants, birds and poems by Roberta Camila Salgado, dimensions variable
Lisson Gallery, 504 West 24th Street, New York
28 October 2020–23 January 2021
Guggenheim Abu Dhabi

Penetrables PN 2 'Purity is a Myth' and PN 3 'Imagetical' are immersive environments that invite viewers to walk barefoot through them. The installation includes sand, gravel, plants and structures resembling favela dwellings. Oiticica incorporates elements from Brazil's marginalized communities, challenging aesthetic hierarchies and ideas of cultural 'purity'.

KEY WORKS

B17 Glass Bólide 05 'Homage to Mondrian', 1965, Tate, London, UK

Tropicália, 1967, Museo Nacional Centro de Arte Reina Sofía, Madrid, Spain

KEY FACTS

Oiticica coined the term Tropicália for a 1967 work exhibited in Rio de Janeiro. The term later lent its name to a radical cultural movement blending popular and avant-garde forms.

Most of Oiticia's work was lost when a fire swept through Rio de Janeiro in 2009. An estimated 90 per cent of the artist's entire body of work was destroyed in the blaze.

HENRIK OLESEN
DENMARK, b.1967

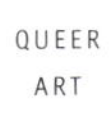

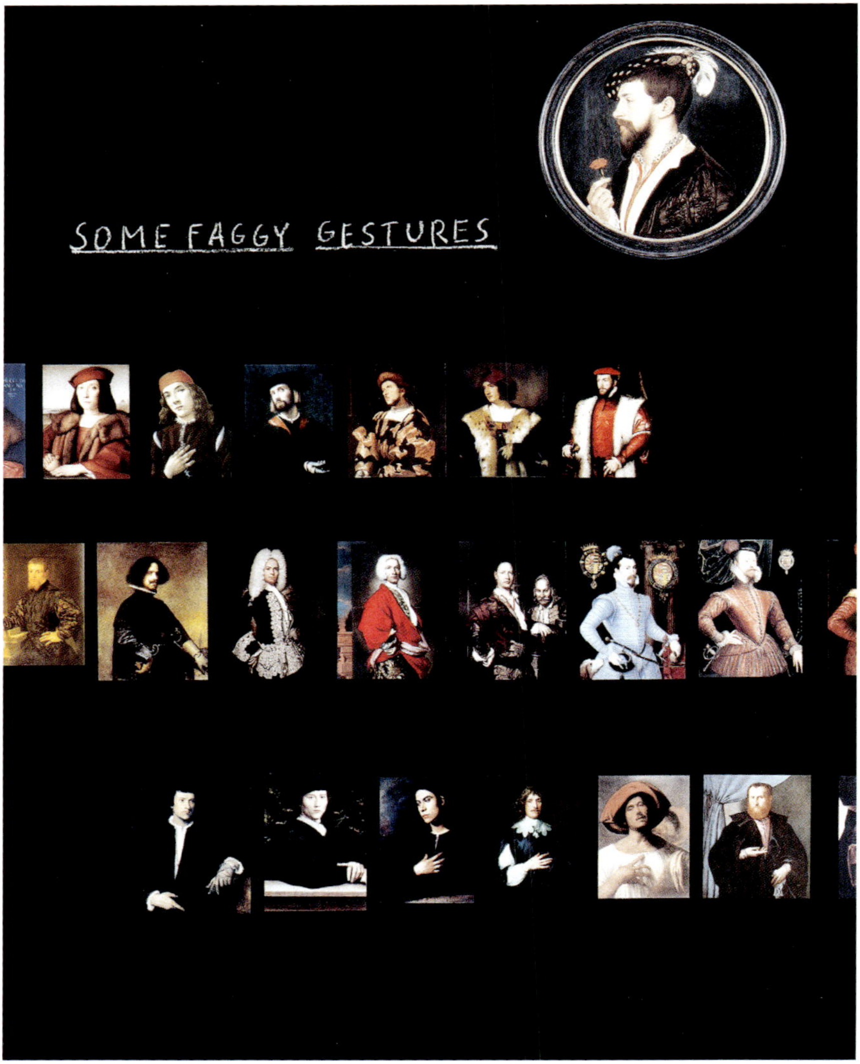

Henrik Olesen is a conceptual artist whose work dissects systems of power, sexuality and representation. Known for his rigorous and subversive practice, Olesen uses archival material, sculptural installations and collages to interrogate how queerness has been excluded from dominant cultural and historical narratives, exposing the mechanisms of heteronormativity as a system of control.

His artistic vocabulary frequently appropriates historical and found imagery, subverting prevailing heterosexual narratives by inserting explicitly queer content. In the artist's book *Anthologie de l'amour sublime* (2003), for instance, Olesen juxtaposed sadomasochistic gay sex and Tom of Finland drawings with other references such as legal, medical and philosophical texts, reframing homoerotic imagery as an integral – rather than marginal – aspect of cultural production.

In *Some Faggy Gestures* (2007) and *American Dykes in Rome* (2007) Olesen playfully reframes Old Master paintings through collage, recoding specific gestures and poses – often interpreted as markers of aristocracy – as signals of queer desire. Through this recontextualization, he invites viewers to question assumptions of heterosexuality and explores how queerness has always been present, though unacknowledged, within visual culture.

Olesen's work interrogates the ways that heteronormativity sustains itself – through cultural systems that define what is 'normal'. His archival work not only retrieves lost narratives, but critiques the way histories are constructed and policed. His titles – some of which reclaim slurs – similarly subvert language as a way of asserting queer presence within a system designed to erase it.

KEY WORKS

Untitled, 2004, Tate, London, UK
A Portrait, 2014, Pinault Collection, Paris, France

KEY FACTS

Olesen's 2011 'Projects 94' exhibition appropriated historic materials to explore the criminalization of homosexuality.

Olesen's *A.T.* (2012) is a 'portrait' of British queer mathematician Alan Turing, juxtaposing his achievements in computing with the state's inhumane punishment for his sexuality.

Henrik Olesen
III – Some Faggy Gestures from 'Some Gay-Lesbian Artists and/or Artists relevant to Homo-Social Culture Born between c.1300–1870',
2007 (detail)
Collage, computer printouts on wooden board, overall dimensions 140 × 600 cm
(55⅛ × 236¼ in.)
Migros Museum für Gegenwartskunst Collection, Zurich

A landmark work in Olesen's career, *Some Faggy Gestures* is a provocative and fragmented exploration of queer identity and embodiment. Across seven panels, the work forms a sprawling collage of images, texts and objects that map a lineage of queerness through time, space and gesture.

XIYADIE
CHINA, b.1963

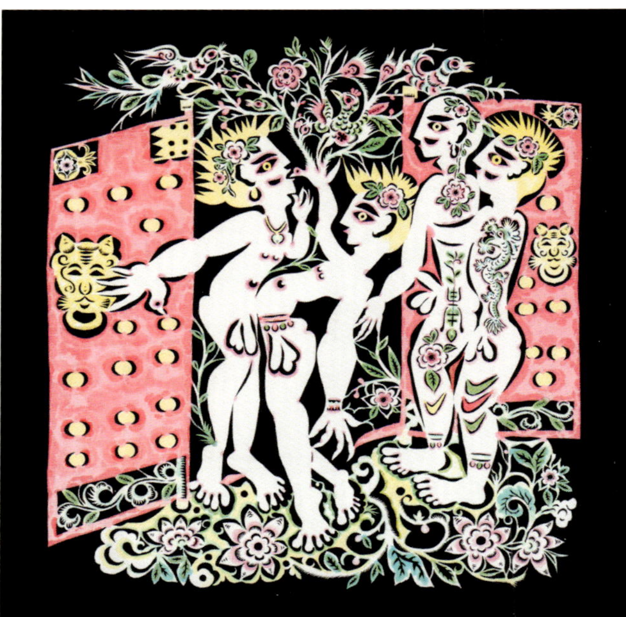

Xiyadie
Gate, 1999
Papercut with water-based dye and Chinese pigments on Xuan paper
141 × 127 cm
(55½ × 50 in.)
Blindspot Gallery,
Hong Kong

Gate depicts four nude male figures sharing a clandestine moment of embrace and voyeurism under a luminously abundant tree flanked by open gates. The motif of gates in Chinese symbolism represents thresholds, transitions and liminality, used here to reinforce themes of queer existence within cultural structures.

Xiyadie is an artist whose work reclaims and queers the traditional folk art of paper cutting. Born and raised in a small village in Shaanxi province, he took on the pseudonym Xiyadie – which translates to 'Siberian Butterfly' – following his move to Beijing in 2005. Although homosexuality was decriminalized in China in 1997, by 2005 there were still no anti-discrimination laws. The societal pressure to conform remained so strong that Xiyadie sought medical advice about suppressing his desire after he moved to Beijing. The doctor, who happened to be gay, told him that he was perfectly healthy and encouraged him to exhibit his work with a local group of gay artists, who promised to protect his identity, resulting in his decision to adopt a pseudonym. Xiyadie has said that the Siberian butterfly, which survives the harshest conditions, symbolizes resilience and the ongoing quest for freedom that underscores his artistic vision.

Paper cutting has deep historical roots in China, dating back to the Eastern Han Dynasty (25–220 CE). Xiyadie uses this ancient technique – typically considered a feminine craft, which the artist learned by watching his mother and other women in his village – to construct scenes of queer eroticism; a practice he began while living in northern China, although he had to keep the subject of his art secret for fear of ostracization. He continues to use the art form to represent gay virility, often depicting the cruising scenes he discovered in Beijing alongside motifs of the natural, fertile world. Using delicate materials such as thin Chinese rice paper, Xiyadie cuts each intricate pattern before dyeing them by hand, in many cases creating multiple versions of each work.

Xiyadie's work is ripe with references to Chinese cultural heritage. The decorations, buildings and clothes reference an ancient past that the national and cultural identity of modern-day China is built on. By situating explicitly queer narratives within this context, Xiyadie explores the potential for harmony as well as tension between queerness and national identity, interrogating what it means to not only be a queer man in China, but a queer Chinese man.

The 1990s saw the emergence of gay social spaces and covert networks in China, yet even after decriminalization, the queer scene is still largely underground. Xiyadie challenges strict heteronormativity embedded in local folk traditions, where depictions of love and fertility are almost exclusively tied to heterosexual marriage. By introducing homoerotic narratives into an ancient, government-sanctioned art form, Xiyadie presents a vision of queerness filled with joy, bliss and possibility within an otherwise oppressive world.

KEY WORKS

Fun, 1990s, Tate, London, UK
Flying, 2000s, Tate, London, UK

KEY FACTS

Xiyadie was formally recognized as a 'living Chinese queer artist' by the Beijing LGBT+ Center, who included his work in an exhibition of queer art in 2010 – an accolade that underscores his significance within China's complex LGBTQIA+ history.

In recent years, Xiyadie has begun exhibiting internationally, including a solo show at The Drawing Center in New York in 2023 and participation in the 60th Venice Biennale in 2024.

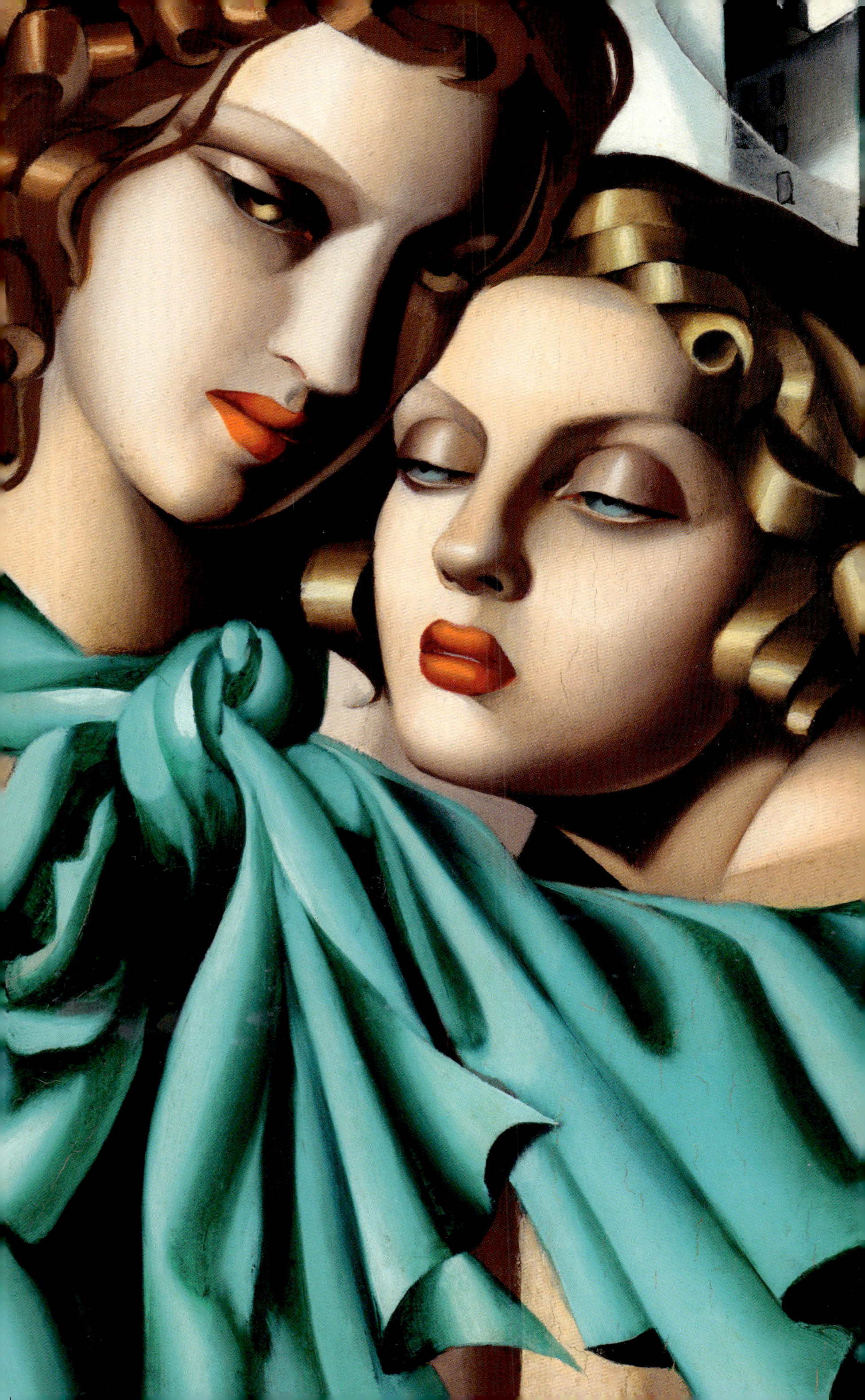

LOVE AND LIBERATION

-

Queer artists repeatedly place love at the
centre of their work because it is inseparable
from justice and survival

-

Queer love is a powerful force, one that has been marginalized, suppressed and misunderstood. Despite facing systemic barriers, it endures, challenging the structures that seek to silence and oppress it.

Expressions of queer intimacy have historically existed under threat: from the criminalization of same-sex relationships to the censorship of queer desire in visual culture. Despite these forces, queer love has always found ways to manifest, subvert and resist. Queer love and desire have fuelled artistic activism across the globe, from shared solidarity in activist movements like ACT UP, to the interventions of artist collectives like Yeguas del Apocalipsis (Mares of the Apocalypse), founded by Chilean artists Pedro Lemebel and Francisco Casas in 1987.

In ancient cultures, evidence of queer intimacy persists, though often overlooked or misinterpreted. From the poetry of Sappho in ancient Greece to the tomb of Niankhkhnum and Khnumhotep in ancient Egypt, these glimpses of love – tender, forbidden or sacred – are part of a long lineage of queer expression.

Audre Lorde famously declared that love – especially erotic and queer love – is a profoundly political and revolutionary act. It is an act of loving both oneself and others, of defying the forces that seek to erase or confine our identities and desires.

Across so many of these artists' works, personal pain and queer devotion become public protest, where love's voice is both joy and weapon. Queer artists repeatedly place love at the centre of their work because it is inseparable from justice and survival. In the face of familial rejection and institutional abandonment, queer communities have long created chosen families. These families are networks of care that resist any biological determinism. This love, built on trust, solidarity and shared survival, reveals alternative ways of both loving and being in the world. In documenting intimacy, these artists are fighting erasure – if love exists, it must be seen. Faced with violence and prejudice, their works remind us that in recounting love – whether current, requited or lost – we are honouring and reclaiming power. Across photography, performance, textiles and sculpture throughout art history, queer artists have developed languages of care and desire. Tenderness might be coded through gesture, repetition, fragmentation or even absence. What is not shown is as powerful as what is made visible.

Queer love has never been merely a private feeling. It is, and always has been, an act of survival within a community – an act of remembering the past and imagining an otherwise. Love, in its myriad expressions – whether platonic, familial, romantic, communal or self-directed – embodies a profound form of resistance and affirmation. Among queer individuals, self-love, in particular, becomes a vital means of survival, often cultivated and articulated through art as a process of self-empowerment, healing and defiance. Queer love is liberation, in every form, at every moment.

KEY READING

bell hooks, *All About Love: New Visions*, New York: William Morrow, 2000

Rachel Smith and Barbara Vesey (eds), *The Love That Dares: Letters of LGBTQ+ Love & Friendship Through History*, London: Ilex, 2022

KEY ARTISTS

Tessa Boffin | Patricia Cronin | Beauford Delaney | Nan Goldin | Jenna Gribbon | Robert Indiana | Doron Langberg | Marie Laurencin | Sabelo Mlangeni | Muhammad Qasim | Gerda Wegener | David Wojnarowicz

ALICE AUSTEN
UNITED STATES, 1866–1952

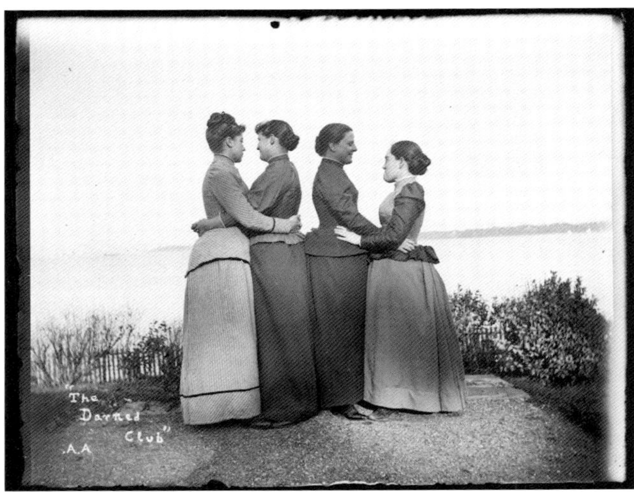

Alice Austen
The Darned Club,
29 October 1891
Glass plate negative
10.2 × 12.7 cm (4 × 5 in.)
Alice Austen Photograph
Collection, Staten Island
Historical Society,
New York

**This photograph of
Austen and three of
her friends embracing
in the garden of Clear
Comfort is one of many
images depicting the
bold and defiant antics
of the photographer's
community. The title
refers to a nickname
given to the close-knit
group of friends by local
men who felt excluded,
which the women found
funny and embraced.**

Alice Austen is celebrated as a pioneer of documentary photography and one of the earliest woman photographers in American history. Growing up in an affluent Staten Island family, she began learning about photography at the age of ten. By eighteen, she was a proficient self-taught photographer with a home darkroom where she developed her own glass-plate photographs. Best known for her street photography, images of New York's immigrant population, photographs of local and international waterways, and private photography of women, Austen went on to produce around eight thousand photographs during her lifetime.

In the late 1860s, Austen and her mother moved into a waterside cottage named Clear Comfort. Now a house museum dedicated to celebrating Austen's photographic legacy, it became a National Historic Landmark for LGBTQIA+ history in 2017. In 1899, Austen met Gertrude Tate who became her partner of fifty-six years, thirty of which were spent living together at Clear Comfort. In 1945 financial ruin forced the couple to sell their home. Tate was able to live with her family, but they would not allow Austen to join her. Austen went to live in a poorhouse, and eventually a nursing home. Tate visited her weekly until Austen's death in 1952.

Cycling was a key part of Austen's life and work. She transported heavy photographic equipment, sometimes weighing up to twenty-three kilos, on the back of her bicycle as she searched for new scenes to document. In 1896, Maria E. Ward published the book *Bicycling for Ladies*, a revolutionary title that introduced Victorian women to bicycling. The book's illustrations were drawn from photographs taken by Austen in a makeshift set on the lawn of Clear Comfort, featuring the gymnast and bloomer-clad model, Daisy Elliott. Ward and Elliott were part of Austen's close social circle – a group of women who rejected societal conventions by living independently, challenging traditional gender roles and embracing sexual autonomy. Elliott's letters from the period reveal that she and Austen were lovers.

Austen's relationship with women, which plays a significant role in understanding her work, has long been omitted from historical narratives. Her inherited wealth meant she didn't need to earn money from her craft and, as such, she was largely considered an amateur photographer. Because her work was not created with public distribution in mind, Austen was afforded the freedom to document the activities of women who chose to live outside of prescribed Victorian limitations; women who pushed the boundaries of gender expectations and found joy in female intimacy. These women wore bloomers rather than corsets, and formed emotional and sexual relationships with one another. Austen depicted them smoking, lounging, embracing and performing athletic movements – all of which contrasted the prevailing notions of restraint, passivity and female modesty.

KEY WORKS

Two People Reclining on a Couch, 1895, Collection of Staten Island Historic Society, New York, USA

Alice Austen and her Bicycle, c.1897, Alice Austen House Archive, New York, USA

KEY FACTS

Austen was the first woman on Staten Island to own a car, driving herself around in an era when female motorists were rare.

In 1951, a young historian discovered a collection of Austen's photographs and helped to publish them. This raised enough money to transfer the 84-year-old Austen from the poorhouse to a private nursing home.

TEE CORINNE
UNITED STATES, 1943–2006

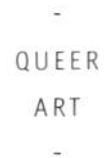

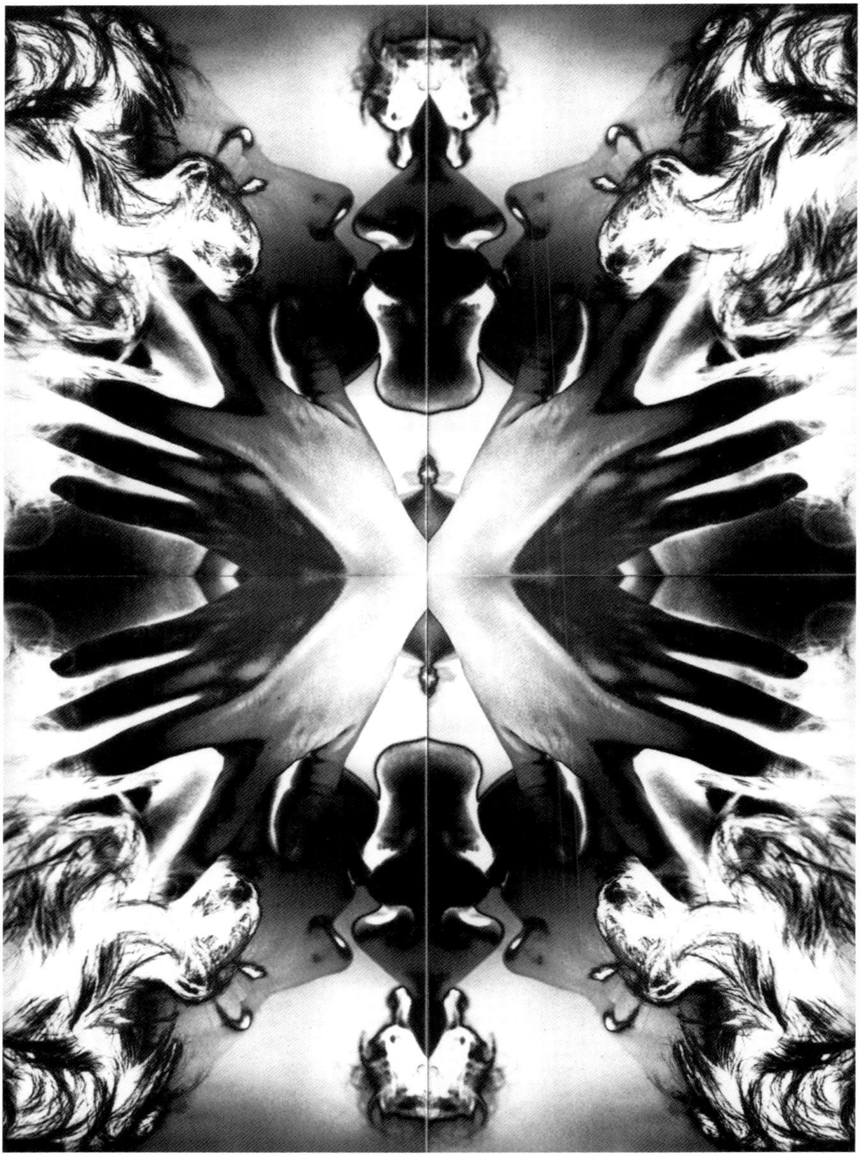

Tee Corinne
Yantras of Womanlove,
p. 20, c.1982
Gelatin silver print
Tee Corinne papers,
Coll. 263. University
of Oregon Libraries,
Special Collections and
University Archives,
Eugene, OR

**Corinne often used
solarization – a technique
whereby a photograph is
briefly exposed to light
during the development
process, causing the
image to wholly or
partially invert – to
present lesbian sexuality
as something spiritual
and transcendent. In
her collection, *Yantras
of Womanlove: Diagrams
of Energy*, the inverted
black-and-white
elements give the erotic
moments she captured
a transcendental
glow, as well as a
sense of anonymity or
universality.**

Tee Corinne was an American artist whose photographs of lesbians and illustrations of vulvas made a significant contribution to the visual history of queer women in the late twentieth century.

Corinne studied art at the University of California, Berkeley, and later earned an MFA at Pratt Institute in New York. During her studies, Corinne had drawn and sculpted men's genitals countless times, but never women's. Following her curiosity, she began producing secret drawings of her own anatomy. By 1974, having left her husband and moved to San Francisco, her art was dominated by labial drawings and images of women having sex. This foregrounding of sexuality was both a manifestation of her self-discovery and a means by which to create a visual presence for lesbian intimacy.

Corinne's line drawings came together in the *Cunt Coloring Book*, which she self-published in 1975. The book reached vast audiences – giving women the opportunity to learn about, reclaim and love their own bodies – and is still in print today. Corinne toured a series of slideshows across the United States. Here, she would showcase her vulva drawings and photographs, alongside depictions of lesbians in historical and contemporary art.

Understanding the potential impact of her work, in an artist statement Corinne described it 'as contributing to a kind of sanity, a witnessing, an affirmation of the fleshy side of lesbianism with more than a whiff of the transcendent'. Her later work notably included explorations of ageing, illness and disability, particularly in lesbian lives. She is recognized for her intersectional approach to choosing subjects, incorporating diverse, multiracial, multigenerational and differently abled queer bodies in her work. She was diagnosed with cancer and continued to create and advocate for greater representation of ageing bodies in art, breaking ground in an area often neglected in queer and feminist discourse.

KEY WORKS

Woman in Wheelchair with Able-bodied Lover, c.1979, University of Oregon Libraries, USA
Isis in the Woods, 1986, University of Oregon Libraries, USA

KEY FACTS

A keen organizer, Corinne inspired many lesbians through her annual workshop, the 'Feminist Photography Ovular'.
In 1981, Corinne co-founded *The Blatant Image: A Magazine of Feminist Photography*.

JEFFREY GIBSON
UNITED STATES, b.1972

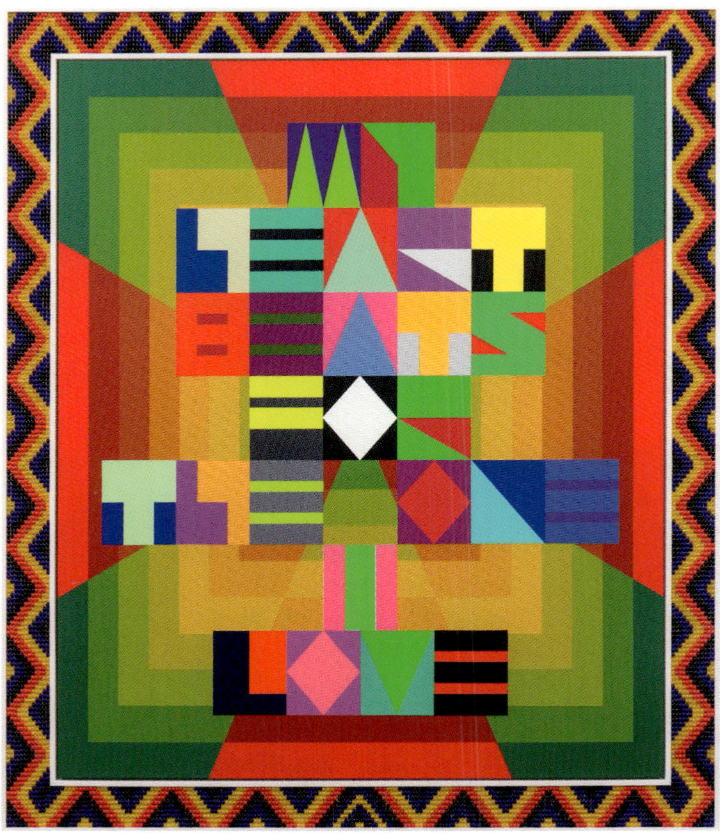

Jeffrey Gibson is a Mississippi Choctaw-Cherokee artist whose
work fuses Indigenous traditions, queer identity and contemporary
materials. Working across textiles, painting, beadwork and sculpture,
Gibson combines the aesthetics of Native American heritage with
influences from queer club culture, fashion, protest movements
and pop music. His work actively resists the historical erasure of
Indigenous and LGBTQIA+ identities, asserting their place within
American cultural history and society.

Born in Colorado Springs, Gibson was raised away from his
Mississippi Choctaw and Cherokee relatives because his father

Jeffrey Gibson
*MY HEART BEATS FOR
THE ONE I LOVE*, 2021
Acrylic on canvas, glass
beads and artificial sinew
161 × 136 cm
(63⅜ × 53½ in.)

Gibson's energetic, text-based pieces assert queer love and desire through his signature use of bold colours, kaleidoscopic patterns and traditional Native American materials such as beadwork and textiles. The phrase itself – borrowed from 'Heartbeat', a disco hit by Taana Gardner released in 1981 (the year the global AIDS pandemic began) – is both deeply personal and universally evocative, embodying themes of longing, resilience and self-expression.

worked for the US military and was often stationed overseas. Throughout his childhood, he sent drawings and letters to his family from Germany, Korea, England and the United States. He studied at the Art Institute of Chicago and earned an MFA from the Royal College of Art, London in 1998.

Gibson's text-based works sit within a lineage of artists who use language as a form of resistance and reclamation – from Glenn Ligon's stencilled text paintings interrogating race and identity to Barbara Kruger's subversive use of advertising aesthetics. However, Gibson's approach is uniquely rooted in Indigenous storytelling and craft traditions. He is also known for creating large textile works, totems and wearable pieces influenced by outfits worn by Indigenous dancers at powwows as well as neon rave aesthetics, combining traditional visual media and techniques, such as Iroquois beadwork, with contemporary queer culture.

In his immersive exhibition, 'POWER FULL BECAUSE WE'RE DIFFERENT' (2024), Gibson presented *Two Spirit People* – a 1992 documentary in which Indigenous artists discuss the term 'two-spirit' as it relates to their lives – accompanied by a four-screen video installation showing material created by more than twenty contemporary two-spirit artists, academics, drag performers and DJs.

Gibson's works are vibrant and celebratory – they reflect a vision of love where queer relationships (romantic, platonic and familial) are integral to survival. By utilizing the visual languages of protest movements and club culture, his work emphasizes the radical possibilities implied by different forms of queer and Indigenous community.

KEY WORKS

Eternal Return, 2014, Philbrook Museum of Art, Oklahoma, USA
I AM A RAINBOW TOO, 2018, San Francisco Museum of Modern Art, San Francisco, USA

KEY FACTS

In 2019, Gibson was awarded a prestigious MacArthur Fellowship, recognized for his innovative fusion of Indigenous craft with contemporary art.

Gibson was selected for the United States Pavilion at the 2024 Venice Biennale – the first time an Indigenous artist has ever been given a solo exhibition in the US Pavilion.

FELIX GONZALEZ-TORRES
AMERICAN, b.CUBA, 1957–96

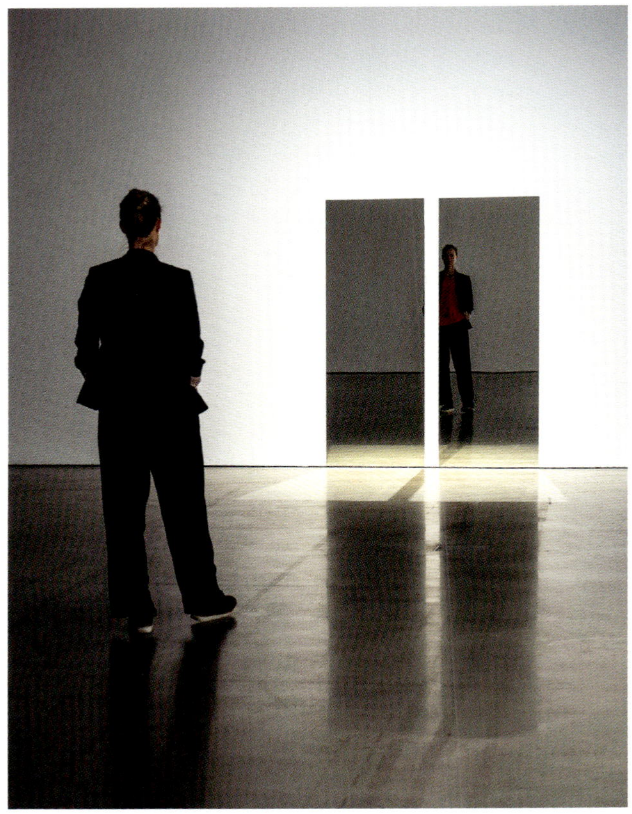

Felix Gonzalez-Torres was an American artist, born in Cuba, whose works offer poignant meditations on love. He moved to New York City in 1979, where his experience as a gay man and immigrant during the AIDS crisis would shape both the form and content of his work. He became known for his use of everyday materials to explore themes of intimacy, impermanence and societal stigma.

Though often associated with its aesthetics, Gonzalez-Torres subverted the traditions of Minimalist art. In contrast to the detached coolness of canonical Minimalism, his pieces often carried coded references to queer experience and loss, challenging the boundaries between public and private, formalism and affect.

Felix Gonzalez-Torres
'Untitled' *(Orpheus, Twice)*,
1991
Mirror
Dimensions variable,
195 × 150 cm
(76¾ × 59 in.)
Two Parts: 195 × 70 cm
(76¾ × 27½ in.) each
Installation view
Bonniers Konsthall,
Stockholm, Sweden.
Private collection

**Conceived in the same
year as the death of
the artist's partner,
Ross Laycock, the two
identical mirrors in this
piece quietly reflect
the surrounding space,
including the viewer.
The title references
the mythological figure
Orpheus, who descends
into the underworld
to retrieve his beloved
Eurydice, only to lose
her again by looking
back. The doubled
mirrors evoke themes
of reflection, absence
and the impossibility
of return.**

Gonzalez-Torres's partner, Ross Laycock, was a central influence in his life and art. In 1988, Laycock was diagnosed with AIDS. The next year, Gonzalez-Torres created a billboard display in New York City to commemorate the twentieth anniversary of the Stonewall Riots, embedding LGBTQIA+ history into the urban landscape. Between Laycock's diagnosis and death in 1991, the couple became known for their activism, using exhibitions to raise awareness of social issues and the human toll of the AIDS pandemic.

Among his best-known works is the candy spill sculpture *'Untitled'* *(Portrait of Ross in L.A.)* (1991). Visitors take pieces of colourfully wrapped candy from the sprawling pile, mirroring Laycock's gradual physical decline as it diminishes. It is a powerful metaphor for loss, love and renewal, with each replenishment an act of remembrance. His work *'Untitled'* *(Perfect Lovers)* (1987–90) – which consists of two clocks, both set to the same time – also concerns love and loss. As the minutes, hours and days pass, the batteries expire at different rates, and the clocks eventually fall out of sync. If one clock stops, they are fixed or replaced. Gonzalez-Torres described this work as 'the scariest thing' he ever did, articulating not only his fear of loss but the passage of time as an inevitable force in all relationships. Iconic in their minimalism, Gonzalez-Torres's pieces resist spectacle while remaining profoundly symbolic. Their quiet repetitions and precise forms are vessels for unspeakable aspects of grief, longing and desire.

Gonzalez-Torres received significant recognition in his lifetime, including a retrospective at the Guggenheim in 1995, a year before he passed away from AIDS-related complications. His legacy continues to shape queer art and theory, offering a vision of love that is both political and poetic; ephemeral yet enduring.

KEY WORKS

'Untitled' *(Public Opinion)*, 1991, Solomon R. Guggenheim
    Museum, New York, USA
'Untitled' *(It's Just a Matter of Time)*, 1992, The Felix
    Gonzalez-Torres Foundation

KEY FACTS

Gonzalez-Torres was a core member of Group Material, a radical
    collective known for community-driven exhibitions.
In 2007, Gonzalez-Torres was selected for the US Pavilion at the
    Venice Biennale – a rare honour as he had died in 1996.

DUNCAN GRANT
UNITED KINGDOM, 1885–1978

Painter and designer Duncan Grant created a profoundly modern
and intimately personal body of work. Born in Rothiemurchus,
Scotland and raised between India and Britain, Grant studied in
Paris before attending the Slade School of Fine Art in London.
Grant was a central figure in the Bloomsbury Group, which rejected
Victorian moralism in favour of artistic freedom, sexual liberation
and unconventional relationships. The group included his cousin,
the writer Lytton Strachey; John Maynard Keynes; Roger Fry;
Virginia and Leonard Woolf; Virginia's sister, the painter Vanessa
Bell; and Vanessa's husband, Clive Bell.

In 1916, two years after the start of the First World War, Britain
introduced conscription, and Grant moved to a house named
Charleston in Sussex, England, along with Vanessa Bell, her two
sons and Grant's lover, David Garnett. Like most of the Bloomsbury
Group, Grant was a conscientious objector – a pacifist who took
an anti-war stance – which meant that he was able to avoid
conscription by working on a local farm along with Garnett.

Almost as soon as they moved to Charleston, Grant and
Bell started to paint every surface of the farmhouse, transforming
it into a living, breathing work of art, and in 1918, they had
a daughter, Angelica, together. Their relationship was marked
by artistic collaboration and deep love for one another, and their
approach to domesticity and family life – eschewing monogamy
and heteronormative structures – was extremely radical for early-
twentieth-century Britain. Grant was in love with Bell but also with
Garnett, and they were both in love with him.

Grant was openly gay despite the legal and social constraints of
the time. The punishment for 'buggery' in Britain had only recently
been reduced from hanging to life-imprisonment when Grant was
born, and six months later the Labouchère Amendment was passed,
which criminalized all male homosexual acts even if there had
been no witnesses, greatly increasing the number of gay men who
were prosecuted. In the 1940s, he formed a lasting and passionate
relationship with Paul Roche, a poet and writer twenty-seven years
his junior, who became a significant muse in Grant's later work.

Having grown up in a period of intense legal and social
persecution of homosexuality, Grant witnessed the slow but

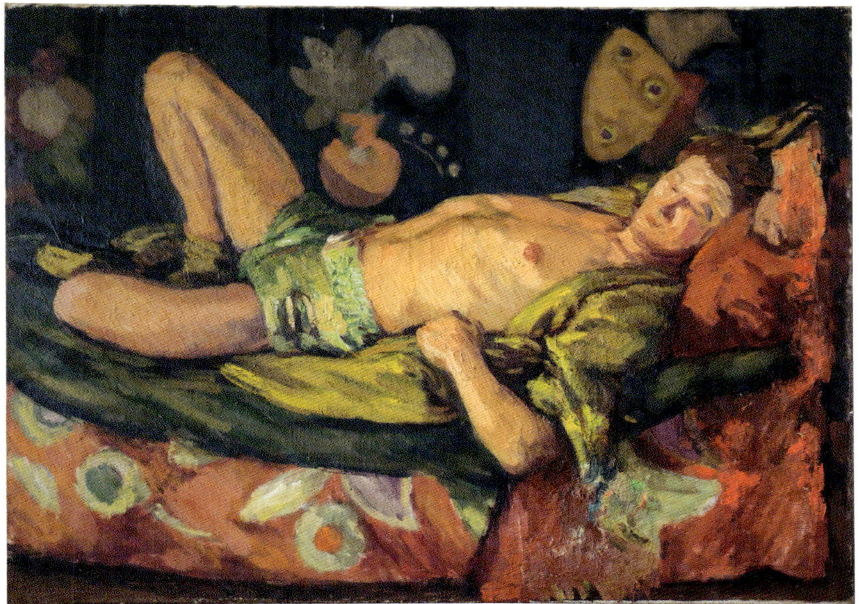

Duncan Grant
Paul Roche Reclining,
c.1945
Oil on canvas
55 × 76 cm
(21¾ × 30 in.)
Charleston, Firle, Lewes

One of Grant's most evocative depictions of male beauty and queer desire, this portrait presents Roche sprawled across a sofa in a pose that recalls classical depictions of reclining nudes. Yet, there is an intimacy and familiarity that speaks to deep affection and attraction.

undeniable shift in attitudes towards homosexuality and the emergence of the modern gay rights movement in the 1970s. He died in 1978, leaving behind a body of work that subtly but powerfully documented queer desire and intimacy. Grant's paintings, including many portraits of his lovers, as well as Vanessa Bell and her children, and hundreds of erotic drawings, demonstrate his personal exploration of love and liberation.

KEY WORKS

Self Portrait, 1910, Charleston, Firle, Lewes, UK
Football, 1911, Tate, London, UK

KEY FACTS

In 1913, Grant, Fry and Bell co-founded the Omega Workshops, a cooperative that produced textiles and other decorative arts.
Grant spent time in France with artists including Henri Matisse and Pablo Picasso.

FRIDA KAHLO
MEXICO, 1907–54

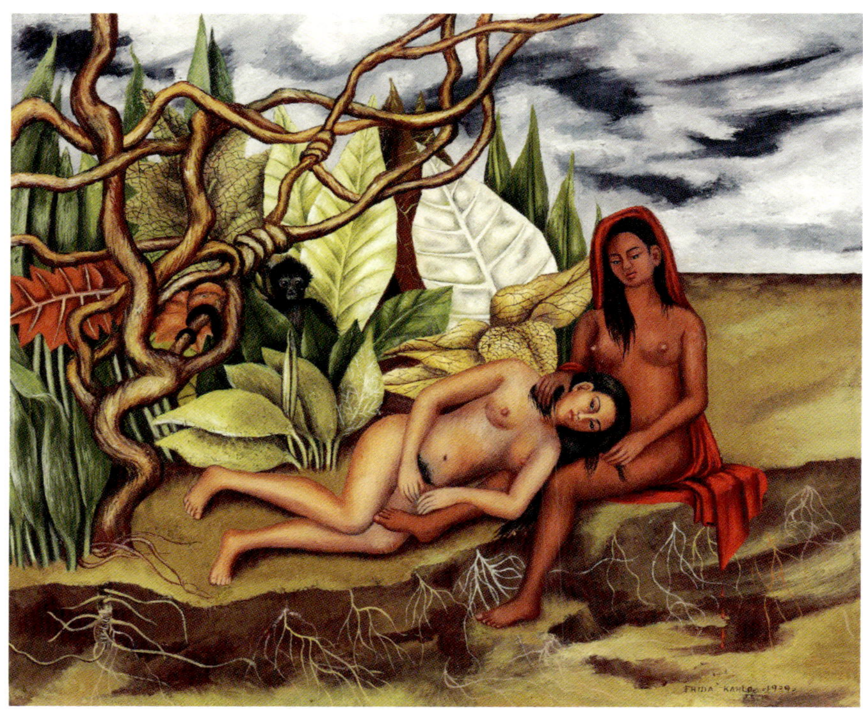

Frida Kahlo is globally recognized as one of modern art's most iconic
and unconventional figures. Born in Coyoacán, Mexico City, to
a German father and *mestiza* mother, of Spanish and Purépecha
descent, Kahlo's life was marked by physical and emotional suffering.
A childhood battle with polio left her with a lifelong limp, and at
eighteen, a near-fatal bus accident resulted in severe injuries that
caused chronic pain for the rest of her life. Initially aspiring to be
a doctor, Kahlo took up painting after her accident, teaching herself
during her recovery. In 1927, she joined the Communist Party,
immersing herself in Mexico's artistic and political circles.

    Kahlo's fluid sexuality is often overshadowed by her tumultuous
relationship with the male muralist Diego Rivera – whom she
married in 1929. However, she was open about her attraction to

women and had relationships with both men and women. Among her rumoured affairs were French performer Josephine Baker, artist Georgia O'Keeffe and Mexican actress Dolores del Río. Yet, for decades, historical narratives largely minimized or erased her queerness, often portraying her as a tragic heterosexual muse rather than a radical and autonomous bisexual artist.

Kahlo's diaries contain candid reflections on her female lovers, while her artworks consistently challenge patriarchal and colonial frameworks. Her paintings frequently feature symbolic elements – monkeys, blood, thorns and broken columns – that speak to pain, sexuality, fertility and endurance. She also used traditional motifs such as Mexican ex-voto panels and Tehuana dress to assert her national and Indigenous identity, while queering the visual codes of femininity.

Over the course of her lifetime, Kahlo produced approximately one hundred and fifty paintings, many of which are deeply personal and politically charged, securing her legacy as one of the most influential artists of the twentieth century.

KEY WORKS

Self-Portrait Dedicated to Leon Trotsky, 1937, National Museum of Women in the Arts, Washington, DC, USA

The Two Fridas, 1939, Museo de Arte Moderno, Mexico City

KEY FACTS

Kahlo famously surrounded herself with exotic pets at Casa Azul, her blue house, including spider monkeys (named Fulang Chang and Caimito de Guayabal), an Amazon parrot called Bonito, a fawn named Granizo, hairless Xoloitzcuintli dogs, chickens, an eagle and more.

Kahlo's first solo exhibition in Mexico (at Galería de Arte Contemporáneo, 1953) coincided with a precipitous decline in her health – but she was determined to be there. She arrived by ambulance on opening night, lying in a four-poster bed that was wheeled into the gallery.

Frida Kahlo
Dos desnudos en el bosque (La tierra misma) (Two Nudes in a Forest), 1939
Oil on metal
25 × 30.2 cm
(9⅞ × 11⅞ in.)
Private collection

This painting was gifted by Kahlo to her lover, the actress Dolores del Río. One figure, bearing the artist's unmistakable features, gazes directly at the viewer while resting her head in the lap of another woman. A small monkey – often a symbol of mischief, protection and devotion in Kahlo's visual language, and a Mexican symbol for lust – watches from the background.

TAMARA DE LEMPICKA
POLAND, 1894–1980

Tamara de Lempicka was a painter whose works have become synonymous with the Art Deco movement. Her sleek, sensual and angular figures, which have an almost sculptural quality, capture the glamour and luxury of modern Europe in the interwar period.

Originally named Tamara Rosa Hurwitz-Górska, Tamara de Lempicka went through several periods of reinvention throughout her life. She grew up in Warsaw, Poland, raised by a wealthy family who converted from Judaism to Christianity soon after Tamara was born, changing their last names to Gurwik-Górska in the process. Her grandmother indulged her with luxurious clothes, and she travelled widely from a young age. In 1916, she married Tadeusz Łempicki, a Polish lawyer. In the wake of the Russian Revolution, the couple escaped to Paris in 1918.

In Paris, Lempicka studied art at the Académie Ranson and changed her name to the aristocratic-sounding Tamara de Lempicka, which helped her navigate Parisian social circles with ease. She quickly found success painting portraits of the wealthy elite. Nobility, entertainers, artists and scientists – as her daughter once said, she painted 'them all, the rich, the successful and the renowned'. In 1928, she divorced her first husband and, after twenty years in Paris, she moved to the United States, where she became a favourite artist among the stars in Los Angeles, eventually marrying one of her wealthiest patrons, Baron Raoul Kuffner de Dioszegh, in 1934.

Lempicka was openly bisexual and had relationships with both men and women. Many of her works explore themes of desire and seduction, celebrating women's physicality, autonomy and erotic freedom. For example, in pieces such as *La Belle Rafaëla* (1927), depicting a reclining nude woman, and *Andromeda* (1929), featuring a nude figure in chains, female desire is central and commanding.

Lempicka's depictions of female lovers and androgynous figures positioned her within the rich, complex history of LGBTQIA+ modernism. Alongside artists such as Romaine Brooks and Claude Cahun (pages 38–39), she created a visual language that celebrated gender fluidity and queer desire, marking her as a radical force in early twentieth-century art.

Tamara de Lempicka
Les jeunes filles
(The Girls), c.1930
Oil on panel
35 × 27 cm
(13¾ × 10⅝ in.)
Private collection

The Girls is among Lempicka's most evocative explorations of female intimacy. Two women are entwined in a sensual embrace, their partially nude bodies, rendered in smooth sculptural forms, meet beneath the rich folds of a single shared garment. The physical closeness, lowered gazes and deep shadows convey an air of secrecy about the encounter.

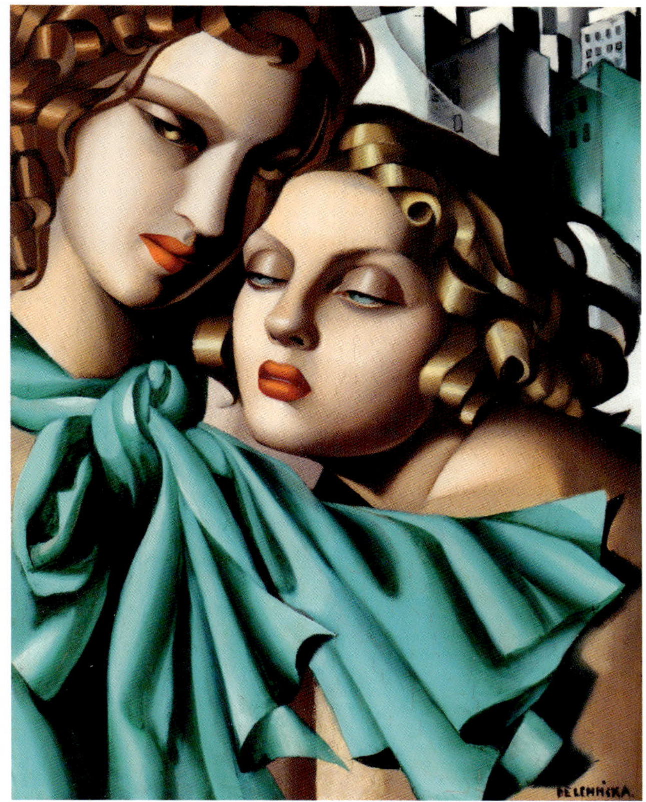

KEY WORKS

Four Nudes, 1925, Private collection
Sleeping Girl, 1930, Private collection

KEY FACTS

Lempicka's final wish was to have her ashes thrown into a volcano. When she died in 1980 in Mexico, her remains were cremated and, per her instructions, scattered over the crater of Mount Popocatépetl – the snow-capped volcano she could see from her home.
Pop icon Madonna counts Lempicka among her favorite painters and has amassed an extensive collection of Lempicka originals.

MICKALENE THOMAS
UNITED STATES, b.1971

Mickalene Thomas is a multi-disciplinary artist working across painting, collage, photography, video and installation. Blending influences from art history, pop culture and personal experience, Thomas challenges the white-dominated canon of Western portraiture, interrogating how Black femininity has been framed, objectified or erased in art and media.

Thomas's practice is deeply personal, often repeatedly returning to figures from her life, such as her mother, Sandra 'Mama Bush' – whom she first began photographing while studying at Yale, and later depicted towards the end of her life – as well as partners, friends and former lovers. Thomas has referred to her mother as the first of her muses, and her work often foregrounds the artist-muse relationship, using it as a framework to explore themes of power, identity, love and legacy, as well as an opportunity to celebrate Black womanhood and queer intimacy. Citing the Black Power Movement and her mother alongside artists such as Carrie Mae Weems and Faith Ringgold as major sources of inspiration in her work, Thomas constructs portraits of Black women that emphasize their agency, beauty and complexity.

Thomas often makes allusions to famous paintings and figures from Western art history, reworking their symbolism through a Black, queer, feminist lens, while taking part in the time-honoured tradition of artists situating themselves within the canon. Her work, *Le dejeuner sur l'herbe: Les Trois Femmes Noires* (2010) reimagines Édouard Manet's picnic scene, replacing the white nude figures with three fully-clothed Black women who meet the viewer's gaze. Her authorship extends to the clothes they wear – having designed the dresses herself. Dressing – rather than undressing – becomes a clear form of agency in resisting canonical voyeurism.

She often incorporates rhinestones, luscious textures and fractured planes of pattern in her work, expanding the language of portraiture and emphasizing abundance, using imagery that speaks of glamour, intimacy and resistance. The spaces her subjects inhabit are often deliberately excessive, and in that regard, celebratory. Domestic interiors are rendered as sites of possession and pleasure, honouring, stylizing and canonizing Black queer love.

Mickalene Thomas
This is Where I Came In,
2006
Rhinestones, acrylic and
enamel on wood panel
182.9 × 152.4 cm
(72 × 60 in.)
Private collection

***This is Where I Came In**
plays with camouflage
and spectacle, featuring
two animal print-clad
bodies intertwined in a
charged embrace. The
title hints at a moment
of return or realisation,
while the rhinestone
sparkle and textured
surfaces heighten the
scene's sensuality and
intimacy.*

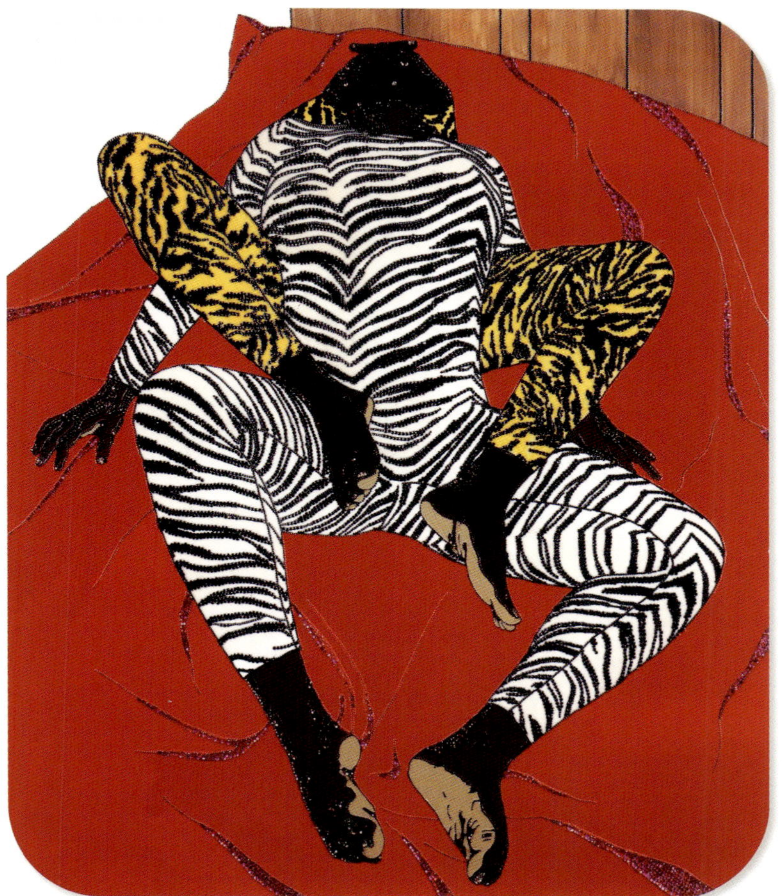

KEY WORKS

Can't We Just Sit Down and Talk It Over?, 2006–7, Art Institute
   of Chicago and Studio Museum in Harlem, New York, USA
Racquel: Come to Me, 2016, Whitney Museum of American Art,
   New York, USA

KEY FACTS

Thomas received the Anonymous Was a Woman Award in 2013.
In 2008, before Amy Sherald's official painting of Michelle
   Obama, Mickalene Thomas created a notable portrait of First
   Lady Obama titled *Michelle O*.

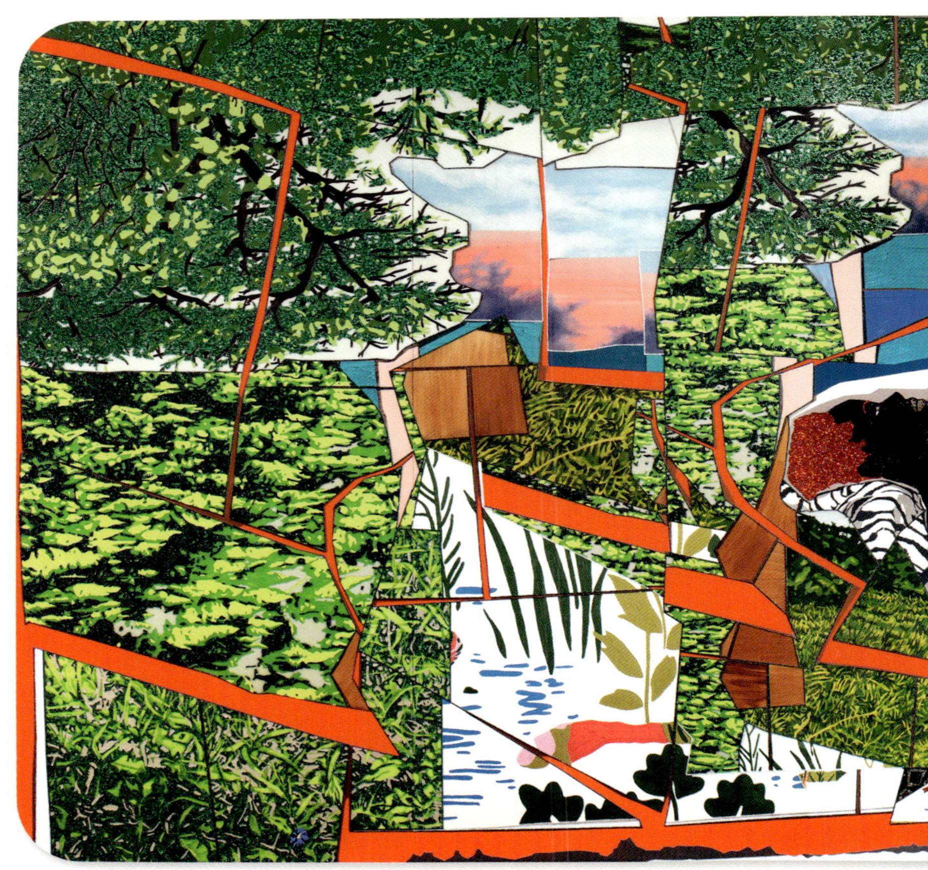

Mickalene Thomas
Sleep: Deux femmes noires,
2011
Rhinestone, acrylic paint
and oil enamel on wood
panel, 274.3 × 609.6 cm
(108 × 240 in.)
Lehmann Maupin
Collections

The large-scale work
***Sleep: Deux femmes
noires*** is rich with art-
historical references.
The two figures recreate
the pose from Gustave
Courbet's 1866 painting
Le Sommeil, in which two
white women embrace on
a bed, causing scandal
at the time.

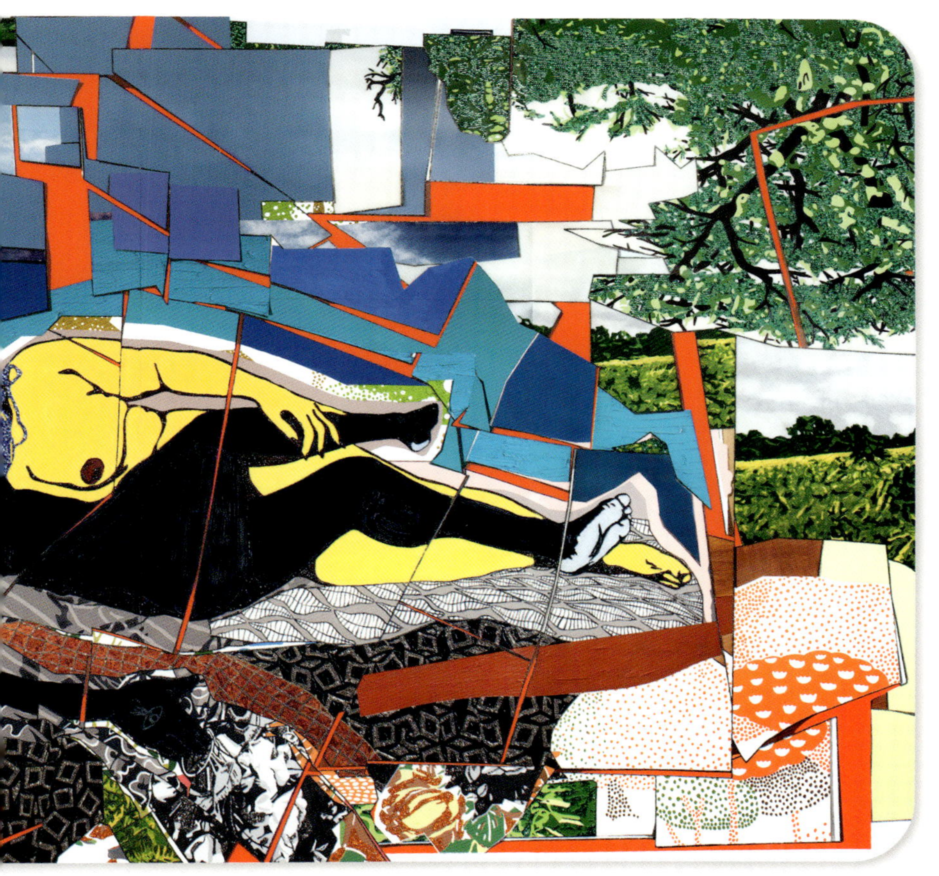

WOLFGANG TILLMANS
GERMANY, b.1968

Wolfgang Tillmans is an artist, activist and documentarian who has spent decades capturing and examining the beauty and complexity of identity and desire, as well as a range of subcultures, within and beyond contemporary queer communities. Known for his radical experimentation in form, Tillmans has worked across genres, from portraiture and still life to abstraction.

Born in Remscheid, Germany, Tillmans began his career in the late 1980s and early 1990s, where he became a key figure in documenting the emerging club scene in Europe. He moved to the UK in 1990, to study at Bournemouth and Poole College of Art and Design, where his experimental approach to photography developed further. Tillmans later moved to London, where he immersed himself in queer nightlife, activism and post-punk youth culture, bringing a diaristic, personal style to communities often under-represented in mainstream media at the time.

Tillmans is an innovative photographic experimenter – combining traditional documentary techniques with abstraction and unconventional processes. His *Freischwimmer* works (2001– present) don't even involve a camera – instead, he manipulates photosensitive paper with a flashlight to create fluid, organic forms. Other notable works, such as *Lighter* and *paper drop*, continued this exploration of photography as a sculptural and physical medium.

Tillmans's work emerged in the wake of the AIDS crisis, a time of immense loss, activism and shifting perceptions of queer desire. Across his practice, Tillmans resists turning queerness into spectacle. Instead, he presents intimacy – whether platonic, romantic or sexual – as ordinary and necessary. His photographs of friends, lovers and everyday moments quietly insist on the legitimacy of queer life. In both his art and activism, Tillmans cultivates a language of openness and care. His work continues to speak to queer resilience, joy and the right to live freely and openly.

Wolfgang Tillmans
The Cock (kiss), 2002

The tightly cropped composition heightens the emotional charge of this image, stripping away external narratives and focusing entirely on the kiss itself. It resists both sensationalism and fetishization, instead offering a sweaty moment of organic, unguarded connection.

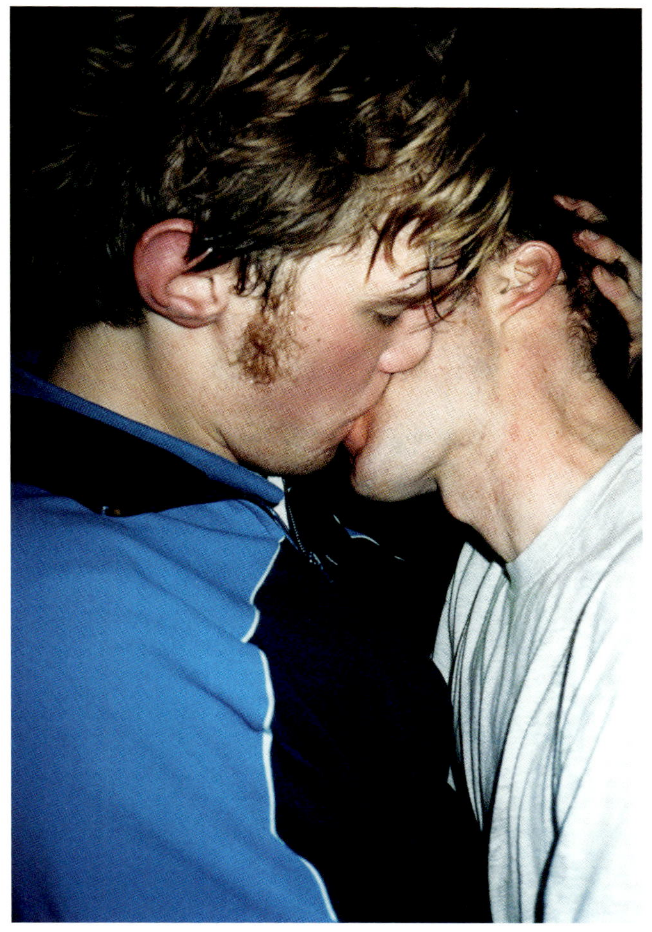

KEY WORKS

like praying I, 1994
Jochen taking a bath, 1997

KEY FACTS

In 2016, Tillmans's track 'Device Control' was featured in Frank Ocean's visual album *Endless*. He has also worked with artists such as Pet Shop Boys, No Bra, Kittin, Salem and Neneh Cherry, contributing album artwork, photography and sound pieces. Tillmans became the first photographer and non-British artist to win the Turner Prize in 2000.

SALMAN TOOR
PAKISTAN, b.1983

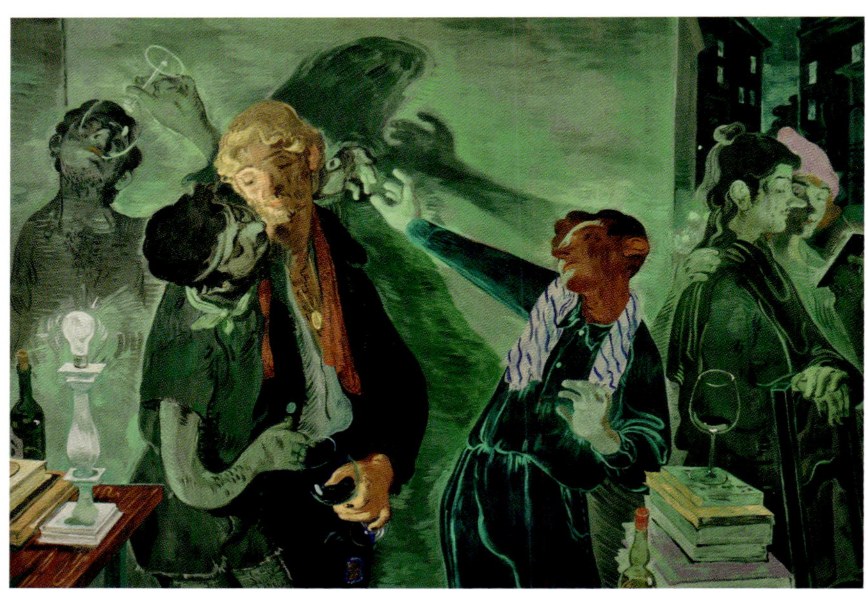

Salman Toor is a Pakistani-American painter whose lyrical and melancholic scenes blend figurative painting traditions with queer storytelling, exploring the tension between home and exile, desire and anxiety, queerness and cultural expectation. He studied painting and drawing at Ohio Wesleyan University, graduating in 2006, before completing his MFA at Pratt Institute in New York in 2009.

Toor's work exists within a long tradition of queer everyday scenes in art. His figures – often a self-referential protagonist surrounded by friends in a bar or domestic setting – navigate the liminal spaces between family expectations and the safety of queer social circles. They are not grand depictions, but quiet, affectionate portraits of queer intimacy as solidarity and kinship, something communal, not only romantic. His world is one of shared spaces and subtle gestures, where love is expressed through unspoken bonds.

Salman Toor
The Green Room, 2019
Oiˡ on panel
124.5 × 180.3 cm
(49 × 71 in.)
Kiran Nadar Museum
of Art, New Delhi

Here, Toor captures a moment of intimacy, coded through light, gesture and atmosphere. His signature green glow bathes the scene, shaping its nocturnal, dreamlike quality. 'I've thought of green as glamorous, poisonous, nocturnal, nostalgic, but not sentimental,' Toor has said. Five figures occupy the space in hushed conversation, their body language suggesting conspiracy and seduction, with a quiet awareness of the world outside.

Often rendered in his signature palette of acidic and emerald greens, Toor's paintings feel dreamlike and otherworldly: at once lush and emotionally charged; unsettling, yet seductive. Light spills from phones, windows or chandeliers, bathing the room in an uncanny glow. He dresses his characters in sheer fabrics, sequins and silk – luxurious, draped garments that seduce the viewer as much as they protect or conceal the figure beneath. This meticulous attention to clothing becomes a kind of second skin, revealing emotional states and personal histories.

While many of his works celebrate community, desire and tenderness, they often carry an undertone of unease, heightened by looming shadows and references to street violence. In *Man with Face Creams and a Phone Plug* (2019), a queer brown figure is searched at an airport checkpoint – highlighting the collision of racial profiling, queer vulnerability and surveillance, speaking to the layered experience of being racialized and queer under scrutiny.

Toor's paintings refuse voyeurism or victimhood. Instead, they centre queer joy, connection and the quiet courage of stepping out into a hostile world. His scenes are tender, fantastical testaments to love and liberation – reminders of the vibrant beauty, resilience and everyday magic of queer life.

KEY WORKS

Bedroom Boy, 2019, Whitney Museum of American Art,
New York, USA
Bar Boy, 2019, Whitney Museum of American Art,
New York, USA

KEY FACTS

On discovering his work, the Whitney Museum gave Salman Toor just six months to prepare his breakthrough solo show, 'How Will I Know' (2020), featuring fifteen intimate paintings of queer South Asian life.

In 2021, Salman Toor illustrated *Jungle Nama*, a verse adaptation of a Bengali folktale by author Amitav Ghosh, blending traditional storytelling with contemporary visual art.

DEL LAGRACE VOLCANO
UNITED STATES, b.1957

Del LaGrace Volcano is a pioneering genderqueer visual activist
and photographer whose work has helped redefine the landscape
of queer representation since the 1980s. Combining portraiture
with political urgency, their practice foregrounds subjects
often excluded from dominant narratives, particularly those
living outside binary understandings of gender and sexuality.
Through photography, Volcano explores embodiment, eroticism
and performance, offering a vital and nuanced depiction of gender
nonconformity. Their images are rooted in both visibility and
resistance, expanding the possibilities for how queer and intersex
lives can be seen and understood.

Volcano was born intersex but assigned and raised female from
birth, which is how they lived the first thirty-seven years of their
life. As a teenager, Volcano moved to San Francisco, supporting
themself with a job as a motorcycle escort before studying at
San Francisco Art Institute from 1979 to 1981.

Often concerned with the politics of representation, they
document queerness and gender variance as lived experience.
Through their visual art, they play with the performative possibilities
of gender, using the body as a site of humour, power, fantasy and
tension. Although their work emphasizes sexuality and eroticism
– as in their 1988 series depicting dykes cruising on Hampstead
Heath, London – their photographs refuse to reduce gender-diverse
and queer subjects to sexualized roles, often capturing them in
candid moments of casual intimacy and laughter.

The importance of Volcano's practice also stems from the urgent
need for intersex visibility. Their work challenges the medical and
cultural silence and stigma that has long surrounded intersex bodies
– the personal cost of which Volcano has spoken candidly about.

A defining work, *Self Portrait with Blue Beard* (1995), captures
Volcano in their London home studio in a moment of personal
exploration. Wearing blue mascara in both beard and hair against
a striking backdrop, the image celebrates experimentation,
self-assertion and joy. Inspired in part by drag-king culture, the
photograph has become a symbol of non-binary identity, queerness
and the radical potential of the 'spaces in between'.

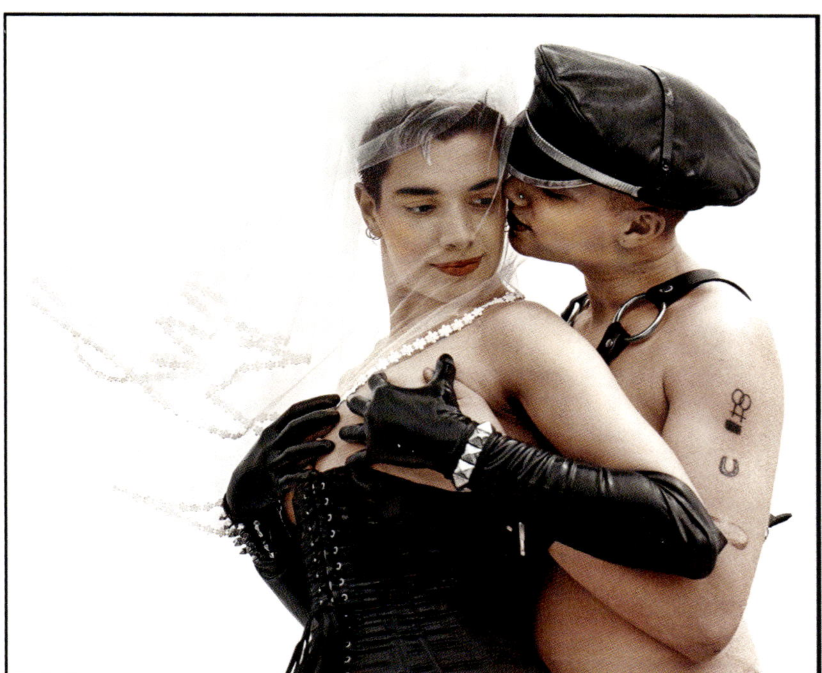

Del LaGrace Volcano
*The Ceremony, Robyn &
Peri, London, 1988*
35mm b/w analogue film
60 × 50 cm
(23⅝ × 19¾ in.)

Twenty-five years before
same-sex marriage
would be legalized in
the United Kingdom,
Volcano humorously
reimagines traditional
wedding portraiture.
Along with Volcano, the
subjects were part of a
group in London's 1980s
lesbian scene known
as the 'Rebel Dykes',
whose aesthetic was born
out of punk, biker and
sadomasochist culture.

KEY WORKS

Self Portrait with Blue Beard, 1995
TWIRL, Kathy Acker, 1997

KEY FACTS

Del LaGrace Volcano's 1991 photobook *Love Bites*, featuring
explicit lesbian sexuality, faced censorship upon release.
It was banned for two weeks in the United States, partially
censored in Canada and controversially received in the UK,
where some lesbian bookstores refused to stock it due to its
BDSM content.

In 1999, Volcano co-authored *The Drag King Book* with gender
theorist Jack Halberstam.

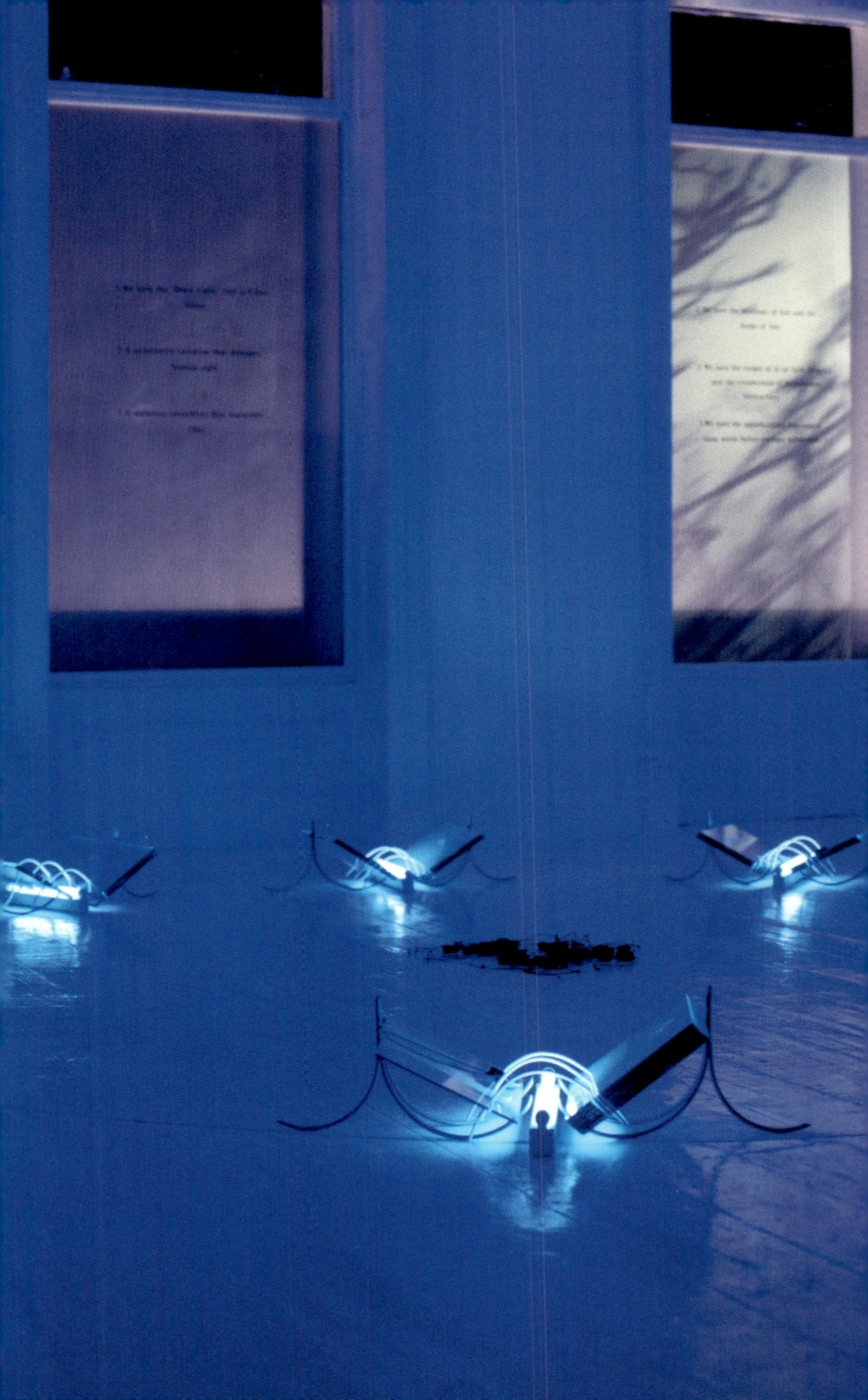

QUEER FUTURES

Queer futures are born from longing, refusal and resilience.
As José Esteban Muñoz wrote, queerness is 'not yet here'
– it exists not only in lived experience but also in the realm of
possibility. It is imagined through dreams of other worlds – worlds
where queerness is not merely tolerated but central. Trans and non-
binary artists are at the forefront of queer futurity, with works that
challenge fixed categories and imagine new forms of embodiment.
Their work often interrogates medical, legal and cultural systems
that regulate the body. Decolonial and Indigenous queer artists may
also reframe futurity not as a break from the past, but as a return
to ways of knowing that predate colonial impositions. Queer artists
have long envisioned what comes next: speculative spaces where
love, fluidity and freedom can flourish, resisting binaries, social
policing and cultural erasure.

A dynamic tension exists between memory and survival in queer
histories. While much has been erased – with lives, communities,
stories and traditions lost to violence – some memories and
narratives remain, carrying with them the possibility of resistance
and survival into the future.

At the heart of this chapter is the belief that queerness is more
than an identity – it is a futurity, a way of imagining beyond the
limits imposed by dominant structures. Contemporary artists are
actively constructing these queer futures through frameworks
such as Afrofuturism, speculative fiction and digital spaces.
In other words, imagining queer futures is a deliberate act of
invention and resistance – distilling utopian values from a life
under heteronormativity. Many of these works foreground
celebration – reaffirming life and community.

Queerness can also be about unbuilding the world we know.
For instance, some queer futurist art depicts environments where
capitalist, heterocentric societies fall into ruin, or where gender
institutions are inverted or collapse. These futures are also born
outside of galleries – they unfold across sound, dance, textiles,
tattoos and protest signs, as well as in community gardens and
DIY publishing projects. Queer futures embody a dual impulse:
both constructing and deconstructing.

Queer futurity is an act of culture-making (or re-making).
The work in this chapter asserts that what is not yet present can
be made 'here' through shared vision. These artworks are not
escapist fantasies – they are soft revolutions, radical propositions
and acts of survival. They emerge in these artists' performance,
paint, photography, archives and digital space. Queer artists have
always provided these – in zines, archives, clubs and pigments;

they have long imagined and built such futures. To envision this queer future is to reshape the present, not escape it. It is to refuse inherited limits, and assert a world where queerness thrives by design. This chapter is a testament to that ongoing work.

KEY READING

Amelia Abraham (ed.), *We Can Do Better Than This: 35 Voices on the Future of LGBTQ+ Rights*, London: Vintage, 2021

José Esteban Muñoz, *Cruising Utopia: The Then and There of Queer Futurity*, New York: NYU Press, 2009

William J. Simmons, *Queer Formalism: The Return*, Berlin: Floating Opera Press, 2022

KEY ARTISTS

April Bey | TM Davy | Nicholas Hlobo | Juliana Huxtable | Kang Seung Lee | Zoe Leonard | Toyin Ojih Odutola | Charmaine Poh | Raqib Shaw | Paul Thek | Michaela Yearwood-Dan | Cajsa von Zeipel

LAURA AGUILAR
UNITED STATES, 1959–2018

Laura Aguilar was a pioneering American photographer who worked to radically reshape the representation of marginalized identities. Born in San Gabriel, California, Aguilar inhabited a complex intersection of identities: Chicana, lesbian, queer and disabled. Her photography became a powerful tool for self-expression and advocacy, giving voice to communities often overlooked in mainstream culture. Although largely self-taught, she pursued formal training at East Los Angeles College in the late 1970s and early 1980s.

In a departure from traditional documentary photography, which often involves outsiders capturing subjects without fully engaging with them, Aguilar's approach was collaborative and introspective, turning the lens on her own community and challenging the power dynamics within photographic representation. Her *Latina Lesbians* series from 1987, for example, included handwritten notes from her sitters, providing personal reflections on their self-perceptions, desires and struggles – an intimate exchange between photographer and subject, which exemplified Aguilar's commitment to emotional depth in her work. In a later series entitled *Plush Pony* (1992), she highlighted the lives of working-class Latina lesbians who frequented a bar of the same name in East Los Angeles.

Aguilar also used self-portraiture to explore her own cultural dualities. In *Three Eagles Flying* (1990), she confronted the tension between US and Mexican nationalism by placing her naked body between two flags – an American flag wrapped around her hips, a Mexican flag entirely covering her face and a rope binding her arms – symbolizing cultural conflict and the tendency for national identity to consume personal identity in contemporary discourse. In her *Grounded* series (2006–7), Aguilar addressed the duality of visibility and erasure, positioning her nude body within the desert landscape to challenge dominant ideals and assert her presence as a large, queer, brown woman. Meanwhile, works such as *Access + Opportunity = Success* (1993) focused on the inequities faced by queer, disabled and Latinx artists.

Throughout her career, Aguilar's work unapologetically centred the bodies and lived experiences of queer, disabled and Latinx individuals. She documented physical, societal and personal

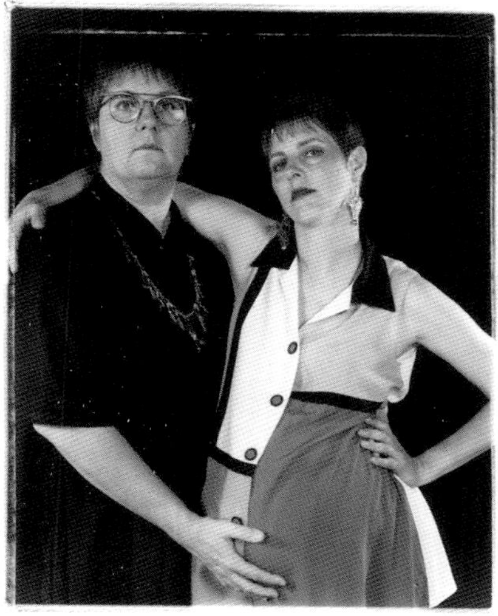 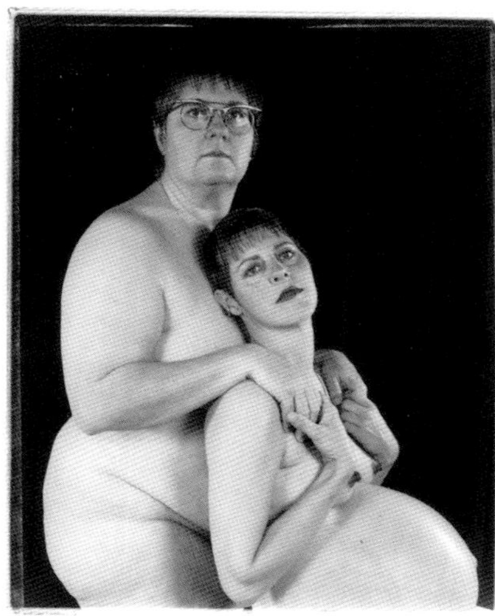

Laura Aguilar
Clothed/Unclothed #30,
1994
Gelatin silver prints,
each 50.8 × 40.6 cm
(20 × 16 in.)

**Through paired portraits
– presenting each
individual both dressed
and nude – Laura Aguilar
explores intimacy,
vulnerability and the
politics of representation,
offering tender,
humanizing portrayals of
her subjects that honour
bodily diversity and queer
visibility.**

vulnerabilities, revealing truths that were often hidden or erased.
Laura Aguilar's photography remains an essential testament to the
resilience and beauty of marginalized communities. She passed away
in 2018, leaving a lasting legacy of empowerment and visibility.

KEY WORKS

Laura A. (from the series *Latina Lesbians*), 1987
Grounded #111, 2006–7

KEY FACTS

Aguilar struggled with auditory dyslexia – a learning disability
that went undiagnosed until her twenties – which made
traditional schooling difficult, while photography gave her
a non-verbal way to communicate.

She began taking nude self-portraits in the desert not as a
provocation, but as a therapeutic practice. Grappling with
depression, body image and identity, Aguilar used the camera
to confront and reclaim her sense of self. She later said, 'If I
could photograph myself in such a way that I could see myself
as beautiful, then maybe I could believe that I was.'

LORENZA BÖTTNER
CHILE, 1959–94

Lorenza Böttner was a Chilean-German artist whose work spanned painting, drawing, photography, dance and performance. Centring her own transfeminine armless body, she explored the intersections of disability, gender identity and social marginalization.

Born in Punta Arenas, Chile, Böttner's's life changed dramatically at the age of eight following an accident that led to the amputation of both arms at the shoulder. Requiring extensive medical treatment after her amputation, she and her mother relocated to Germany, where she encountered the stigma and exclusion often imposed on disabled individuals. She rejected the prosthetic arms that doctors prescribed her, and learned to paint and draw with her mouth and feet, also developing a passion for classical ballet, jazz and tap dancing – disciplines that would later influence her performative works.

Böttner studied at Kassel School of Art, where she produced a graduate thesis provocatively titled 'Behindert?' (meaning 'Disabled?') that critically examined the medicalized gaze she had experienced as a disabled person. During this period, she began to openly embrace her identity as a transgender woman, using her art to express and affirm her femininity: depicting herself as erotic, nurturing and defiant.

As a painter, Böttner's artworks directly resulted from street performances. She painted in public, in real time, using her mouth and feet in acts she called 'danced painting' and 'pantomime painting'. This method placed her in a lineage of mouth-and-foot artists often associated with public spectacle, where disabled artists were expected to perform to entertain an able-bodied audience – a tradition Böttner radically subverted. Her performances were not passive displays, but confrontational assertions of selfhood. By creating her work publicly, she confronted the viewer's gaze, not as a spectacle but as a political subject reclaiming her body on her terms.

Böttner was closely affiliated with the Disabled Artists Network, and advocated for the inclusion of mouth-and-foot artists within institutional and art-historical frameworks. Diagnosed with HIV in 1985, Böttner passed away from AIDS-related complications in 1994.

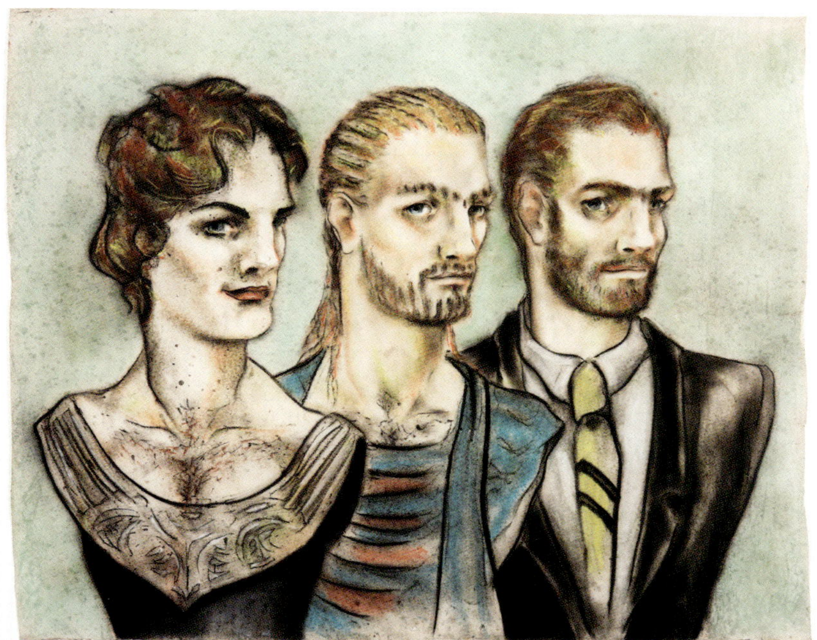

Lorenza Böttner
Untitled, undated
Pastel on paper
137.2 × 170.2 cm
(54 × 67 in.)
Private collection

Drawn in soft pastel on a large scale, the three differing styles of dress in these self-portraits suggest a shifting 'performance' of identity. However, they share a unified gaze – defiant and tender.

Böttner's legacy speaks to a future in which trans and disabled artists are no longer marginalized. Through her refusal of invisibility, Böttner envisioned a world in which bodily diversity is both accepted and celebrated.

KEY WORKS

Kain Karawahn, date unknown, private collection
Face Art series, 1983, Leslie-Lohman Museum of Art,
    New York, USA

KEY FACTS

After recovery from her accident, Böttner rejected the use of
    artificial arms or the label of 'disabled'.
Although Böttner never achieved widespread fame during her
    lifetime, she did receive some recognition – such as modelling
    for the photographer Robert Mapplethorpe. However, she felt
    that much of the attention she received was exploitative of
    her disability.

DANIELLE BRATHWAITE-SHIRLEY
UNITED KINGDOM, b.1995

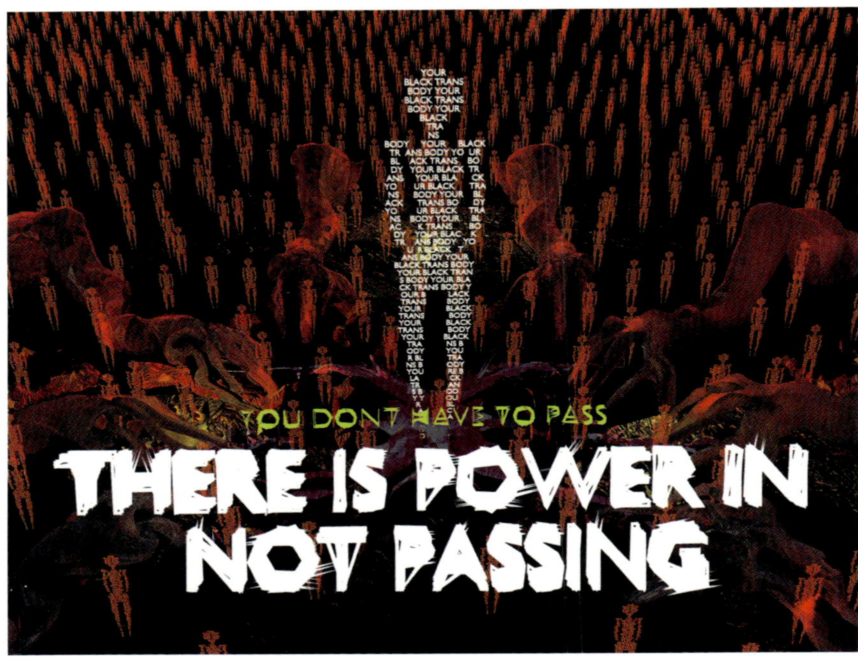

Danielle Brathwaite-Shirley is a British artist and game developer whose work reconstructs Black trans histories through interactive digital archives. Describing herself as a 'Virtua Trans Myst', she creates immersive, speculative worlds that not only document Black trans lives but emphasize the need to actively protect and celebrate them. The term 'myst' is a playful nod to 'Myst' (1993) a classic adventure-puzzle video game, in which players explore an immersive, strange world. Brathwaite-Shirley creates her own 'mist', a soft fog that drifts through her digital world – an ethereal force that shields Black trans existence from harm.

Brathwaite-Shirley works across animation, sound, performance and coding, rejecting traditional institutional models in favour of participatory, community-driven digital spaces, where guests are invited to contribute stories to her archival projects. In doing so, she insists that Black trans people must be at the centre of their

Danielle Brathwaite-Shirley
'THERE IS POWER IN NOT PASSING'
Part of the installation
WE ARE HERE BECAUSE OF THOSE THAT ARE NOT/ BLACKTRANSARCHIVE. COM, 2020
Print on PVC

The phrase 'there is power in not passing' (where 'passing' means to be perceived as the gender you identify with) refers to the idea that not conforming to societal expectations of gender can be a radical source of strength.

own narratives – not subjects of academic study, but the architects of their archival, digital and physical futures.

In games such as *GET HOME SAFE* (2022) and *INTO THE STORM* (2022) Brathwaite-Shirley explores what it means to move through the world when safety is never guaranteed. Players try to get home, walking the streets alone at night or navigating inhospitable terrain at the end of the world, experiencing the heightened awareness and dread that so many Black trans people face daily. These games prompt urgent questions: What must change for the outside world to become a truly safe space? What structures must be dismantled? What new structures must be built? Some suggestions for these she digitally constructs in her games, such as spas designed to cater for Black trans people, which function as real meditative space.

Brathwaite-Shirley's work exists within a broader lineage of Black trans artists and activists whose activism has reshaped the broader LGBTQIA+ rights movement – a lineage whose existence she emphasizes in her work. Through speculative storytelling, Brathwaite-Shirley not only archives Black trans lives but envisions alternative futures where they thrive.

KEY WORKS

I CANT REMEMBER A TIME I DIDNT NEED YOU / Blacktransair.com, 2020, Victoria and Albert Museum, London, UK
PIRATING BLACKNESS / Blacktranssea.com, 2022, Arts Council Collection, London, UK

KEY FACTS

Brathwaite-Shirley collaborates with a group of Black trans coders and developers using tools like Blender and GIMP to rapidly create digital assets. A unique rule in their process is that once an element is created, it cannot be deleted, ensuring that all contributions, regardless of perceived imperfections, make it into the final work.

Alongside her digital practice, Brathwaite-Shirley stages participatory performances that demonstrate her belief in the power of real-world experiences and offline encounters.

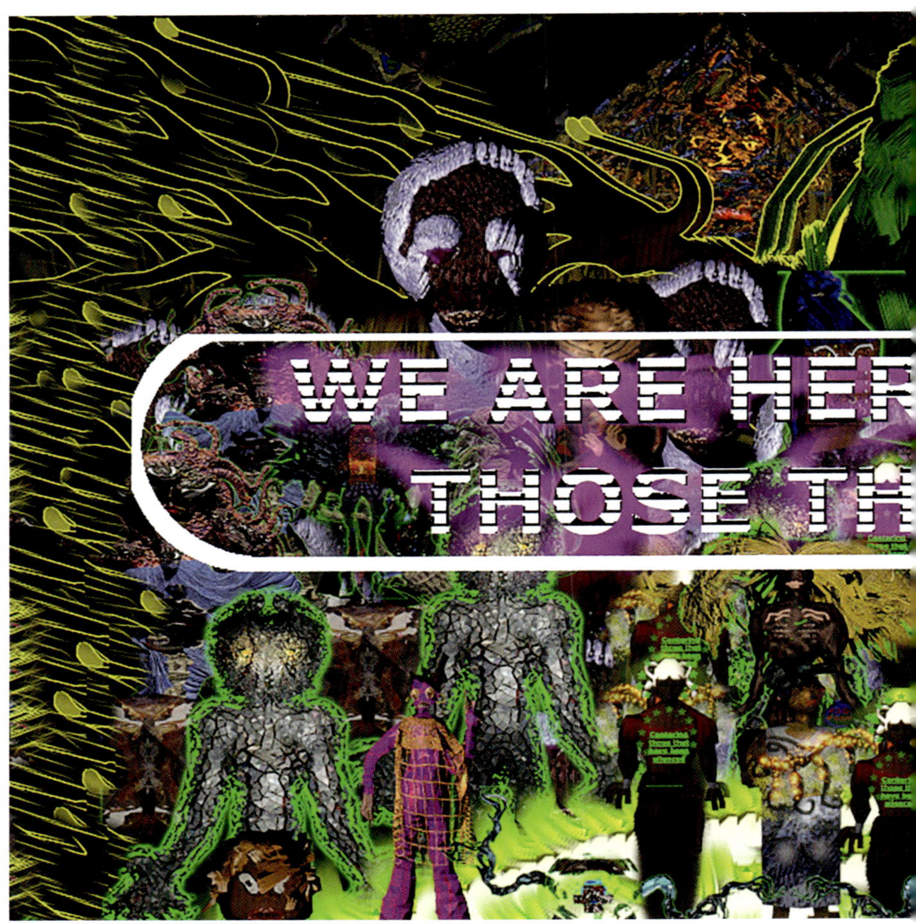

Danielle Brathwaite-Shirley
*WE ARE HERE
BECAUSE OF THOSE
THAT ARE NOT/
BLACKTRANSARCHIVE.
COM, 2020*
Interactive archive

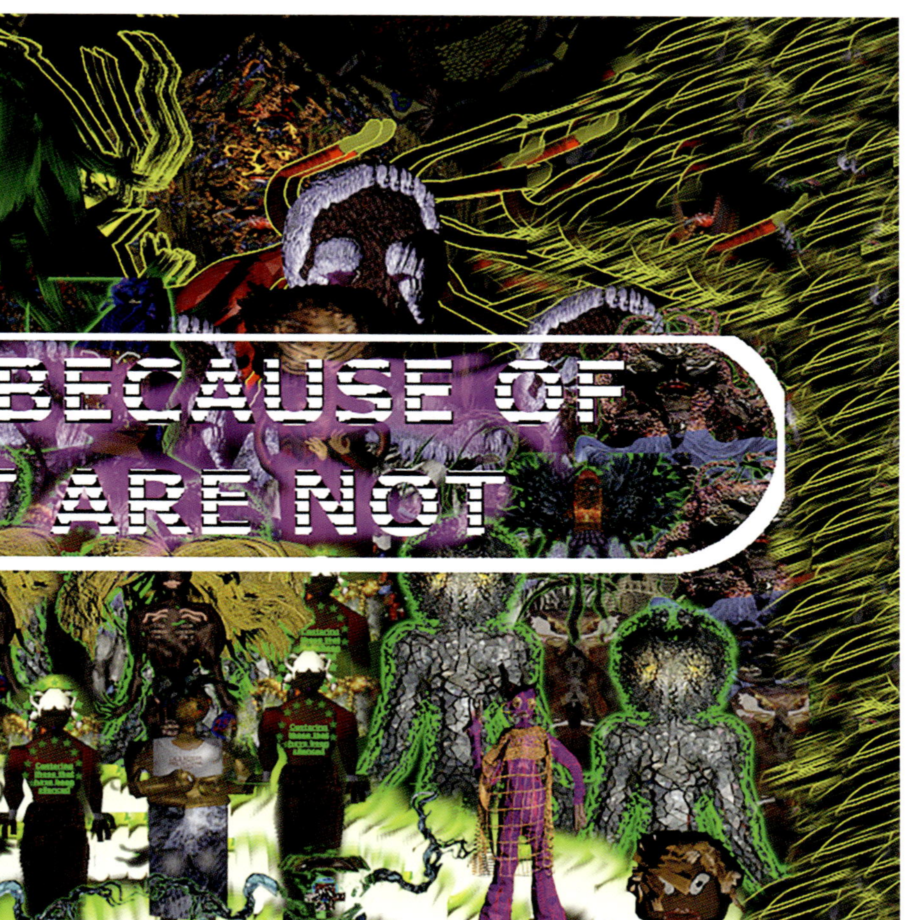

Since 2020, blacktransarchive.com has served as an evolving digital archive, structured like a video game that asks users to navigate history based on their identity – whether they are 'BLACK AND TRANS', 'TRANS' or 'CIS'.

By embedding gaming mechanics into the archive, Brathwaite-Shirley disrupts the idea of history as neutral or static, instead presenting it as interactive and shaped by those who engage with it.

HAMAD BUTT
PAKISTAN, 1962–94

Hamad Butt was born in Lahore, Pakistan, and moved to England with his family as a young child. He spent the 1980s studying at various London art schools, predominantly Goldsmiths. Although his studies overlapped with those of the group that became known as the Young British Artists (YBAs), he did not identify with the aesthetics of Brit Art. Instead, he pursued his own politically nuanced artistic language, incorporating ideas relating to the queer and immigrant experience in Thatcherite Britain. Butt died of AIDS-related pneumonia at the age of thirty-one, only four years after graduating. In his short life he was prolific in drawing, painting and printmaking, but he is best known for his sculptural installations built around hazardous materials such as bromine and chlorine gas.

Transmission (1990) was Butt's first sculptural installation. Nine books made of glass rest on steel stands. An ultraviolet light illuminates each book from below, making visible an image of a triffid etched onto each of the open pages. Triffids are a fictional species of plant taken from *The Day of the Triffids*, a 1951 novel written by John Wyndham. When a meteor shower blinds most of the human population, the triffids, which are venomous, carnivorous and capable of moving around autonomously, decimate the population. In Butt's piece, the triffid is employed as a motif representing terror and powerlessness in the face of the seemingly inescapable and fatal transmission of HIV. Wyndham's post-apocalyptic novel is about building the world anew after it has ended – a process no doubt familiar to Butt, as it was to a whole generation of queer people who lost loved ones during this period.

The fact that triffids are made dangerous by blindness emphasizes the role of visibility in the history of AIDS, a disease which was rendered doubly hard to detect by the lack of testing available in the 1980s and the atmosphere of shame that was constructed around it. The ultraviolet lights Butt used to illuminate the image in his work are dangerous to look at, so viewers are given protective goggles before being allowed to approach the work, further associating visibility with the possibility of harm. This drive to confront his viewers reveals the artist's preoccupation with the future, the unknown hurdles one must navigate in order to survive, and what state it will be in if we get there.

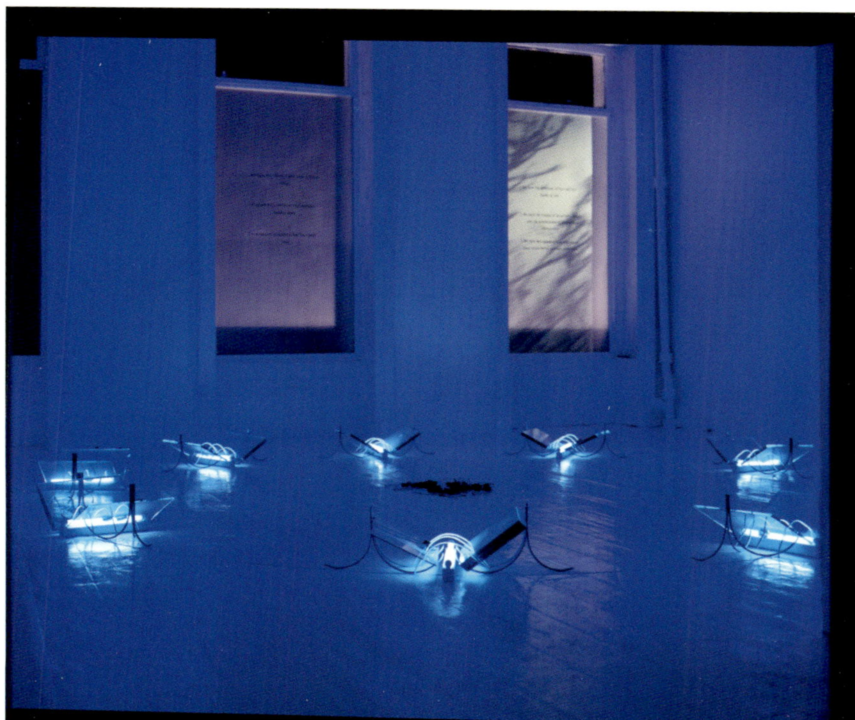

Hamad Butt
Transmission, 1990
Etched glass, steel, rubber
tubing, wires, bulbs and
ultraviolet light
Dimensions variable
(up to 4 metres, 13 feet
in diameter)
Installation view,
Goldsmiths College,
London, 1990
Tate, UK

Transmission **is centred
around a circle of nine
glowing glass books, each
emitting ultraviolet light
that would damage the
audience's eyes if viewed
directly.**

KEY WORKS

No Title – Figures with Muzzles, c.1984, private collection
Familiars (Cradle, Substance Sublimation Unit and Hypostasis),
   1992, Tate, London, UK

KEY FACTS

Nine months after his death, Butt's work *Familiars* (1992) was
   included in Tate's 'Rites of Passage' exhibition alongside
   artists like Joseph Beuys, Louise Bourgeois and Mona Hatoum.
A trained biochemist turned artist, Butt often incorporated
   hazardous or deadly chemicals into his work.

JESSE DARLING
UNITED KINGDOM, b.1981

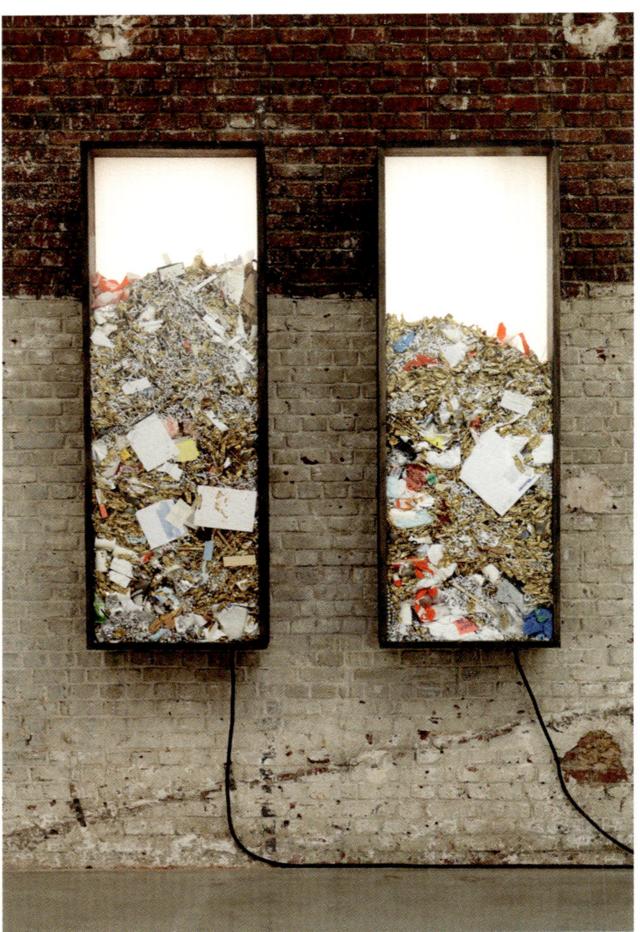

Jesse Darling
Reliquary (for and after Felix Gonzalez-Torres, in loving memory), 2022
Light boxes, leftovers of installations by Felix Gonzalez-Torres (candy wrappers, light bulbs, beads...), each lightbox 200 × 70 × 40 cm (78¾ × 27⅝ × 15¾ in.)
Installation view, Palais de Tokyo, Paris, 2023
Centre national des arts plastiques, Paris

The two illuminated vitrines in this piece are filled with remnants from Felix Gonzalez-Torres's installations. These fragments – such as shredded exhibition catalogues and institutional documents – are typically discarded, but in Darling's piece, they are elevated into artefacts of intimacy and remembrance. The work echoes Gonzalez-Torres's own approach to assemblage and memory, emphasizing the relationship between the personal and the collective.

Jesse Darling is a multidisciplinary artist whose works explore how socio-political forces shape and reshape bodies with a focus on themes of gender, sexuality, disability, love and companionship.

Born in Oxford and educated at Central Saint Martins and the Slade School of Fine Art in London, Darling spent several years living and working in Berlin before returning to the UK to take up a teaching position at Oxford University's Ruskin School of Art.

Darling's work addresses the failures of modernity and capitalism, and the ongoing legacies of colonialism. By exploring the history of technology and the production of ideology – the objects and ideas with which we make sense of the world – he considers vulnerability, intuition and community as alternative starting points for imagining new forms of collective existence.

Within his sculpture and installation, these ideas are articulated through the inclusion of everyday objects: from hazard tape, barbed wire and crowd-control barriers to plastic carrier bags, household blinds and medical equipment. These mundane objects are imbued with emotional resonance and charged meaning, transforming the ordinary into allegorical reflections on the issues impacting society as a whole. The seemingly simple sculptural compositions embody a dynamic tension, balancing fragility with resilience. Darling's sculptures often take utilitarian objects associated with power or masculinity and present them as vulnerable or absurd. In his Turner Prize-winning show, for example, Darling mounted hammers in glass cases but bound them up with ribbons and bells, in turn transforming these macho tools into almost camp, impotent relics.

Through his practice, Darling examines the complexities of identity – drawing from both personal lived experience and broader historical narratives. His work addresses the ongoing tensions between individual agency and systemic pressures, inviting reflection on how identity is shaped by external forces and how it can be reclaimed or redefined.

KEY WORKS

Equestrian Statue, 2015, Government Art Collection, UK
Brazen Serpent, 2018, Arts Council Collection, London, UK

KEY FACTS

A core theme in Darling's practice is what he calls 'the fragility of what we take for granted'. Having experienced illness and disability, Darling addresses the transient nature of the body, and his works often allude to mortality and decay.

In 2023, Darling became the first transgender artist to win the Turner Prize, one of the leading awards for contemporary art in the United Kingdom.

ZILIA SÁNCHEZ DOMÍNGUEZ
CUBA, 1926–2024

Zilia Sánchez Domínguez was a pioneering Cuban artist renowned
for her undulating shaped canvases that blur the line between
painting and sculpture. Born in Havana, Cuba, she grew up
surrounded by art, with her mother and amateur painter father
playing an influential role in her early development, as well as her
childhood neighbour, the prominent Cuban artist Víctor Manuel
García Valdés.

At university Sánchez Domínguez initially enrolled in
architecture but soon shifted her focus to fine arts, studying
painting for five years. She later went on to study art restoration.
Amidst the political unrest of 1950s Cuba, culminating in the
Cuban Revolution which ended in 1959, she immersed herself in
the burgeoning cultural scene of the resistance, working as a set
designer and painter for revolutionary theatre groups.

In 1960 Sánchez Domínguez relocated to New York City, where
she would further develop her iconic style – three-dimensional,
shaped canvases stretched tautly over wooden armatures, which
she referred to as 'skin'. This technique, combined with a minimalist,
often monochromatic palette, became the hallmark of her work.
Informed by her earlier studies in architecture, painting and
restoration, her distinctive approach to painting on structured
canvas surfaces incorporated a sensuality that set her apart from
her male peers.

From the 1990s, Sánchez Domínguez's work has been discussed
through the lens of 'queer formalism'. This term is used to describe
work that explores identity and desire using abstract visual forms
rather than figuration or obvious representation. In creating three-
dimensional, sculptural canvases, Sánchez Domínguez disrupts rigid
minimalist aesthetics, conjuring a sense of intimacy through the
physicality of her work. Notable works such as *Las Amazonas* (1968)
and *Troyanas* (1967) alluded to classical myths and archetypes
of powerful women, reflecting Sánchez Domínguez's fascination
with gender, power and identity. These works explored themes of
femininity and strength while also addressing cultural histories and
narratives of resistance.

Zilia Sánchez Domínguez
Lunar V (Moon V), c.1973
Acrylic on stretched
canvas
189.9 × 201.9 × 25.4 cm
(74¾ × 79½ × 10 in.)
Private collection

**These sculptural
canvases, which recall
the curves of the female
body, were referred to
by the queer Cuban poet
and critic Severo Sarduy
as 'erotic topologies',
which Sánchez
Domínguez adopted
as the title of her most
prominent series.**

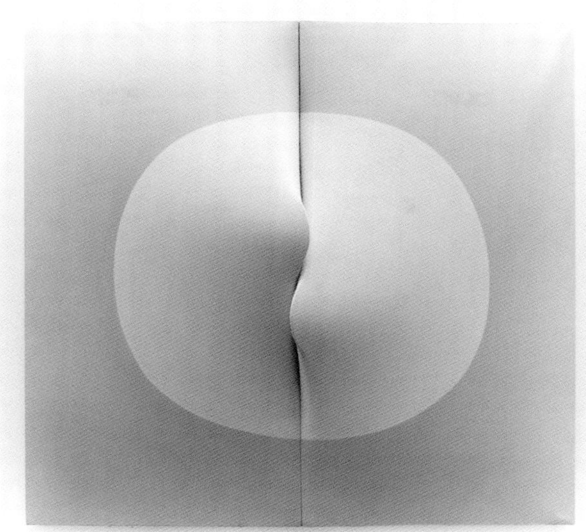

In 1971, Sánchez Domínguez and her partner, Victoria Ruiz,
relocated permanently to Puerto Rico, where she continued her
artistic practice and became a crucial figure in feminist and anti-
colonialist movements.

KEY WORKS

Antigone, 1970, Museum of Modern Art, New York, USA
Sin título (from the series *Topología erótica*), 1970, Pérez Art
　Museum, Miami, USA

KEY FACTS

Sánchez Domínguez contributed her graphic design skills to
　the literary journal *Zona de Carga y Descarga* and later taught
　at various institutions, passing on her revolutionary approach
　to art.
During the 1950s, Sánchez Domínguez was involved with the
　avant-garde collective Los Once (The Eleven), a group of
　painters and sculptures credited with introducing new ideas
　and non-figurative practices to Cuban art.

NICOLE EISENMAN
FRANCE, b.1965

Widely considered one of the most significant artists of her time, Nicole Eisenman has developed a distinctive practice of painting and sculpture that fuses humour, social critique and an unflinching exploration of identity, intimacy and community. Taking inspiration from art history and popular culture, Eisenman reimagines familiar forms through a queer and feminist lens, challenging the conventions of representation and power structures.

Born in Verdun, France, and raised in the suburbs of New York, Eisenman studied at Rhode Island School of Design, graduating in 1987. Early exposure to feminist and queer art movements shaped her practice, which blurs the boundaries between personal and political narratives. Her work derives from various artistic traditions, with inspirations moving fluidly between Renaissance painting, German Expressionism, underground comics and contemporary pop imagery, creating compositions that are at once subversive and deeply human. By blending historical influences with contemporary concerns, Eisenman continues to redefine the possibilities of figuration, queer joy and resistance.

Eisenman's work frequently depicts gatherings including the dreamlike leisure of large-scale paintings *Beer Garden with Ash/ AK* (2009) or *Another Green World* (2015). These scenes offer alternative visions of belonging, where outsiders, queers and misfits form their own communities. At times, her work veers into darker critiques of alienation, masculinity and the failures of late capitalism, balancing absurdity with biting social commentary.

Eisenman's work gestures towards queer futures as lived, tangible possibilities. Her worlds are collective, unruly and resolutely non-normative. Figures in the paintings often display a range of emotions – bored, bruised, ecstatic or disaffected – but they are never idealized. Instead, they form communities grounded in mutual understanding, care and shared experience, existing in the present as speculative spaces for connection.

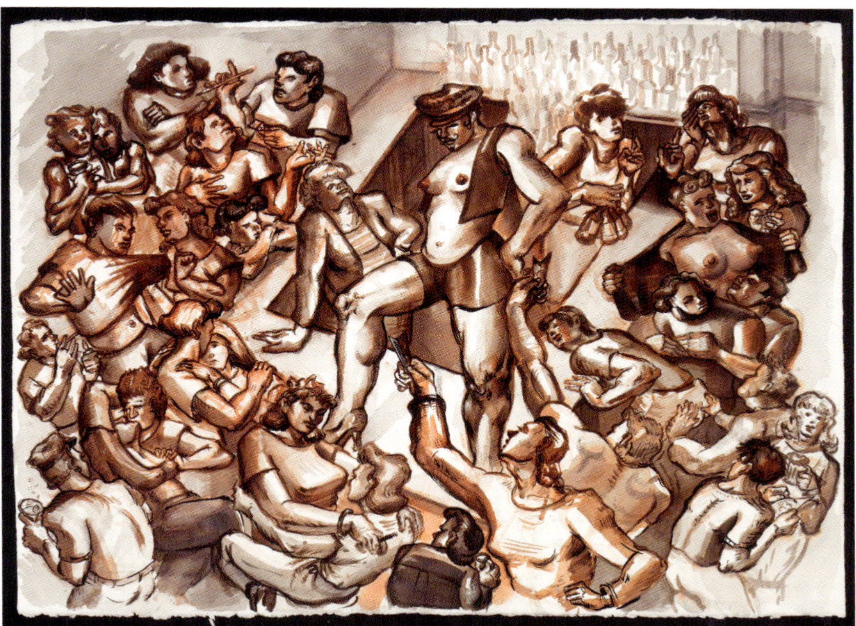

Nicole Eisenman
Trash's Dance, 1992
India ink on paper
55.9 × 76.2 cm
(22⅛ × 30 in.)
Hort Family Collection

Eisenman's intricate ink drawing *Trash's Dance* depicts a bawdy bar scene in which a central leather-clad figure performs for a writhing lesbian crowd who flirt, kiss, grind, fight and collapse into a euphoric communion.

KEY WORKS

Betty Gets It, 1992, private collection
Morning Studio, 2016, Institute of Contemporary Art, Miami, USA

KEY FACTS

Beyond her studio practice, Eisenman has been a key figure in queer artistic activism. In 2005, she co-founded Ridykeulous, a feminist art collective with artist A.L. Steiner, using humour and provocation to critique sexism, misogyny and homophobia in the art world.

Over the years, Eisenman has been recognized with numerous accolades, including a MacArthur 'Genius' Fellowship in 2015 and participation in major exhibitions such as the Whitney Biennial.

FRANCESCA GALLIANI
ITALY, b.1962

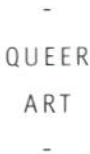

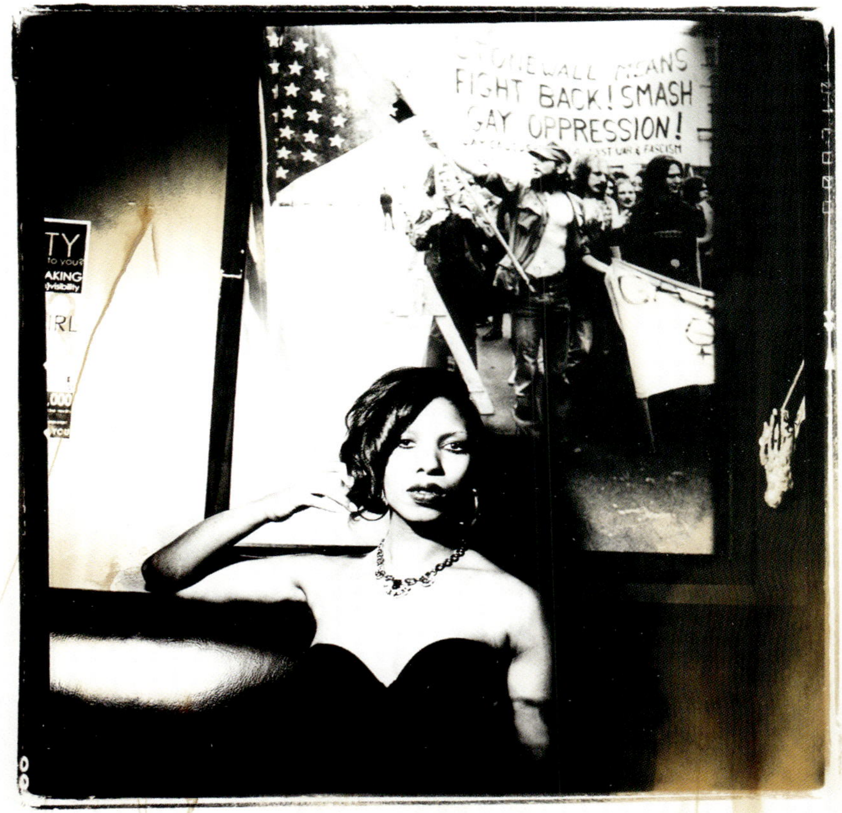

Italian artist Francesca (Frankie) Galliani is known for their distinctive photographic style and mixed media painted works. Often depicting transgender people, LGBTQIA+ activists and queer nightlife, they describe their work as a 'celebration of the diverse'.

Born and raised in Milan, Italy, Galliani moved to the United States in 1982 at the age of nineteen where they completed a BFA at Corcoran School of Art in Washington, DC. Since then, they have primarily lived in America, with their work exhibited extensively on an international scale.

Francesca Galliani
Fight Back, NY, 2014
Manually toned gelatin
silver print
50 × 50 cm
(20 × 20 in.)
Collection of the artist

**Galliani has been
photographing
transgender subjects
since the 1990s, often
in bars and night-time
spaces. Here the subject
poses in front of a large
image of a historical
Pride march that hangs
on the wall of a New York
gay bar.**

Central to Galliani's work is analogue photography, which allows them to manipulate their prints in the darkroom. They then further modify their prints with hand painting and collage, resulting in images which embody a strong punk and DIY aesthetic, channelling the visual language of the underground club scene that Galliani became part of when they moved to New York City in 1990. During this period, they began photographing transgender subjects, which they have aligned with their own self-discovery as a queer non-binary person. Depicting beauty, power, vulnerability and dignity, the work becomes an unapologetic expression of existence, presenting audiences with the opportunity to connect on an authentic and intimate level with their subjects.

Galliani's painted works – which include painted books and mixed media assemblages, as well as both large and small-scale canvases – use a limited palette of black, white and sometimes reds. As in their photography, the figurative elements from their painted and collaged works are used to confront themes of social justice, gender identity and queer resilience; often emphatically placed within stark and seemingly violent abstract planes. In the 2000s, Galliani's images appeared in many editorial contexts and fashion campaigns, and later they began producing their own screen-printed and painted t-shirts, bringing their bold aesthetic and LGBTQIA+ subjects to a mainstream audience. Believing passionately in the role of artists to create change, their work promotes human rights for all.

Galliani's practice embraces experimentation, self-invention and hybridity. Their wearable art and painted books expand these artistic ideals into the everyday, emphasizing the resilience and persistence of queer self-expression in all aspects of life.

KEY WORKS

Nudi 94, 2011, collection of the artist
The Eagle, 2014, collection of the artist

KEY FACTS

In 1995, Galliani won the European Kodak Award with an image made from cut and collaged negatives that were printed by hand and manually manipulated in painterly ways using toners.
Galliani has reinterpreted their artworks for major brands, including a Levi's 'Blue' campaign featuring painted fashion photography that appeared in magazines all over the world and was exhibited at the Triennale Museum in Milan.

GORDON HALL
UNITED STATES, b.1983

In an essay on the 2016 North Carolina 'bathroom bill', which made
it illegal for anyone in the US state to use a public bathroom unless
it matches the gender on their birth certificate, Gordon Hall writes
about an object they encountered that winter, known as 'the slant
step'. This object was bought in the 1960s by two artists, William
Wiley and Bruce Nauman, who were fascinated by the slant step
because, although clearly designed for something, its function was
a mystery. Hall argues that the slant step can be used as a lesson,
or rather as a teacher, in conversations about gender, objects and
personhood: 'I want to learn what it seems to already know – I can't
always know what I am looking at.'

As a sculptor, writer, performance artist and sculptor, Hall's
conceptual work and site-responsive sculptures speak to pressing
issues – particularly those facing queer and trans people – using
minimalist sculpture and thoughts about objects to interrogate,
among other things, visual classifications of personhood. Their
sculptures often take the form of meticulously crafted objects that
resemble furniture or utilitarian design, rendered in often muted
tones and refined materials. At first glance these pieces (such as
a set of interlocking concrete panels that form a bench, or a life-
sized wooden clothes valet studded with nails) appear sleek and
functional. Yet each is purposefully ambiguous in nature: 'drained
of use', but nevertheless 'suggestive of function'.

A trained dancer, Hall treats the objects they create – all of
which are neither totally abstract, nor fully figurative – as performers
themselves during movement performances. In doing so, they test
out ways of using and interacting with objects, opening up different
possibilities in how we are able to relate to the physical world
around us.

In their influential essay *Object Lessons* (2013), Hall critiques the
tendency to identify works as queer only when they feature explicit
LGBTQIA+ subjects or symbols. They refer to this as the 'glitter
problem', instead putting forward a vision of future queer art,
theory and life that is de-linked from the necessity of obviously
legible representation.

Gordon Hall
End of Day, 2021
Poplar, brass and
steel nails
121.9 × 32.4 × 45.7 cm
(48 × 12¾ × 18 in.)
Private collection

Once a traditional men's
clothes valet, Hall has
encrusted this 'oddly
gendered' item with
silver nails, creating the
appearance of scaly skin.
By altering its ability
to perform the task it
was designed for and
adorning it in a particular
way, Hall challenges the
viewer's understanding
of it as a useful and
gendered object.

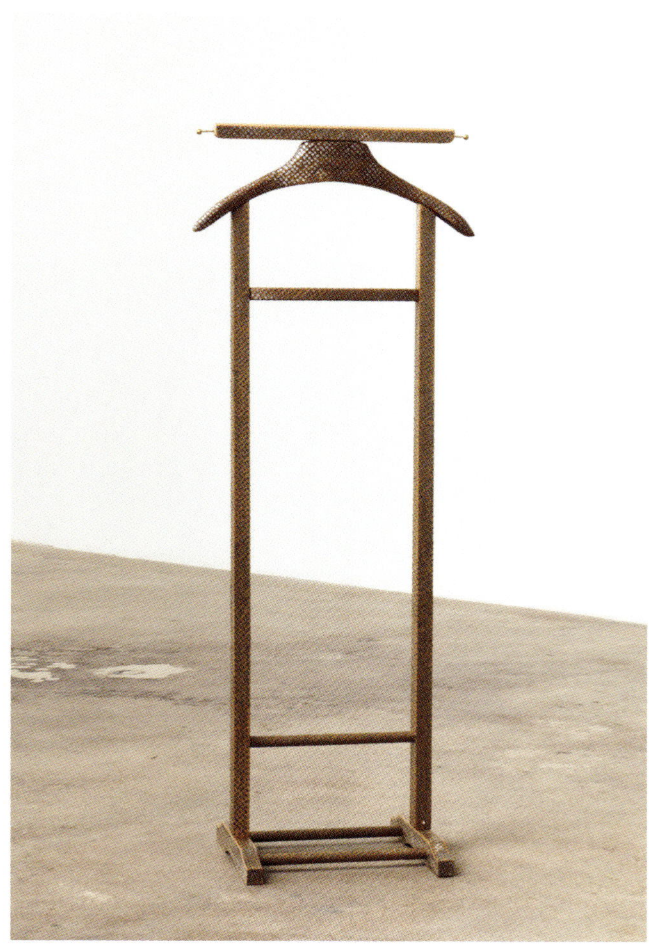

KEY WORKS

The Number of Inches Between Them, 2017–21, Museo de Arte
    Contemporáneo de Monterrey, Mexico
Brothers and Sisters, 2018, collection of the artist

KEY FACTS

Hall has taught at Rhode Island School of Design and
    elsewhere; they consider both teaching and sculpture
    as spaces for learning and unlearning.
Hall founded the Center for Experimental Lectures in 2011 –
    a platform for artists to present performative lectures.

KEITH HARING
UNITED STATES, 1958–90

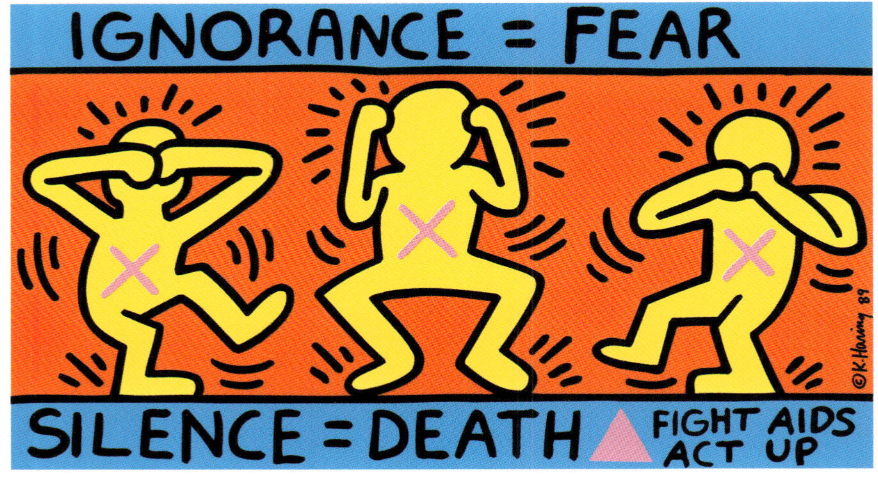

Known for his instantly recognizable visual language that bridged the worlds of street art, activism and pop culture, Keith Haring's bold, rhythmic linework and vibrant colours transformed public spaces into powerful messages about love, joy and resistance. Through murals, drawings and prints, he tackled themes of queer identity, the AIDS crisis, racism and state violence – using art as a tool for both celebration and protest.

Born in Reading, Pennsylvania, and raised in nearby Kutztown, Haring studied at the School of Visual Arts in New York City from 1978, where he experimented with video, installation, collage and performance alongside his now-iconic line drawings.

Committed to public engagement, Haring led art workshops for children and collaborated with social service organizations, believing art should be democratic and accessible. He embraced public art, creating hundreds of murals in clubs, subways and city streets to reach the widest possible audience.

Haring's work is grounded in utopian ideals – not just in his bold, dancing figures, but in how his works expressed hope for

Keith Haring
Ignorance = Fear, 1989
Offset lithograph poster
61 × 110 cm
(24 × 43¼ in.)

The phrase 'Ignorance = Fear, Silence = Death' was popularized by ACT UP (AIDS Coalition to Unleash Power), a movement that redefined public discourse on HIV/AIDS.

a better future. During the AIDS pandemic and rising conservatism, Haring promoted love, mutual aid, collective care, radical joy and empathy to so many.

His 1989 work *Ignorance = Fear, Silence = Death* epitomizes his activism during the AIDS crisis. Created in the final year of Haring's life, as he battled the disease himself, the work is both a call to action and a warning against societal complacency. The three figures – marked with pink crosses – gesture in a manner reminiscent of the proverb 'see no evil, hear no evil, speak no evil'. reinterpreted here as an indictment of political inaction and silence surrounding the pandemic.

Over the course of his career, Haring created more than fifty large-scale public artworks worldwide, many for hospitals, orphanages and charities. His work was exhibited in over one hundred exhibitions, cementing his status as one of the most influential artists of his generation. Haring passed away in 1990 at the age of thirty-one, but his legacy endures – his art continues to serve as a vibrant testament to activism, accessibility and joy.

KEY WORKS

Untitled, 1982, Rubell Museum, Miami, USA
Once Upon A Time (bathroom mural), 1989, LGBT Community
  Center, New York, USA

KEY FACTS

In 1986, Haring opened the Pop Shop in Manhattan's SoHo,
  selling posters, T-shirts and other affordable items featuring
  his designs. This initiative, supported by his mentor Andy
  Warhol, extended his belief that art should exist beyond
  galleries and museums.
Diagnosed with AIDS in 1988, Haring established the Keith
  Haring Foundation in 1989 to support AIDS organizations,
  children's programmes and arts education.

KILUANJI KIA HENDA
ANGOLA, b.1979

Kiluanji Kia Henda is a self-taught artist whose practice encompasses photography, performance, video, sculpture, theatre and installation. Growing up in the aftermath of the Angolan Civil War, his work grapples with themes of conflict, post-colonialism and identity.

Kia Henda's artistic journey began at a young age. With access to a video camera, he created stories and short films with his siblings and neighbours. He was later trained within the Southern African documentary tradition, first by his brothers Cassiano Bamba and Afonso Laixes – both of whom died during the Civil War – and later by photojournalists Carlos Louzada and John Liebenberg. Raised in a family of photography enthusiasts, he developed a deep belief in the power of photography as a tool for change.

Through his lens, Kia Henda interrogates the interplay between fact and fiction, often using photography as a 'pliable fiction' that challenges dominant political and historical narratives. By blending history with fiction, Kia Henda reconfigures it to centre marginalized perspectives and, in doing so, creates space to imagine alternative futures free of colonial legacies and stringent identities.

Humour and irony are central to Kia Henda's approach, providing accessible entry points for audiences to engage with complex political messages. His practice extends fictional narratives through various media, inviting viewers to question what is real, and also how histories and realities are remembered, staged and constructed. His large-scale installations and sculptures often bring these themes into physical form, extending his critique of historical power structures into the realm of the material.

Kiluanji Kia Henda
Redefining The Power (with Pamina Sebastião), 2011
Photograph on matte paper mounted on aluminum. Edition of 5
150 × 100 cm
(59⅛ × 39⅜ in.)

Kia Henda's ongoing project *Homem Novo (New Man)* explores the ways in which post-colonial Africa grapples with its past, specifically the legacy of colonial statues and public monuments. In this work, he reclaims empty plinths in Angola's cities, inviting friends and community members to perform in the spaces once occupied by these monuments. This act of re-appropriation becomes a potent statement on re-imagining the future of national identity.

KEY WORKS

Redefining The Power III (series 75 with Miguel Prince), 2011
Under the Silent Eye of Lenin, 2018, Zeitz MOCAA, Cape Town, South Africa

---

KEY FACTS

Henda won Angola's National Prize of Art and Culture in 2012.
In 2017, Kia Henda became the first African artist to receive the Frieze Artist Award.

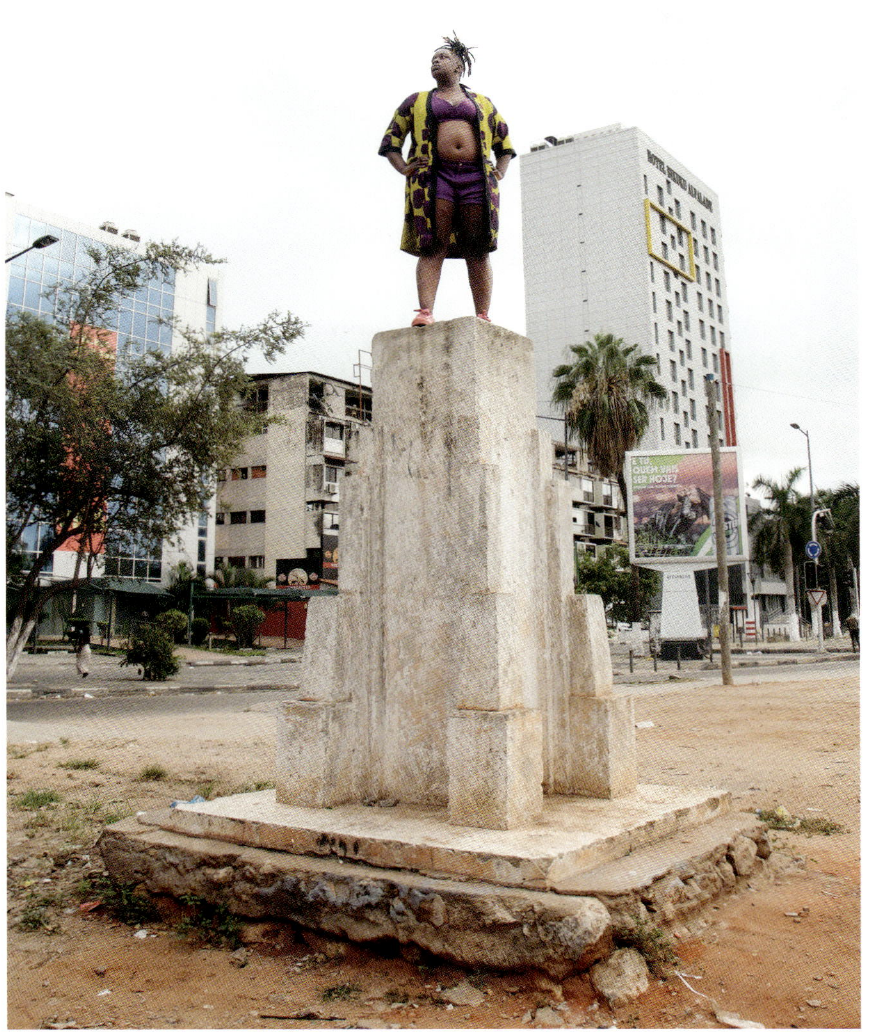

NADIA HUGGINS
TRINIDAD AND TOBAGO, b.1984

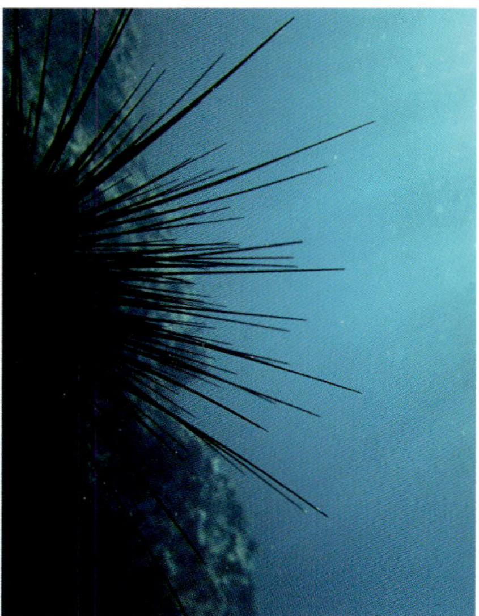

Nadia Huggins
Transformations No. 1,
2015
Digital photograph
76.2 × 118.1 cm
(30 × 46½ in.)

In the *Transformations* series (2014–16), underwater self-portraits are paired with marine organisms. Through this process Huggins articulates the transformative power and solace found through being weightless in the water, creating what she describes as 'a lasting breath that defies human limitations'.

Nadia Huggins is a self-taught artist who was born in Trinidad and Tobago, and raised in St Vincent and the Grenadines. Growing up as a queer woman of East Indian and Portuguese descent, in a mixed class family, she felt a persistent sense of otherness. Photography, particularly self-portraiture, thus became a means of self-discovery as she navigated the expectations for young women growing up within a small island community.

All of Huggins's work is a response to her environment. By foregrounding the Caribbean landscape, she explores the nurturing qualities of the natural world, in particular the healing power of the ocean. Through an ecological lens, conscious of the fact human development is shaped by interactions with interconnected environmental systems, she presents the ocean as a source of liberation and discovery. The work serves as a reminder, however, that things must flow both ways, positioning our relationship with the ocean as one of reciprocal care and responsibility. This ecological sensitivity extends into her activism: in 2018 she co-founded One Drop in the Ocean, a group dedicated to raising awareness about global plastic pollution.

By situating the body within the ocean – an environment that is at times safe and comforting, at times threatening and unknown – Huggins introduces ambiguity in how we are perceived, particularly in relation to our gender. In the series *Circa No Future* (2014– present), she creatively photographs young boys' interaction with the sea in order to consider the pressures of Caribbean adolescent masculinity. *Is that a buoy?* (2015) is a double self-portrait, showing her head breaking the surface of the water – a work she says is concerned with 'the ambiguity of the body in the sea', born out of her experience of being misgendered by people due to her baldness.

KEY WORKS

Resurfacing II (from the series *Circa No Future*), 2015
Transformations No. 6 (from the series *Transformations*), 2016

KEY FACTS

Huggins first picked up a camera as a teenager, and quickly discovered that photographing herself was an effective way of asserting her identity.
In 2018 Huggins was selected for the New York Portfolio Review.

RENE MATIĆ
UNITED KINGDOM, b.1997

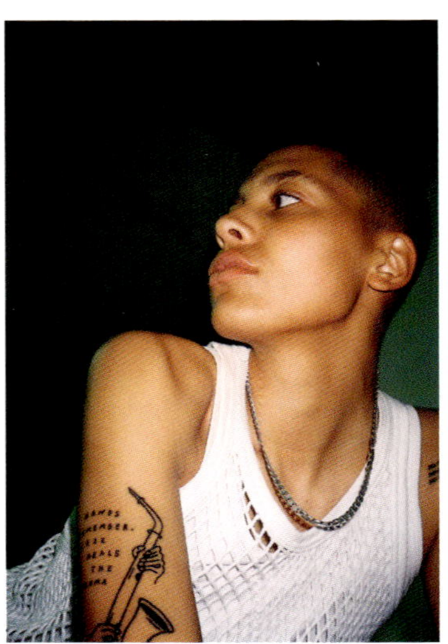 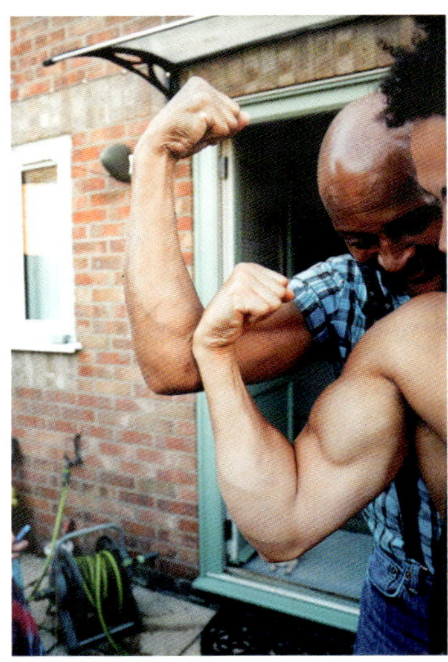

Rene Matić is a British artist working primarily in photography, video, writing and installation. Documenting the world around them and sharing intimate moments from life, their work is a heartfelt exploration of Britishness, 'a love letter to England'. Interested in the complex relationship between West Indian and white working-class culture in Britain, specifically through the lens of skinhead culture, they take inspiration from dance and music movements such as northern soul, ska and two-tone. Tracing their own relationship with identity, as a queer mixed-race person, Matić celebrates their close-knit community and the spaces they come together in, finding liberation through love. Matić's work considers the way in which families shape us, from the family we are born into to the chosen family we work hard to keep safe.

Central to Matić's practice is a concept they refer to as 'rudeness', inspired by the rude boy subculture that originated in 1960s Jamaica and started to appear in England in the late 1970s. For Matić, 'rudeness' incorporates ideas of the 'in-between'

Rene Matić
Kai in White, 2019
Inkjet print, framed;
unframed dimensions:
25 × 16.9 cm
(9⅞ × 6⅝ in.)

Rene Matić
*Paul and Zac in the
Garden, Peterborough*,
2022
Inkjet print, framed;
unframed dimensions:
40 × 26.5 cm
15¾ × 10⅜ in.)

**Matić's photographs
feature the people they
love captured through a
distinctively tender gaze.
Here we see the artist's
friend, the poet and
model Kai-Isaiah Jamal,
and their father and
brother, Paul and Zac.**

– existing in-between races, gender, class – and a defiant refusal to adhere to structures that do not feel relevant. Posing questions and challenging racist, classist and heteronormative structures, their work asks us to reimagine what core concepts such as body, self, family and home mean to us and the value they hold.

Taking inspiration from artists and writers such as bell hooks, Nan Goldin, Derek Ridgers and Patti Smith, whose works all seek to understand community and belonging from the perspective of the outsider, Matić's work speaks almost directly to José Esteban Muñoz's idea of queer futurity: 'the socially symbolic performative dimension of certain aesthetic processes that promote a modality of political idealism ... in a counternarrative to political nihilism.' Matić's world is inhabited by people close to the artist, depicted through a tender and loving gaze. In an increasingly bleak world Matić turns to love 'as a way of surviving and trying to find a way out of this kind of chaos'. Through Matić's lens we find a future filled with dance, love, intimacy and belonging.

KEY WORKS

Mia and Cait Snogging I, 2020
VE Day, Skegness III, 2020

KEY FACTS

In 2021, Tate bought fifteen photographs from Matić's series 'flags for countries that don't exist but bodies that do', making them one of the youngest artists to be acquired for Tate's collection.

Although photography is central to their practice, Matić received no formal photographic training and doesn't consider themselves a photographer. Instead, they refer to their approach as 'imaging' – imaging things in whatever format that might take.

AD MINOLITI
ARGENTINA, b.1980

Merging Latin American geometric abstraction with queer and feminist theory, Ad Minoliti is celebrated for their playful and vibrant practice, which spans painting, sculpture, mural work and immersive installation, and uses the visual language of abstraction as a conceptual tool to resist fixed binaries and narratives.

Trained as a painter at Prilidiano Pueyrredón National Academy of Fine Arts in Buenos Aires, Minoliti pursued research at Buenos Aires's Centro de Investigaciones Artísticas from 2009 to 2011. Their work builds on the legacy of Argentina's Grupo Madí and AACI – two concrete art movements that used geometry and colour to challenge authoritarian norms during and after the Argentine military dictatorship. Minoliti sees abstraction as a space of radical potential. By applying feminist and queer theories to this visual language, they reimagine what abstraction – and society – can be.

Minoliti's works are known for their flat, organic shapes that overlap photo-realistic backgrounds. Minoliti's influences include children's books and cartoons. These are explicitly cited along with the sources they use for their colour schemes, which deliberately reference different forms of political activism. For example, a recurring shade of green alludes to Argentina's abortion rights movement, and the combination of black, pink and baby blue refers to the Black trans pride flag. Characters in the works are intentionally indeterminate. For example, in *Biosfera Peluche* (2021–2) – an artwork which took as its point of departure Biosphere 2, an artificially closed ecological system built in the 1980s to explore the possibility of space colonization – the artist transformed two UK galleries into an immersive environment that featured animal furries (hybrid creatures that reference cartoons and internet subcultures) and brightly painted murals. Minoliti gave their furries gender-neutral names and clothing, which they designed in collaboration with fellow artist Lam Hoi Sin.

Minoliti's painted figures sit between machine, animal and human – blurring fixed categories. The idea of a 'biosphere' for Minoliti is a rich metaphor as a sealed, alternative world.

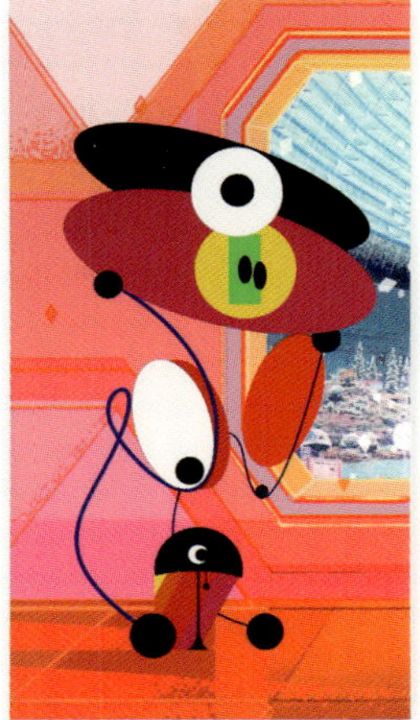 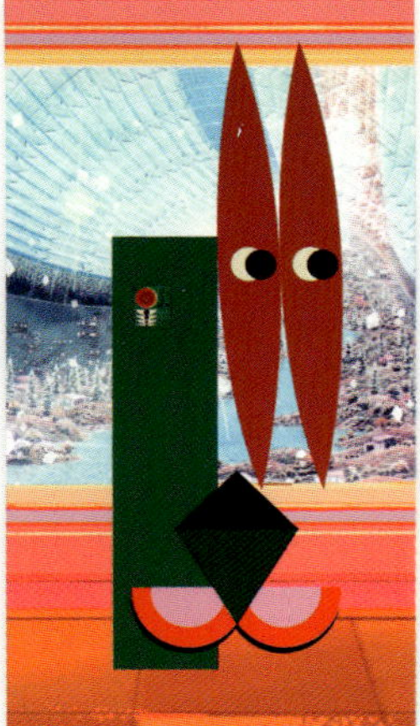 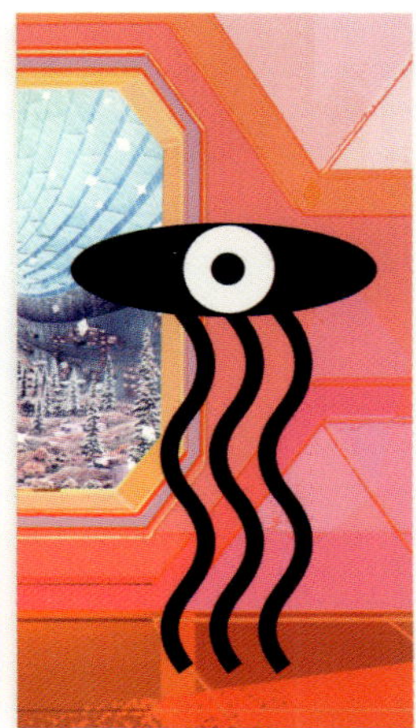

Ad Minoliti
Abstraccion geometrico-galactica, 2019
Unique eco-solvent inkjet print on canvas
150 × 250 cm
(59⅛ × 98½ in.)
Three panels: each
150 × 80 cm
(59⅛ × 31 ½ in.)
KADIST collection

In ***Abstracción geométrico-galáctica***, Mimoliti constructs a utopian, pictorial space where biomorphic forms and saturated colour fields conjure non-binary cosmologies. Spanning three panels, the work envisions a world in which gender is fluid, painting becomes a speculative tool, and all forms of life are honoured in their multiplicity.

They describe nature itself as queer, pointing to organisms like fungi, which exist outside the animal-plant binary as a microcosm, as emblems of that potential. Minoliti does not depict a real future; they imagine an alternative one – where all beings, regardless of form, are welcomed.

Despite the density of its ideas, Minoliti's art remains light, humorous and welcoming. While criticizing patriarchal norms and cisheteronormative thinking, their visions of queer futurity are colourful and joyous.

KEY WORKS

The Feminist School of Painting, 2018, commissioned by the 13th Gwangju Biennale
Queer Deco, 2021, Taguchi Art Collection, Japan

KEY FACTS

Minoliti represented Argentina at the 2019 Venice Biennale.
Minoliti is a co-founder of PintorAs, a feminist painters' collective.

2400 BCE: Royal servants Khnumhotep and Niankhkhnum are buried together in Egypt, depicted embracing – often cited as the first recorded same-sex couple.

600–570 BCE: Sappho of Lesbos writes lyric poetry expressing love between women; her name and island inspire the terms sapphic and lesbian.

200–300 CE: The Kama Sutra in India describes homosexual acts between men and between women and introduces a 'third nature' concept for people with same-sex desire.

342 CE: Christian Roman emperors Constantius II and Constans impose the death penalty for male-male marriage, outlawing same-sex unions in the late Roman Empire.

900s: In Baghdad's flourishing Abbasid court, homoerotic poetry thrives. Poets like Abu Nuwas write openly about same-sex love and desire, influencing Arabic art and literature for centuries.

700s–1100s: Across Europe, Christian penitentials – handbooks for priests administering penance for sins – detail same-sex acts among sins, reflecting the Church's increasing regulation of queer behaviour and desire.

1200s: Medieval illuminated manuscripts, including illustrated Bibles and bestiaries, feature intimate same-sex imagery and gender-fluid figures.

1500s: Renaissance artists in Italy such as Michelangelo, Leonardo da Vinci and Titian create works with homoerotic undertones.

1533: The Buggery Act is passed in England, overriding the ecclesiastical courts and making homosexual sex a capital offence – the first civil anti-sodomy law in the country.

1700s: Japanese artist Miyagawa Chōshun produces Shunga (erotic art) depicting male-male intimacy.

1867: German lawyer and writer, Karl Heinrich Ulrichs, delivers one of the first public speeches advocating for gay rights, pioneering early LGBTQIA+ activism in Europe.

1885: The UK's Criminal Law Amendment Act (Labouchère Amendment) outlaws 'gross indecency' between male persons, a vague charge used to prosecute any homosexual behaviour.

1895: Oscar Wilde is tried and convicted for 'gross indecency' in a highly publicized trial in London.

1897: Magnus Hirschfeld founds the Scientific-Humanitarian Committee in Berlin, the world's first LGBTQIA+ rights organization, to lobby against Germany's 'sodomy law'.

1914: Marcel Duchamp adopts the female persona 'Rrose Sélavy', challenging gender and identity norms in avant-garde art.

1920s: Lesbian bar, Le Monocle, opens in Paris.

1931: Dora Richter undergoes gender affirming surgery at Magnus Hirschfeld's clinic in Berlin, becoming the first known transgender woman to have a vaginoplasty.

1953: US President Eisenhower signs Executive Order 10450 banning homosexuals from federal employment, deepening the Cold War 'Lavender Scare'.

1954: The English computer scientist Alan Turing dies, possibly taking his own life, after being convicted for 'gross indecency' in 1952 and being subjected to a course of oestrogen injections intended to suppress libido.

1956: Thailand decriminalizes homosexuality.

1967: The Sexual Offences Act is passed in England and Wales, legalizing homosexual acts in private between consenting adults who are more than twenty-one years old.

1967: The Nuestro Mundo Group, the first gay rights organization in Latin America, was founded.

1969: The Stonewall Riots erupt in New York City on 28 June, as LGBTQIA+ patrons of the Stonewall Inn resist a police raid, sparking a wave of activism and becoming a turning point in the modern queer rights movement.

1970

1972: Sweden becomes the first country to allow transgender people to legally change their gender.

1978: Artist Gilbert Baker debuts the Rainbow Flag at San Francisco's Gay Freedom Day Parade.

1978: Harmony Hammond curates 'A Lesbian Show' in New York.

1980: The Great American Lesbian Art Show (GALAS) opens at the Woman's Building in Los Angeles, spotlighting lesbian artists and launching satellite exhibitions across the US.

1981: The US Centers for Disease Control and Prevention (CDC) reports the first cases of a rare pneumonia in gay men – the dawn of the AIDS crisis.

1985: Schwules Museum, the world's first museum dedicated to LGBTQIA+ history and culture, founded in Berlin.

1987: Leslie-Lohman Museum of Gay and Lesbian Art founded in New York, having existed in earlier forms as a private collection and informal gallery space since the 1970s.

1987: ACT UP is founded in New York City to demand urgent action on the AIDS crisis through direct action and civil disobedience.

1988: Section 28 becomes law in the UK, banning the 'promotion of homosexuality' by local authorities and sparking widespread protest.

1989: Denmark enacts the world's first registered partnership law, granting same-sex couples nearly all the rights of marriage.

1990

1990: South Africa holds the first Pride march on the African continent in Johannesburg.

1990: World Health Organization removed homosexuality from its list of mental illnesses.

1991: Derek Jarman's 'Queer' exhibition at Manchester Art Gallery, Manchester, UK is met with strong backlash in the British press.

1995: 'In a Different Light' at Berkeley Art Museum and Pacific Film Archive (BAMPFA), University of California, Berkeley, is widely recognized as the first North American institutional exhibition exploring queer sensibilities and explicitly using the word 'queer' in exhibition materials.

1998: Ecuador became one of the first countries in the world to constitutionally ban discrimination based on sexual orientation.

2000

2004: 'Queer Visualities' at Art Gallery of York University, Toronto, is one of the first museum-level art exhibitions to use the word 'queer' in its title.

2008: California Supreme Court legalizes same-sex marriage, but the decision is later overturned via a popular vote on a constitutional amendment.

2013: Russia passes a federal 'gay propaganda' law, banning positive depictions of LGBTQ relationships to minors.

2014: The Sunpride Art Foundation is founded in Hong Kong to 'raise awareness and respect for the LGBTQIA+ community through art'.

2017: 'Queer British Art 1861–1967' at Tate Britain, London, marks the 50th anniversary of the partial decriminalization of male homosexuality in England.

2018: India's Supreme Court strikes down Section 377 of the colonial-era penal code, decriminalizing consensual gay sex.

2022: Same-sex marriage becomes legal nationwide in Mexico.

2023: Uganda's president signs the Anti-Homosexuality Act, one of the harshest anti-LGBTQ laws in the world, imposing life imprisonment for same-sex acts.

GLOSSARY

Afrofuturism: a cultural and artistic movement that combines elements of science fiction, historical reimagining and African diasporic culture to explore Black identity, challenge colonial narratives and imagine liberated futures.

Androgyny: a blending or ambiguity of traditionally masculine and feminine characteristics.

Anti-gay laws: legislation that criminalizes or discriminates against people based on their actual or perceived sexual orientation. These laws have historically ranged from prohibitions on same-sex relationships to restrictions on expression and civil rights.

Avant-garde: a term used to describe artists or movements that are experimental, radical or ahead of their time. Avant-garde work often challenges artistic convention.

Ballroom Culture: an underground LGBTQIA+ subculture, originating in Black and Latinx communities in 20th-century New York, where people compete in performance-based categories like voguing, runway and realness. It offers space for self-expression, belonging and chosen family.

Bloomsbury Group: a group of early 20th-century British writers, artists and intellectuals known for their radical ideas about art, sexuality and society.

Butch: a queer identity often associated with perceived masculinity, particularly within lesbian and gender-diverse communities.

Chosen Family: a network of supportive relationships formed by mutual care and trust, often in place of or alongside biological family. Chosen families are especially significant in queer communities where traditional structures may reject or exclude people.

Cisgender: a term used to describe someone whose gender identity aligns with the sex they were assigned at birth.

Coding: the use of symbols, gestures or imagery to convey hidden or layered meanings – often used by marginalized communities.

Collage: an art technique involving the assembly of different materials. This may include paper, photographs or fabric, and then application onto a single surface.

Conceptual Art: an art movement first emerging in the 1960s, where the idea behind the work is considered more important than the finished object. It often challenges traditional notions of authorship, value and the role of art.

Dada: an early 20th-century avant-garde art movement that emerged as a reaction to the horrors of the First World War. Dada artists embraced absurdity, chance and anti-establishment values, challenging traditional aesthetics and logic.

Documentary Photography: a photographic genre that aims to capture real-life events, people and environments.

Dyke: a slang term for lesbian. Once used as a slur, it has been reclaimed by queer women at various points throughout history.

Fa'afafine: the third gender identity in Sāmoan society, referring to people assigned male at birth who embody both 'masculine' and 'feminine' traits. Fa'afafine are a respected part of Sāmoa's social fabric, existing outside Western gender binaries.

Fabulation: a way of storytelling that mixes truth and fiction to imagine new realities. It has been used by queer and marginalized artists to rewrite, or reinterpret, history and create space for political fantasy.

Female Gaze: a way of seeing that centres female experience, desire and subjectivity in contrast to the traditional 'male gaze'.

Feminist Art: art that addresses issues of gender inequality, patriarchy and female experience. It emerged as a political movement in the 1970s.

Femme: a queer identity that embraces femininity as a conscious, political expression rather than a passive or traditional role. Often used in contrast to butch, 'femme' can subvert, exaggerate or reclaim traditional femininity.

Futurity: a concept that refers to the potential of what is to come, often used in queer and critical theory to imagine alternatives beyond current systems of power, normativity and oppression.

Gender: a social and cultural system that organizes people based on masculinity and femininity. It is distinct from biological sex and can be fluid, multiple and self-defined.

Heteronormativity: the assumption that heterosexuality is the default or 'normal' way of being.

Hijra: a Hindi term with ancient origins referring to a particular group within Hindu culture who would be called transfeminine or transgender in Western terms. Hijra are legally recognized as belonging to a third gender in India, Pakistan and Bangladesh, although some Hijra campaign for recognition as women and access to gender-affirming healthcare.

Homophobia: prejudice, discrimination or hatred directed at people who are lesbian, gay or otherwise non-heterosexual.

Intersectional Feminism: a feminist approach grounded in the concept of intersectionality. It recognizes that gender is shaped by its entanglement with other identities and systems of power – such as race, class, sexuality, disability and migration status – and calls for a feminism that addresses multiple forms of inequality at once. The term was popularized by scholar Kimberlé Crenshaw in 1989.

Intersectionality: a framework for understanding how different systems of oppression – such as racism, sexism, homophobia and classism – interact and overlap. It emphasizes that social identities and structures of power are interconnected, and that experiences of inequality cannot be understood in isolation.

Intersex: a term describing individuals born with physical sex characteristics that don't fit typical definitions of male or female. Intersex people may have variations in chromosomes, hormones or anatomy, but not everyone with intersex traits identifies with the term.

LGBTQIA+: an acronym for Lesbian, Gay, Bisexual, Transgender, Queer or Questioning, Intersex and Asexual, Aromantic or Agender, with the '+' representing groups such as non-binary, gender fluid or pansexual people, whose identities may not be adequately or entirely represented by the listed letters.

Male Gaze: a term coined by the feminist theorist Laura Mulvey in 1975 to describe how women are often presented from a heterosexual male perspective. It critiques the objectification of women.

New Queer Cinema: a film movement of the early 1990s marked by radical, experimental approaches to storytelling and representation. It centred queer perspectives, rejected respectability politics and tackled issues such as AIDS.

Non-binary: a gender identity that doesn't fit within the traditional categories of male or female. Non-binary people may identify as both, neither, or as something entirely different.

Pride: a celebration of LGBTQIA+ identity, community and history that combines festive parades with ongoing activism and protest.

Queer: originally used as a slur against LGBTQIA+ people, queer has been reclaimed as an empowering term to describe non-normative sexual and gender identities. It also signifies a political stance that challenges fixed categories and celebrates fluidity, resistance and community.

Queer Formalism: an artistic approach that explores how form, style and materials convey queer ideas and emotions, demonstrating that how a work looks or is made can be as political as its subject matter.

Speculative Fiction: a literary and artistic genre that imagines alternative realities, futures or worlds. It includes science fiction, fantasy and utopian or dystopian visions.

Street Art: visual art created in public spaces, often without official permission.

Subculture: a group that exists within a larger culture but with distinct values, norms or aesthetics.

Transgender: a term for people whose gender identity differs from the sex they were assigned at birth. It can encompass a wide range of experiences and expressions.

Transphobia: prejudice, fear or discrimination directed at transgender people.

Two-Spirit: a term used by some Indigenous North American cultures to describe people who embody both masculine and feminine spirits. It is a sacred, cultural identity.

Visual Activism: the use of art and imagery as a tool for political or social change.

FURTHER READING

Amelia Abraham (ed.), *We Can Do Better Than This: 35 Voices on the Future of LGBTQ+ Rights*, London: Vintage, 2021

Hongwei Bao, *Queer China: Lesbian and Gay Literature and Visual Culture Under Postsocialism*, New York: Routledge, 2020

Hongwei Bao, Diyi Mergenthaler and Jamie J. Zhao (eds), *Contemporary Queer Chinese Art*, London: Bloomsbury Academic, 2025

Clare Barlow, *Queer British Art: 1867–1967*, London: Tate Publishing, 2017

Jan Christian Bernabe and Laura Kina (eds), *Queering Contemporary Asian American Art*, Seattle: University of Washington Press, 2017

Anne Marie E. Butler and Sascha Crasnow (eds), *Queer Contemporary Art of Southwest Asia, North Africa*, Bristol: Intellect, 2024

Judith Butler, *Gender Trouble: Feminism and the Subversion of Identity*, New York: Routledge, 1990

Anne Carson, *If Not, Winter: Fragments of Sappho*, New York: Vintage, 2002

Nadim Choufi and Yasmine Rifaii (eds), *I Will Always Be Looking For You: A Queer Anthology on Arab Art*, Beirut: Haven for Artists, 2025

Zorian Clayton, Lydia Easton and Hannah Kaluznick, *Calling the Shots: A Queer History of Photography*, London: Thames & Hudson, 2024

Flora Dunster and Theo Gordon, *Photography – A Queer History*, London: Ilex, 2024

Andrew Gayed, *Queer World Making: Contemporary Middle Eastern Diasporic Art*, Seattle: University of Washington Press, 2024

David J. Getsy (ed.), *Queer: Documents of Contemporary Art*, Cambridge, MA: The MIT Press, 2016

Harmony Hammond, *Lesbian Art in America: A Contemporary History*, New York: Rizzoli, 2000

Brenda S. Helt and Madelyn Detloff (eds), *Queer Bloomsbury*, London: Bloomsbury Academic, 2016

Diarmuid Hester, *Nothing Ever Disappears: Seven Hidden Histories*, London: Penguin, 2024

bell hooks, *Art on My Mind: Visual Politics*, London: Penguin Classics, 2025

Peter Horne and Reina Lewis, *Outlooks: Lesbian and Gay Sexualities and Visual Cultures*, London: Routledge, 1996

Jonathan D. Katz, *About Face: Stonewall, Revolt, and New Queer Art*, New York: Monacelli, 2024

Jonathan D. Katz, *Hide/Seek: Difference and Desire in American Portraiture*, Washington, DC: Smithsonian Institution Press, 2011

Jonathan D. Katz and Johnny Willis (eds), *The First Homosexuals: The Birth of a New Identity 1869–1939*, New York: Monacelli, 2025

Jon Key, *Black Queer and Untold: A New Archive of Designers, Artists and Trailblazers*, Montclair, NJ: Levine Querido, 2024

David Leddick, *Intimate Companions: A Triography of George Platt Lynes, Paul Cadmus, Lincoln Kirstein, and Their Circle*, New York: St. Martin's Press, 2000

Catherine Lord and Richard Meyer, *Art & Queer Culture*, London: Phaidon, 2013

Audre Lorde, *Sister Outsider: Essays and Speeches*, London: Penguin Classics, 2019

José Esteban Muñoz, *Cruising Utopia: The Then and There of Queer Futurity*, New York: NYU Press, 2009

Quentin Petit Dit Duhal, *Art Queer: Histoire et théorie des représentations LGBTQIA+*, Joinville-le-Pont: Double ponctuation, 2024

Alex Pilcher, *A Queer Little History of Art*, London: Tate Publishing, 2017

Christopher Reed, *Art and Homosexuality: A History of Ideas*, New York: Oxford University Press USA, 2011

Maura Reilly, *Curatorial Activism*, London: Thames & Hudson, 2018

Gemma Rolls-Bentley, *Queer Art: From Canvas to Club, and the Spaces Between*, London: Frances Lincoln, 2024

Legacy Russell, *Glitch Feminism*, London: Verso, 2020

James M. Saslow, *Pictures and Passions: A History of Homosexuality in the Visual Arts*, New York: Viking, 1999

William J. Simmons, *Queer Formalism: The Return*, Berlin: Floating Opera Press, 2021

Rachel Smith and Barbara Vesey (eds), *The Love That Dares: Letters of LGBTQ+ Love & Friendship Through History*, London: Ilex, 2022

INDEX

Illustrations are in *italics*